Walled-In

Walled-In

Arctic Housing and a Sociology of Walls

Lisa-Jo K. van den Scott

Foreword by Patsy Kowtak Kuksuk

LEXINGTON BOOKS

Lanham • Boulder • New York • London

Published by Lexington Books
An imprint of The Rowman & Littlefield Publishing Group, Inc.
4501 Forbes Boulevard, Suite 200, Lanham, Maryland 20706
www.rowman.com

86-90 Paul Street, London EC2A 4NE

British Library Cataloguing in Publication Information Available

Library of Congress Cataloging-in-Publication Data Available

ISBN 978-1-66695-989-5 (cloth : alk. paper)
ISBN 978-1-66695-990-1 (electronic)

♾™ The paper used in this publication meets the minimum requirements of American National Standard for Information Sciences—Permanence of Paper for Printed Library Materials, ANSI/NISO Z39.48-1992.

Dedicated to Krass and Estelle Kestin, lovers of knowledge of all kinds. To Jeff, my beloved. To Debbie and Will, the trees from which my apple does not wish to roll far. And to my graduate students.

Evening in the Arctic
Spreads your soul wide
Wide across the sky
When the moon swallows the land
Yawns before you
Red and swelling
Ready to hold your heart
Or break it
Depending on how you hold your breath
Or break the cold night air around you
The moon receives its share of reverence
And when the moment passes
Try to repack the contents of your heart
Fit them home where they once were
Lovingly or harshly
As the moon dictates.

Contents

Foreword

By Patsy Kowtak Kuksuk

First of all, I want to thank Lisa-Jo for writing this book. It gives an in-depth view of one who wanted to get to know the people (Inuit), how we live, and how we interact as a family.

To deeply know something, you have had to live it personally for the majority of your life; to be born into it. One may study it and understand it, but to have lived it is to fully understand it. This speaks to the importance of work that invites reflections on lived experiences. By learning from people about what their own lives are like, we can make better policies in service to communities.

I have been involved with housing for many years now. The first time was around the age of 12. I was sort of understanding the English language when people were looking for people (voices?) who can speak to those who had authority over the new way of living. These authority figures had control over resources such as funding for houses, schools, and so on. I didn't know what it was and all I was told was, "you say whatever you want when it comes to helping *inuuqatitit* (your people)." So, then, I became a housing board member.

My family did not know how to live in a wooden constructed house until I was nine years old. Before that, we had lived in igloos. We did not know the luxury of having to turn on a light switch, but we also lost some luxuries. Living in the wooden houses meant learning how it was to live in a cold house with windows all frosted up in ice, rather than being able to move into a brand-new spotless white home when it was time, as we could when we lived in igloos. How so white it would be and looking so new! We had to live in another kind of home; one that cannot be moved nor replaced for years. I found the constructed home colder than an igloo, and so much darker. However, they were roomier.

Since "Housing" became my full-time career in 1989, and having been my passion since the age of 12, it became more and more obvious to me that more and better houses need to be built. Over my life, I have wrestled with the question of what I can do to achieve that? From the 1990s on, I noticed much improvement has been made. The houses are built more culturally orientated, such as having cold porches for hunting clothing, skins that need to be in a cool place, and as a place to store country food.

From the time constructed homes have been built, there has always been a shortage which resulted in a number of nuclear families living under one roof because no houses are available. There are many disadvantages to this, such as family disagreements, abuse, taking turns sleeping when there are no beds/ rooms available, spreading of viruses such as TB (and recently COVID-19), and other diseases. Where I work, we gather all the information available, such as overcrowding, where there are most needs for homes, and so on, so we can use these to try and get more funding to build homes. Funding is always an issue as we can only build so much based on the amounts that are received. Today, we have a total of roughly 3,000 families that need a home across Nunavut. These families could be a couple, a family with one, two, three, or four children, or even more.

Inuit need to try and get more people to be independent and not be so dependent on the government. But how do we do that?

1. Education (including training opportunities for youth)
2. Jobs
3. Reduce the cost of living in the north
4. Create awareness of the realities of northern, Inuit life.

We must continue working together to achieve these.

As you read this book, remember we are part of the same human family, and I hope you can see both the impact of the current housing situation and our resilience as Inuit, as people.

Acknowledgments

First and foremost, I must thank participants, whose generosity and support are truly humbling. They welcomed me into their homes, encouraged me in my work, and taught me how to do research with them. I would also like to thank the Elders for their guidance and those members of the community in Arviat who were of particular support; Aja, Oka'naaq, Diane Angma, Ujarak Appadoo, Gara Mamgark, Elizabeth McClintock, Marvin McKay-Keenan, Angela Mukjungnik, Margaret and Karen Panigoniak, and Katelyn Sularayok. Ujarak and Karen both also were my research assistants and were invaluable.

Gary Alan Fine, Wendy Griswold, Steven Epstein, and Daniel and Cheryl Albas have all been tremendous mentors. Gary Alan Fine adopted me intellectually, and I could not have been luckier. Thank you also to my own graduate students who inspire as a matter of routine.

Many other mentors have played a role. Andrea Doucette for being pivotal in my transition into a tenure-track job. Thank you also to Savina Balasubramanian, Charles Edgley, Clare Forstie, Scott Gryder, Albert Hunter, Stacy Lom, and Nick Sula. For reading drafts, my heartfelt thanks to Julia Christensen, Stephen Crocker, Thomas Gieryn, Stacey Hannem, Steven Kleinknecht, Stephanie Peña-Alves, Antony Puddephatt, Carrie Sanders, Deana Simonetto, Karen Stanbridge, Eviatar Zerubavel, and especially Allison Surtees. I also owe a debt of gratitude to the various reading groups who have commented on my work over the years. These include Northwestern University's Ethnography Workshop, the Culture Workshop, the Comparative-Historical Workshop, the Urban Workshop, as well as McMaster's writing group, spearheaded by Dorothy Pawluch.

I would also like to thank the Integrated Chronic Care Service (ICCS), Dr. Huang, Dr. Sarah Pegrum, Dr. Erin Hoffe, and Michelle Geldart.

Finally, I would like to thank my family; my nieces and nephews, Camille, Carmel, Emilie, Emma, Hélène, Kathleen, Luke, Nico, Samuel, Simon, and William. To the utter shock and amazement of my childhood-self, I absolutely treasure my sister, Cheryl, and my brother, Jordan, and am eternally grateful for their love and support.

My parents, as fellow sociologists, have given me intellectual shoulders to stand on. I only hope that by following in their footsteps I do not muddy the waters of their stellar reputations. Despite my having been a wretched child to raise, they suffered through reading many drafts of this work. I thank them from the bottom of my heart.

Thanks are most due to my most beautiful beloved, Jeff. This work, or any other work in my life, simply would not have been possible without him.

This research was accomplished with the assistance of the Government of Canada and The Graduate School at Northwestern University. This research was also supported by the Social Sciences and Humanities Research Council. The publication of this monograph was supported by the Publications Subvention Program at Memorial University.

Introduction

Whenever I share that I am writing a book about the sociology of walls, I am met with confusion and a questioning look that says, "what could possibly be interesting about walls?" I never expected to be enthralled by the role of plain, old, boring walls of buildings. And yet, they have captured my imagination. However strange it seems, when asked what kind of nut I am, the only possible answer is that I am a wall-nut.

I first moved to Arviat, Nunavut, Canada, in 2004. As I built friendships within the community, I began to visit my friends' homes. I was struck by the dramatic difference in how they treated their walls. Lucia[1] had almost blank walls, with a small cross perched high up, monitoring the room (see figure A.1). Lily, whose walls I will discuss in more detail in the second chapter, had created a colorful mosaic of traditional scenes along her walls (see figure A.2). As I discovered how walls become tools of the powerful, I became both horrified by the reality of colonization and awe-inspired by the resilience and agency of *Arviammiut*, the people of Arviat.

In this book, I present a sociological theory of walls, a conceptual approach people can use to understand people's relationships with their walls, as well as to shed light on the use of housing in colonization practices, and the strength with which Inuit in Arviat resist, reimagine, and refuse to allow their culture to be bound by their walls.

I begin with a statement about my positionality. Then, I discuss symbolic interaction and Indigenous methods as frameworks for this study. I give some background about the built environment, Arviat's sociohistorical context, the relocation *Arviammiut* experienced, and then an outline of following chapters. Because this book centers the everyday lived experience of *Arviammiut* today, I pick up where the histories (e.g., Bennett & Rowley 2004) leave off, while still setting the scene of colonization and resiliency.

1

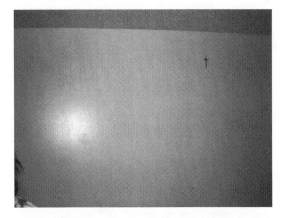

Figure A.1   Almost Blank Wall.

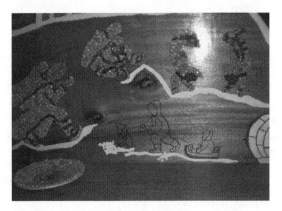

Figure A.2   Lily's Wall.

POSITIONALITY

I am an immigrant to Canada, half Jewish, half Dutch. I came to Canada when I was two years old, but, living in a rural area, I grew up as an outsider to New Brunswick culture (I still don't know how to play the local card game "45s"). As a non-Christian, there were homes I was not allowed to enter. As adults, my spouse and I moved to Arviat when he was invited to be the music teacher. I had no intentions of becoming a researcher at the time. I found myself in a warm, hospitable community where we shared a mutual appreciation of sewing and needlework skills; I had been cross-stitching since I was 12. In addition, I have a disability and often walk with a cane. I was delighted to find myself embraced by a group of people who did not view that disability as a negative. As an ethnic Jew, and as a Bahá'í, I connected with the sense of loss and suffering. As a human being, I connected with fellow human beings in the love and laughter it takes to survive Arctic winters. I felt more welcomed in Arviat than I had yet experienced.

I will always be, however, an outsider in fundamental ways in Arviat. I am neither Inuit nor Indigenous, and, obviously, can never be. It has been my honor, however to find myself among Inuit and to have received their encouragement to transition from friend into the role of researcher. Early in my time, I became involved in projects with Elders. After living in Arviat for two years, I obtained a research license from the Nunavut Research Institute (NRI) and, with the guidance of my Inuit friends and Elders around me, I undertook my first research with them (van den Scott 2009). I work to center Inuit experience in my work, and to reflect on the impact of my role in the field, and their lives.

INTERPRETIVE METHODS AND SYMBOLIC INTERACTION

As a sociologist, I approach my research from a symbolic interactionist perspective (van den Scott 2019), an approach that recognizes participants as experts in their own lives. This perspective allows for us to look at the social world with a view to process and meaning-making. I am neither a story-teller, nor a knowledge-keeper. Rather than sharing Inuit knowledge, I am showing what can be gained by *respecting* their knowledge. I honor their narratives as offering depth of understanding to all of us through a new perspective about how people and groups interact with their walls and the role of power in built environments. In this sense, I work toward a decolonizing methodology that emphasizes story-telling, or storywork (Archibald 2008).

As a matter of course, symbolic interactionists generally do not seek generalizability. Rather, they acknowledge that there are generic social processes (Prus 1987) through which we accomplish our everyday lives, including how we navigate structural constraints and our sociohistorical contexts. As a simple example, think about how, when we make a mistake while speaking, we engage in some form of work to compensate; we laugh, or correct ourselves, or perhaps we blush. Goffman calls this "saving face" (Goffman 1959). We all work to save face, however it might look very different in various contexts. Once we know, however, to keep an eye out for saving face, we can then study it.

Once we know that walls are symbolic and representative of power structures, which we may resist, reinvent, or reimagine, then we can attend to this aspect of walls in other contexts as well. As Kublu et al. (2017) stress, the importance is in the specific. This approach develops concepts that may apply elsewhere as well. As Chelsea Vowel encourages, we move toward a "deeper understanding of one another's concerns and beliefs" (Vowel 2016, 2). Symbolic interaction privileges research methods that focus on everyday lives. Like standpoint theory, symbolic interactionists begin from the position of respecting participants, regardless of the group, as experts in their own lives, as knowledge-keepers, and as valuable to work with in understanding humanity.

I do not try to speak for *Arviammiut*. I use extended quotes to let participants speak for themselves. I'm interested in identifying patterns that may help us understand how societies, more broadly, work. It would be a shocking disservice to exclude any group from our attempts to understand people and humanity. *Arviammiut* helped me look upon *walls* as an object of interest. In doing so, one can see ordinary walls through new eyes as extraordinary in the lives of ordinary people (Berger 1963). As we looked at the walls together, this book emerged.

INDIGENOUS METHODS

I embrace the two-eyed seeing approach (Bartlett, Marshall & Marshall 2012) championed by Elder Albert Marshall. He and Murdena Marshall stress the importance of multiple perspectives. While one eye stays trained on Indigenous ways of knowing and being, the other eye seeks to weave together this knowledge with "contemporary sciences."

Non-Indigenous researchers, however, have broken a sacred trust. Rather than working with Indigenous groups, they have turned their scientific gaze on them in ways that make them subjects, that "other" them, and that see them only as exotic beings so as to either romanticize or fetishize them. There has been a push within interpretive sociology to move away from the term "subjects." Rather, interpretivists use the term "participants," as I do here, to indicate that knowledge-seeking is a collaborative effort between participant and researcher (even the distinct roles can be challenged, depending on the research model, such as in community-based action research). The term "participant" indicates that the participant is a fully respected person with agency and knowledge. The researcher approaches the participant in an attitude of learning, seeking mutual relations with an awareness that the participant is the expert (Coultard 2014). I have worked, from my position as a white researcher, to decolonize my own thinking and to eliminate othering from my work. In particular, I work to deconstruct *white possessive logics* (Moreton-Robinson 2016) as I consider my conversations with participants and my experiences in Arviat. Any failings in this regard are mine as I continue to work toward truth and reconciliation from my end.

I seek here to expose colonial ideologies (Younging 2018) and to convey how they are represented in the built environment. In addition, I work to highlight and honor the resiliency with which *Arviammiut* maintain and grow their knowledge system and ways of being (Kablu et al. 2017), as an Indigenous knowledge system that has existed and flourished over vast periods of time (Younging 2018).

Inuit are an ethnically distinct Indigenous group in Canada. They have their own unique history, experience, and relationship with colonialism. Too often, Inuit find their unique experiences subsumed under the broader umbrella of Indigeneity in Canada. Doing research among Inuit, as with any group, requires on-the-ground time to find out what Inuit, themselves, consider ethical research. It is important to attend to their distinct and specific experiences. As Kublu et al. (2017) remind us, Inuit are a heterogeneous group, diverse in the ways of all groups. I strive to honor that diversity in demonstrating the various patterns that emerged from the research.

The everyday lived experience of Inuit, rather than traditional knowledge, comprises most of the focus of this book. Regardless of the formality or longevity of knowledge, any knowledge—even everyday knowledge—is relational (Kublu et al. 2017); hence the context of colonization permeates this book. Inuit navigate their everyday lives through colonial spaces, continuing and building relational knowledge amid a built environment that echoes colonial power relations. The theory and concepts I offer in this book do not work to solve a problem among Inuit, nor do they try to explain anything. Rather, these are concepts that work toward making sense of reality, a key part of Indigenous research (Smith 2021).

I came to Arviat with an attitude of learning and encountered generosity of spirit and acceptance in a way I had not previously experienced. Mark Kalluak, an Elder from Arviat, describes the importance of *tunnganarniq*, open-heartedness, for Inuit:

> *Tunnganarniq*, or open heartedness, was a core expectation for all Inuit. It means being approachable and being open to assisting anyone at any time. It describes people who do not withhold the giving of proper advice and instructions for a full and meaningful life. (Kalluak 2017, 44)

This resonates with the spirit in which Elders asked me to do this research. Everyday diverse experiences among *Arviammiut* teach us ways to think about people's walls, ways to lead meaningful lives in these built environments, even when those built environments may be hostile.

HOW I CAME TO RESEARCH IN ARVIAT

I first moved to Arviat with my spouse when he became the music teacher at the local high school. I lived there for five years and learned to speak Inuktitut (although it is a bit rusty now). I soon found work as a substitute teacher and then as an instructor at Nunavut Arctic College. Knowing Inuktitut helped me to teach English. I was fortunate to already be considered a member of the community when I began to transition into the role of researcher. As such, I was able to consult with both the Elders and my Inuit friends as I made the decision to become a researcher. The formation of good-faith, reciprocal (Coulthard 2014; Fine 1996), trust-based relationships (Archibald 2008; Smith 2021) benefited not only the participants, myself, and my research, but adheres to recommended practices in working with Indigenous communities (Brook & McLachlan 2005; Caine et al. 2009; Castleden et al. 2012; Smith 2021; Wong et al. 2013). My research consisted of ethnography, 50 formal interviews, as well as innovative uses of photography and cognitive mapping.

I built trust-based relationships and friendships, initially, to embed myself in the community as a resident and an active participant, learning the language as well as involving myself with sewing seal skin boots and spending time with Elders. In my first year in Arviat, I was invited to sit on the Sivulinut Elders Society to help navigate the bureaucracy of applying for grants, as well as to support research within and coming into the community. I was the first non-Inuk, first non-Elder on the council, but we served each other well. I found acceptance in a form I had never experienced before.

It was thus that I became quickly involved in the affairs of the community. Soon after, I volunteered at the drop-in center (now closed) and taught cross-stitch. The next day I had a young girl at my door wanting to learn more. The following day there were three of them. Over my five years of living in Arviat, I had over 150 children come through my living room to participate in what developed into a funded after-school program, including a few sleepovers where 15 sleeping bags lined my living room floor with girls ranging in age from 7 to 13. Children, whom the teachers defined as unable to concentrate, would stitch with deep concentration for hours on end. Eventually, at the request of the children, we also did math, creative writing, photography, and cooking. By involving myself with the children, I inadvertently made many ties within the community. Above all, I was able to show that I could have a full, crazy, messy house "just like an Inuk," as one of the Elders said when she dropped by with some paperwork and saw 10 girls hanging out at my house. Eventually, after my long involvement with the Elder's council, the Sivulinut Society, and the relationships the community and I built together, the Elders asked me to become a researcher in the community.

I supplemented my ethnographic field notes with 50 formal in-depth, open-ended qualitative interviews. I performed the majority of these in participants' homes. In all cases, I encouraged story-telling (Archibald 2008). I felt this was very important as when I had lived there in the past, some who had participated in other research projects told me afterward that they had merely told the researcher what he or she thought the researcher wanted to hear. To overcome this in my own work, in addition to supplementing interviews with ethnographic data as well as informal conversations, I took pains to make the interviews as relaxed as possible. After several of the interviews, participants told me that it had been "fun" and referred to it as a "visit" and hoped that I would come back again soon, either to interview or to visit.

While it is commonplace for researchers to pay participants in Arviat, I felt uncomfortable doing this and could not afford it at the time. In the first place, it is documented that research involving money in the North is not necessarily reliable (Collings 2009). In the second place, I felt that it was more consistent with Inuit traditional practices to bring gifts. Arviat is known for its sewing. When interviewing women, I would bring several choices of fabric with me, based on what I already knew of the participant. At the start of the interview, I let them know that my research was only partially funded and I could not afford to pay for interviews (the common rate being $50–75/hr) and asked if that was okay. At the end of the interview, I pulled out the fabric as a gift, thanking them for participating. This is consistent with traditional practices around knowledge-sharing. When interviewing men, I would bring fabric in case they wanted it for their wives or sisters, as well as harmonicas and guitar strings.

When interviewing Elders, I was the most nervous about not having money. They understand that *qablunaaqs* show respect for the worth of something, even knowledge, with money. All the Elders whom I approached agreed to be interviewed for free. One Elder pushed my hands away, when offered the gift, telling me that I was a friend and did not need to pay or give her gifts for her stories. This heartened my hopes that I was not offending them (Collings 2009), and also deeply touched me. In the end, I showed her the intended gift, some fringe that was highly valued in the community and extremely hard to come by, and she relented and accepted the gift. As I left, she gave me a *kunik* (nose kiss), as she had done on a few other occasions.

While many participants were confused as to my interest in walls and space and place, they were eager to help me with my schooling, as well as to share their lived experiences within and without their homes. Not all researchers are accepted with open arms (Caine et al. 2009; Collings 2009). The Elders supported me in my work and I owe a debt. This book is the fulfillment of my promise to those Elders.

In addition, the vetting process of the NRI is extensive. My proposal was shared with all of the main organized groups in Arviat, including the District Education Authority, the Hunters and Trappers Organization, Church leaders, and even the managers of the local stores. They all had the opportunity to provide feedback. I am honored to have been able to work with *Arviammiut* on my research.[2] The community and I, together, have figured out something fascinating about walls and the concepts I introduce in this book can help others to study walls in other settings. The first chapter covers sociological concepts; however, you can skip this if you are more interested in reading about everyday experiences.

THE BUILT ENVIRONMENT

Groups that experience massive change, a "culture crash" (van den Scott 2017), or the sociological concept "identity foreclosure" (van den Hoonaard, D. 1997), find themselves struggling to build new authentic selves within unexplored terrain, be it physical, symbolic, or social terrain—or some combination thereof. For many groups, this involves a process of sedimentation— into different routines, different ways of being and thinking, and different performances of identity from before. In order to accomplish identity-work and build new, resilient, and authentic selves, people must negotiate different sets of limitations, exigencies, and contingencies in their everyday lives. This can be especially challenging for Indigenous groups in hostile environments (Snipp 2013; Stewart 2015). In this book, I examine this experience from the perspective of Inuit of Arviat, Nunavut, Canada.

How do Inuit materially achieve giving new meaning to their built environment without losing cultural identity? This is a story about how a displaced group, in the throes of a culture crash, moves through a novel built environment and struggles with performing traditions in authentic ways while removed from the locus of knowledge of these traditions. Credibility of identity performance hinges on place and the ways in which place can and cannot be overcome. The complexity of our relationship with the built environment and its overlapping symbolic significance create a constellation of intertwined meanings, influenced by the local and the more structural power relations in a given situation.

I engage with the literature on space, place, and power to demonstrate that the built environment must be considered from the aspect of technology studies, Indigenous studies, and culture. The built environment is part of physical, symbolic, and social landscapes over which boundaries are affirmed or broken down. Geographies of knowledge and identity emerge as key components of place, emplacement, and the built environment, where layered, contextual meanings of identity performance play out. Within the battle for distinct identity in the face of massive change, macro forces have great influence, and yet resistance exists at the grassroots level (Scott 2008; see also Coburn 2015; Kino-Nda-Niimi Collective 2014; Simpson 2017).

Walled-off, or perhaps more accurately "walled-in," from past knowledge means having to come to terms with the new structures and built environment. Inuit do so through performance of knowledge linked to traditional identity. The new landscape, including a geography of knowledge, is an ambivalent landscape. Walls and structures force certain forms of docility. The system Inuit face today is one that rewards a willingness to be disciplined.

The disruption of life-as-it-was, the culture crash, leaves a group grasping for continuity of identity and traditions, while at the same time, it threatens collective memory and continuity of practices. Traditional knowledge becomes a resource for identity performance, aided by what transforms into a "wow factor" of many traditional practices in comparison with colonizing practices, such as exotic foods.

Loss of place, sense of self, and norms is devastating. As a result, Inuit develop strategies to access previous conceptions of identity from which they are geographically, symbolically, or socially separated to perform new-yet-traditional authentic selves which reaffirm Inuitness. They agentically invoke strategies to navigate presentation of the self when the locus of family traditional knowledge is located, not where you inhabit, but where you visit.

ARVIAT—A BRIEF OVERVIEW

Arviat, Nunavut, Canada is a small Inuit hamlet comprised of roughly 2,500 inhabitants. From the time when I first moved to Arviat, in 2004, to the time I finished my last data collection in 2012, the population grew from roughly 2,000 to 2,500,[3] approximately half of whom are under the age of 15. The hamlet is accessible only by airplane, although at certain times of the year one can make the arduous journey to other communities by snowmobile or dog team, the closest hamlet being roughly 210 kilometers away as the crow flies. The runway and roads are dirt in the summer and compacted snow in the winter. There are approximately 450 inhabited houses within the clutch of buildings that make up Arviat although that number does increase slightly every year. Aside from a handful of transient *Qablunaaq* (Western or "Southern" people from south of Churchill, Manitoba, usually white but not always), the population is almost entirely Inuit, comprised of both *Ahiarmiut* (inland) and *Padlirmiut* (coastal) tribes.

This book is interested in the lived experience of Inuit today. The built environment reifies their sociohistorical context, one of brutal colonization. I give a brief history to establish colonization as the context for *Arviammiut*'s lived experience; a diverse and heterogeneous experience within the overall intergenerational trauma of a colonial history. Additionally, it is not sociology's goal to arbitrate or to find some absolute truth. Rather, *Arviammiut* explicitly declare colonization as a present, relevant, and oppressive force— so it is. This book is about their experience, narratives, and resiliency.

Frank Tester defines colonialism as "a process of coming to see and define 'Others' as primitive, in need of the benefits of Western-European civilization and living with unexploited resources and opportunities" (Tester 2017, 21). This book acknowledges the tragedy of the colonial experience in the North and seeks to eradicate this othering view of Inuit, highlighting their resiliency in the face of colonialism, their ingenuity, and their ability to perform resistance in everyday life.[4]

Arviammiut have been living in houses for approximately 50 years. Arviat is one of the very last Inuit settlements to be created, and it therefore had an accelerated, unusually rapid colonization process. As such, even among Inuit, this group is experiencing a unique, historically situated social moment (Gilleard & Higgs 2002). Other Inuit communities, such as those on Baffin Island, have had a much longer exposure to Western culture and a more gradual colonization process. Arviat, however, had its first sustained contact with Westerners starting in the early 1920s, when the first trading post was established in the area followed by Catholic and Anglican missionaries' beginning to focus on this area in earnest.

The isolation of Arviat is profound and extreme in many ways, though the airplane out serves as both a bridge and a barrier (Simmel 1994). *Arviammiut* use their isolation to help maintain their traditions. Inuktitut is still the language of the streets with all but 175 (which include Western residents) citing Inuktitut as their first language and 460 citing Inuktitut as their only language, as of the 2021 census; numbers which have not changed a lot in 10 years, although population has increased substantially (Stats Can 2023). Subsistence hunting provides much of the meat in town, and some still sew with animal skins, albeit much more rarely than before.

Arviammiut now live in houses, imported from "the South" (i.e., Western mainstream culture) and constructed according to the cultural beliefs and practices of a different cultural group, a colonizing group with power and influence. Inuit remain marginalized in Canadian society and feel their status as a minority and stigmatized group despite the population of the hamlet being approximately 98% Inuit. Julia Christensen (2017) has contributed to studies of the Inuit housing crises and houselessness. John Kyser (2011) argues for the importance of hearing from stakeholders, particularly around cultural design considerations in Indigenous housing. His work includes several First Nation groups, but no Inuit groups. Similarly, Patrick Reid Stewart

(2015) is an Indigenous architect who interviewed other Indigenous architects around the world about how they incorporate Indigenous world views into their architecture. Andrea Proctor and Keith Chaulk (2013) have a chapter about Nunatsiavut land-use in *Reclaiming Indigenous Planning* (2013). Inuit, particularly in this corner of Nunavut, however, have not garnered as much attention. I seek to expand this work by learning from Inuit in Arviat about the specific cultural incompatibility of their homes.

Relocation

The rapid process of colonization in Arviat began in earnest around the 1950s. In the late 1950s and the 1960s, the government relocated many Inuit in the name of more easily dispensing aid and medical care in the face of a famine and a tuberculosis outbreak, although the motives the government claims should not obscure the violence and abuses of this relocation. The Royal Canadian Mounted Police (RCMP) settled *Arviammiut*, the people of Arviat, many by force, into the hamlet only in the last half-century. As resources built up, more and more also chose to remain permanently in Arviat. Before that, a nomadic way of life with ingenious and creative survival-based technology provided the basis of Inuit identity. They lived in *igluit*, snow houses, and *tupik*, caribou-skin tents, depending on the season. These structures developed independently from those of other Indigenous groups in Canada. Putting anything on the inside walls of an *iglu* would threaten its long-term structural stability. Priests encouraged Inuit in the area to put crosses up in their tents, but other than that there was little culture of display (for more on *iglus*, see Kershaw, Scott, & Welch 1996; Lee & Rienholdt 2003).

In the late 1950s, the caribou herd migrated and the *Ahiarmiut* were faced with a government-defined famine. This scourge affected the *Padlirmiut* as well, but not to as great a degree. The government decided that the best way to "take care of" the suffering Inuit (Thomas & Thompson 1972) and to provide them health and educational services, was to sedimentize them (Dawson 2003; Thomas & Thompson 1972; Williamson 1974). There is some debate about the degree of famine, given that some women report that there was plenty of food at that time, and can point to where their belongings were bulldozed, along with the meat they were drying (Kuksuk, p.c. 2021).

Colonial governmental practices walled-in *Arviammiut*, into a symbolically *Qablunaaq* built environment. Once the authorities rounded up the nomadic Inuit forcing them to live "off the land" in the newly created town thatpersists today, they introduced Inuit to permanent structures (Dawson 2003; Marshall 2006). This ended the period that Damas (1988) calls the "contact-traditional horizon" when Inuit lived rather autonomously from others. The Inuit of the area, now *Arviammiut*, began living in foreign structures and have lived in them for roughly 50 years. At first this took the form of "matchbox houses" made of plywood, with no electricity or running water. Houses as small as 240 square feet accommodated whole families (Tester 2017). These homes created unsanitary conditions along with other issues such as lack of access to food. The famous "famine" may be as much a reflection of these issues as any other. By the mid-1960s, prefabricated homes began to replace matchbox houses, improving several aspects of the living environment. Mark Kalluak, an Elder from Arviat, was a key component of the push for better housing in the 1960s and 1970s (Tester 2017). Figures A.3 and A.4 depict the contemporary community as it was in the 2010s.

Today, the binary construction of "South" and "North" pervades. Involved groups, to varying degrees, particularly emphasize this division, considering themselves to be arrayed in a binary fashion across the North/South divide, which quite often stands for the Inuk/*Qablunaaq* divide. The danger arises when these binaries are accepted at face value when, in fact, all parties have both "Northern" and "Southern" interests.

The RCMP, missionaries (both Catholic and Protestant), and the Canadian Federal Government are part of a large social construction of the governmental institutions of the "South" in Arviat. Another "Southern" group is the Hudson's Bay Company, precursor of today's "Northern," a general store. These groups all had some role in the introduction of housing to Inuit. Due to their common goals and close working relationship (ignoring their

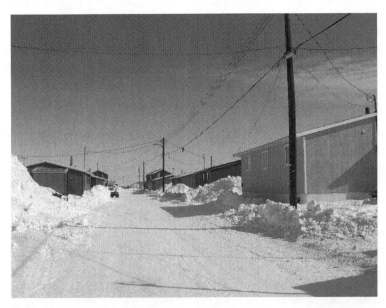

Figure A.3   Housing in Arviat Today.

Figure A.4 A House in Arviat Today.

motivations), one could argue that the RCMP, missionaries, and the Canadian federal government could often all be lumped together from the perspective and experience of Inuit. Much of the work carried out in the North was done by an amalgamation of these groups in one form or another, either formally or informally. More importantly, *Arviammiut* often lump these groups together, especially when considering the recent past. The Hudson's Bay Company had entirely different interests and a widely differing definition of the situation from the others from the "South." However, when it benefitted it, the company would also act in conjunction with other Southern groups.

Missionaries were among the first to use permanent structures as displays of power and institutional "truth," much like the Hudson's Bay Company's trading post walls proclaimed a "truth" about capital, trade, and the abstract worth of goods. The health center and other buildings followed with the cooperation and help of the church, often run by missionaries. These buildings were impressive centers of power which doled out health services, education, and other kinds of help. Buildings clearly and quickly conveyed the material resources of the church. For the missionaries, these buildings were key in establishing themselves as a dominant institution.

The Canadian government is responsible, however, for deciding on the form of permanent housing (today mostly prefabricated houses) that would be shipped to Arviat. It also put in place much of the material infrastructure existing today, either directly or indirectly. This is in addition, of course, to other travesties that accompany colonization, such as assigning identifying numbers, rather than names. These numbers were stamped on dog tag-like identification tags (*ujamiit*) which Inuit could either wear around their necks or sew onto their clothing.

The Hudson's Bay Company was also among the first to set up permanent structures, especially in areas outside of the communities where they had trading posts. For white traders, these structures meant safety from the elements, separation from the Inuit as interactions with Inuit were mediated by the traders' ability to go indoors and away from them, and a way to store and protect goods—especially from theft. This must have seemed very odd to Inuit at that time, who did not work within an economy where goods could be hoarded by one person or group with no expectation of sharing.

At the time of the introduction of Southern structures, there were the *Ahiarmiut* and the *Padlirmiut* in the area. *Padlirmiut* were originally from about 100 to 150 miles west of Arviat, while *Ahiarmiut* were from the area around Ennadai Lake. Many people in Arviat now call themselves *Tahiuyamiut*. Although the government treated them as one group, they were, and still are, two distinct groups from the perspective of the Inuit, despite living together in one community and intermarrying. Anthropologists play up this division extensively. In reality, the internal boundaries, while still present, are weakening alongside a heightened awareness of the external boundaries.

The Government of Nunavut, the territorial government, is also a contemporary player. Under this umbrella are several relevant social groups alternately dedicated to preserving "traditional" culture, promoting Inuktitut, and bringing Nunavut up to par (however problematically they may define that) with the rest of Canada. The most relevant branch of the territorial government is the Nunavut Housing Corporation, which battles endlessly the Northern housing crisis of overcrowding. Homelessness, in its various guises, has been a consistent problem in colonial settings in the North (Christensen 2017). In addition, a report from Arviat showed that in 2006, 25% of dwellings needed "major repair" (Aarluk Consulting Inc. 2011). This has only increased.

Most governmental institutions have been taken over either by local *Arviammiut* or by the territorial Inuit government, keeping in mind that many advisors are Southern. In particular, the religious institutions, especially in their day-to-day operations, are in the hands of local laymen and volunteers. These laymen and volunteers are striving to meet the goals and ideals laid out for them by the Southern institutions.

Today, there are four churches in town; Catholic, Anglican, Glad Tidings (Pentecostal), and the Christian and Missionary Alliance (an evangelical Protestant denomination). Although health services, education, and other governmental services are no longer dispensed through the church, *Arviammiut* still feel obligated to attend the services regularly. At this point, the community does not perceive any fundamental differences among the churches, and individuals move back and forth easily, although at the time of my research the Glad Tidings Church drew the biggest crowd. There are services and singing almost every day of the week, except when these activities would compete with Bingo nights. Sundays, however, tend to be Bingo-free.

Territorial branches of the government are now also in Inuit hands. This results from 20 years of Inuit leaders' researching, resisting, and challenging the status quo. Following this resourceful and successful movement, the federal government granted Inuit self-governance in 1993 and, in 1999, Nunavut became its own territory and self-governance came into effect, with ongoing financial aid from the Canadian government. While some institutional structures necessarily bureaucratically mirror those in the South, Nunavut prides itself in doing several things differently, such as having a non-partisan political structure. One of these differences is a dedication to a decentralized government (Hicks & White 2005). In this way, each hamlet hosts some branch of the territorial government and the jobs and revenue can be shared by all. While they have been successful in many ways, often the top jobs end up seated in Iqaluit, the capital, and communicate from a distance with the rest of the department. In addition, this means a great deal of traveling for meetings which is costly, both financially and environmentally. Being a larger community in the territory, Arviat has retained the headquarters of the Nunavut Housing Corporation, Nunavut Arctic College (though many top administrators are located elsewhere), and the Curriculum and School Services division of the Department of Education.

Larger buildings (relative to homes) represent various levels of government in the community. The government has an interest in defining those buildings as centers of power and maintaining them. These include the school, hamlet office, health center, post office, and the "Blue Building," which houses the Department of Education and the Nunavut Housing Corporation. Within these buildings, some families find legitimacy as experts, while those outside the buildings often do not have their local knowledge legitimated. The Education Department, for example, hires elders to advise. One of these, a "young elder" in his early 50s at the time of this work, has an office, which provides him the clout to practice Inuitness in a more Southern interior context. The post office is also a particularly interesting space where the structure and decoration of the walls mimic the Southern post office, though it is now located in a corner of the Northern Store. One can walk off the ice road in the Arctic tundra into a space which could be a post office anywhere in Canada.

While many would advocate studying the institutions, I work to upend power structures that silence grassroots-level *Arviammiut*. I privilege, instead, their experiences of spaces, houses, and institutions and regard them as experts in their own lives. They are the ones negotiating a new built environment. In this sense, I take up the urging of Dorries et al. (2019), who examine the urban and non-urban in their edited volume about another Indigenous group, prairie First Nations, to politicize how urban spaces are produced—and further, I argue that by attending to how walls are *used* reveals resistance, resilience, and the messiness of contested spaces and how they are instantiated in the built environment.

Although there are no nomadic Inuit remaining in this area, *Arviammiut* still value traditional *iglu*-building and hunting skills and incorporate them into the everyday fabric of the community through conversation, consumption of traditional foods, and participation in these activities. These elements are deeply woven into the *Arviammiut* Inuit identity, an identity which *Arviammiut* strive to reinforce through the engagements they have with their built environment. Much of this performance of identity involves the struggle for authenticity within *Qablunaaq* walls and spaces.Outline

Permanent housing, and thus permanent walls, has only been introduced to Inuit people of Arviat (*Arviammiut*), in the far North of Canada, within the 50 years prior to this study. The first public houses were "matchbox houses" with no running water or power and a honey bucket for a toilet. Today most of the houses are prefabricated houses modeled on the ideals of the Canadian South with its emphasis on the nuclear family. This book examines how *Arviammiut* relate to their walls and use their walls to express identity, as a locus for collective memory, for storage, and for privacy. I attend to changing conceptions of public and private, space and place, symbolically connected interior spaces, and how the divisions of rooms have affected the transmission of family as well as cultural and gendered knowledge. Walls also mediate their experience of "outside," "nature," and the weather.

Walls have brought many cultural changes. Inuit, however, have agency and exercise that agency in how they give meaning to walls, how they develop a relationship with those walls, and how they use their walls. For example, the display of old photographs taken by early explorers, ripped from the books or even photocopied, is a way that Inuit reclaim their past. In addition, by prioritizing the display of family photographs over the display of art, they are expressing their cultural values and personally claiming a stake in the community. Living within the walls, apart from the locus of traditional knowledge, impacts how Inuit not only perform identity-work, but also relate to their own sense of ethnicity, creating an awareness of knowledge and identity as interlinked. While agency was once spread through human and non-human components, colonization has disrupted this. Inuit, however, work through their agency within their built environment to restore the sacredness of the relationship between place, non-humans, and humans (Watts 2013).

I argue that walls are boundary objects, cultural objects, and technical objects. I have organized this book into three parts, prefaced by a chapter on the theory and sociological relevance of walls, explaining walls as various kinds of objects. This initial chapter will be of more interest to those who wish to look at their own walls in a new way, to examine power relations in the built environment, or those who wish to deepen their understanding of sociological aspects of space and place.

Each of the three parts thereafter establishes in a brief introduction how walls function as a certain kind of object, followed by two empirical chapters, which demonstrate the usefulness of that theoretical approach. These can be read without the theory-laden first chapter. The first part introduces walls as boundary objects, objects through which a group or groups negotiate a relationship with another group or groups. The first chapter in this part, chapter 2 of the book, discusses a geography of knowledge. In addition, this chapter lays out the class structure in Arviat and familiarizes the reader with the layout of the community. Inuit knowledge is deeply tied into the land, while Western or *Qablunaaq* (Southern) knowledge is tied into the hamlet. *Arviammiut* link their knowledge and identity closely. By living within Southern walls, walled-in culturally, Inuit, as individuals, as families, and as communities, must negotiate their identities and the meaning of traditional and Western knowledge in creative and resourceful ways. The next chapter addresses the challenges walls present to traditional ways of transmitting family knowledge. Children are no longer a captive audience. This has gendered implications. Where "woman's work" was honored and given space inside, and "men's work" happened outside in front of the house, the unintended consequence of the spatial arrangement is that women's work is not being passed on to the daughters in the same way men's work is being passed on to the sons. Of course, like anywhere in the world, there is heterogeneity in the degree to which this happens.

The next part introduces walls as cultural objects. The first empirical chapter, chapter 4, examines how Inuit apply the value of interpersonal relationships through the use of their walls. *Arviammiut* predominantly display family photographs on their walls, prioritizing these over Western concepts of art, for example. This is one way in which Inuit bring their culture inside the walls and appropriate the walls for their own cultural uses and displays. This helps to locate the individual within the family, and the family within the community. Small gifts displayed on the walls also help to create symbolically connected interior spaces, achieving what I call *spatial fusion*, which further reinforces interpersonal relationships as a dominant Inuit value. Culture perseveres through agentic use of the walls. The second empirical chapter in this part discusses how Inuit resist within *Qablunaaq* spaces through food consumption practices. I trace the different treatment of traditional foods and store-bought *Qablunaaq* foods and the role of resistance in each case.

The final part introduces walls as technological objects. Here, I introduce the concepts of passive and active engagements to study both how walls impact Inuit culture as well as how Inuit agentically resist and transform inside spaces. The first chapter of this part, chapter 6, focuses on a passive engagement; changing notions of public and private. I discuss the ways in which walls influenced these notions, I also touch on issues of overcrowding and how that conflicts with the expectations houses have imposed on Inuit. The next chapter of this part examines the use of the walls as storage, moving from items that are stored long-term, such as out-of-date certificates, to items that are used daily, such as phone numbers or keys. These uses of the wall display pride in and a fostering of the Inuit values of being resourceful, creative, and adaptable. Something becomes beautiful here because it demonstrates these Inuit values.

In all, I hope to honor participants by clearly communicating the role of power in the built environment of their houses, and giving voice to their oppressed experiences, while at the same time celebrating their agency, resilience, and strength. I know that I cannot do justice to their generosity of spirit and kindness as they encouraged me throughout this process.

NOTES

1. All names are pseudonyms unless otherwise stated.

2. For a more complete discussion on transitioning from friend to researcher and the role of reflexivity, see van den Scott (2018).

3. Statistics Canada (2007) puts the population at 2,060 in 2006, while the territorial government web page estimates the population at roughly 2,500. Statistics Canada (2023) listed the population count from the 2021 census as 2,864.

4. I offer here a very brief outline of colonial history to provide the context for the life stories of participants. For more historical information, see Bennett and Rowley (Eds.) (2004), Damas (2004), Eber (1975), and Tester and Kulchyski (1994).

Chapter 1

A Sociology of Walls

Walls are one of the most mundane parts of the landscapes that shape our lives. They intrude in utterly profound ways. In the negotiation of everyday life, being virtually invisible in our minds, walls have a dramatic impact. Walls construct an immediate sense of place and define our relationship to others. Picture yourself in a coffee shop. You know immediately by looking at the walls around you if you are in a locally owned, quirky coffee shop or a corporate chain. Now imagine yourself in an office. The walls communicate the formality of an office space. Say, you imagine yourself in a doctor's office. You are stuck in the waiting room, while the doctor has a series of examination rooms, private offices, access behind the receptionist's desk and office area, and perhaps a coffee break room; it is clear that she has more power than you do in that space. Not only that, the walls guide how you are able to access the doctor through her main waiting room and then the waiting, still separated by walls, in her examination room. Walls are fundamental to the shaping of social, spatial, and symbolic dimensions of our lives.

Many areas of the social sciences and humanities have touched on walls, such as space and place, built environments, urban sociology, and work on the meanings and uses of the home. There exists, however, no comprehensive theory of walls. I pull from empirical and theoretical work across the social sciences and humanities to explore the various meanings of walls and create a theoretical framework through which we can take into account the walls in our lives, and our positions with relation to those walls. I view this work from a symbolic interactionist perspective. That is, I am interested in cocreated meanings and how we socially construct the meanings, uses, and symbolism of walls. Cultural studies, as well as science and technology studies, offer theoretical leverage on the materiality of walls. Walls distribute power, define roles, reflect culture, and so we can use these different approaches to examine them empirically.

In addition, theorizing walls helps to explain what is going on in my field site, Arviat, an Inuit hamlet in Nunavut, Canada. Over my time in Arviat, it became obvious to me that the impact of walls is particularly salient. This venue is much more rewarding for developing sociological theory than is the case with a field site where people have found peace with their walls and take them for granted. The aggressively colonized population of Arviat was only recently relocated and "walled-in" and are now coming to terms with their new homes and built environment. This housing, like most Indigenous housing in Canada, is inadequately designed and often does not take cultural design into consideration (Kyser 2011). Inuit in Arviat have been in their permanent homes since the early 1960s. While the physical reality of walls creates barriers, their social reality, by contrast, creates bridges across which people create and reify private and collective meanings. As you get into the meat of this book, you will see that my empirical site of Arviat has an extreme relationship with walls. For now, let's talk theory. I pay attention to walls because of their mundaneness set in juxtaposition with the profoundness of their impact and impingement on daily life. So, let's theorize walls!

SPACE AND POWER

Understanding space and place is crucial in studying the roles of walls in the built environment. Walls are located in space and divide space. They create physical boundaries that mirror social boundaries. Border walls are an obvious example of this, but so are the walls of our homes. Who is inside which houses delineates the social boundaries of families. Any theory of walls must, therefore, begin with a grounding in space and place that leads to a discussion of *boundary work*. Boundary work describes the work people do to define and reinforce social groupings and meanings around social identities (Gieryn 1983).

Contemporary foci of space and place studies engage with ideas around power and recursiveness. So, taking a space-based approach, our conversation about walls and the built environment begins with a discussion of the recursiveness of space and place; the ebb and flow of how we both shape and are shaped by space and place. We already know that in urban sociology, place and power dominate the conversation. I begin inside and move outward, from the built environment of the home to the community, and to the boundaries between community and the land itself, be it countryside, forest, or tundra. In the case of Arviat, walls interrupt life-as-it-was and separate Inuit from the tundra, which contributes to the social meaning of their walls.

In studying the built environment, urban sociologists have taken the "built" part of the built environment quite literally. It is only in contrast to the built environment that nature is considered within the context of the social construction of nature. Gary Alan Fine's (1998) work on how mushroom collectors define and think about the outdoors and nature makes it clear that we consider nature and urban settings in juxtaposition with each other. Rurality still consists of built forms, such as small towns, and the contrasts they present with the city. There have been many dichotomies developed to investigate these contrasts, such as Ferdinand Tönnies' *gemeinshaft* and *gesellschaft* ([1957] 1964), or Emile Durkheim's mechanical and organic solidarity. The undeveloped, or even the agriculturally developed, land surrounding both rural and urban areas exists in tension with the more traditionally conceived notion of a built environment. The land, however, offers its own problems of meaning. Land that falls outside the built environment remains undertheorized. Ultimately walls, or the lack thereof, define what is in the purview of urban or rural sociologists. Walls domesticate and create non-nature.

RECURSIVENESS AND SPACE/PLACE

The use of space can be read as expressing something about a particular society. We can talk about the meaning of how groups use space, for example, and investigate how Xhosa beer-drinking rituals spatially reflect status (McAllister 2004), or how contemporary Inuit homes are spatially an inadequate cultural "fit" (Dawson 2004) because sleeping together was (and still is for many) a spatial expression of Inuit closeness. Mauss and Beuchat (1979) note that the Inuit, pre-sedimentization, used space differently according to the season. In the winter, the space inside iglus was larger so that they could accommodate social and ritual behaviors, reflecting Inuit practices. Rapoport (1982) also stresses that meaning is transmitted through the built environment. As Bedouins became more sedimentized, their use of space became more specialized (Lawrence & Low 1990). We can "read" this as an expression of their changing culture.

In looking at space and place, however, its reciprocal nature continually presents itself. One cannot simply read spatiality and stop there. Lawrence and Low's (1990) seminal literature review of the built environment and spatial forms from an anthropological perspective draws out the interactive relationship of the built environment as "people both create, and find their behaviour influenced by [it]" (Lawrence & Low 1990, 454). Built forms both represent and reinforce social forms and patterns. Anthony Giddens (1990) calls this *structuration*, where the individual and society reciprocally shape each other, while Pierre Bourdieu (1977) stresses that the built form formalizes the role of action in the meanings and structures present in space and time. In short, place influences us, and we influence the construction of place. It is a back and forth relationship.

The built environment also represents power dynamics in each society. Look around a classroom and see how we have organized the power dynamics in that room. The students are organized into rows by virtue of the placement of desks, and the professor stands at the front of the room pontificating. Professors may work to resist and disrupt this hierarchy by putting chairs in a circle. Architecture is political! For Edward Soja (1989), while the use of space reflects human agency, the built environment also *teaches*, rather than simply expresses. Factories, for example, teach capitalist notions and discipline workers at the same time. Deyan Sudjic (2005) notes that buildings can also represent democracy; the history of buildings is political in nature and linked with power, money, and politics.

The built environment not only expresses power, it is a tool for power. Places communicate and reinforce power relations as a fundamental component of the exercise of power. Urban and non-urban spaces alike can become messy sites of colonial contestation (Dorries et al. 2019). As colonial studies scholar A. D. King states:

> in a Foucauldian sense, the socially constructed environment is not simply an unpeopled "landscape" acquiring an "imperial imprint" but becomes a disciplinary terrain, a mechanism for inducing new practices, an arena around which new discourses are created, a resource for some, a weapon for others, with which to harass, reclassify, categorize and control. (1989, 15)

Resistance, however, always exists. While dominant powers are busy organizing and controlling people, local peoples renegotiate and reinterpret their built environment. *Arviammiut* creatively and agentically bring their culture indoors, demonstrating resilience and resistance, rather than learn all that their homes are trying to teach them about how to conform to mainstream Canadian culture. Meaning, agency, and use are constantly constituted through interaction. In all cases, recursiveness plays a role.

Now that we have established that the built environment is both recursive and implicated in power relations, not only as an expression of power, but as a tool for power, let us consider how scholars have approached the built environment. We will walk together, if you will, from inside our homes to the edge of the communities we live in, pausing along the way to point out relevant elements to a theory of walls.

The Home

The spatial ecology of power and identity begins in the home. Houses not only structure behavior in the home, but also represent varying forms of power to different groups that occupy homes, such as in homes designed by a colonial power and imposed on others. There are also various experiences for different members within a household. A child's experience will not be the same as an adult's experience. The built environment sets the tone of a space, transforming it into a specific kind of place, conveying certain messages about power. Who gets the biggest bedroom? Walls define spaces, and in our use of walls, we define places.

Houses are intimately linked with identity, which is especially apparent in our living spaces. Homes are what Sherry Turkle (1995) calls *evocative objects*. They are objects that cause us to think; they provoke reflection about the self and identity. The built environment of the home embodies different metaphors for different people, based on their contextual circumstances (Harré 2002). We communicate about our social class by how we maintain and decorate our walls. We reflect our class aesthetic in the art we choose. We locate ourselves within families with the photographs we display, often curated by the women of the home. Not only do we express ourselves, but we read a lot into another person upon seeing the inside (or even the outside) of their homes for the first time.

The built environment of the home engenders norms around which we operate. Thin walls can be a challenge. The 1950s and early 1960s saw an academic interest in conceptions of privacy and the home. Elmer Johnson's study (1952) includes a story of a husband on one side of the wall asking his wife to pass the ketchup, and the wife on the other side of the wall passing ketchup to her husband as an accidental disruption of enacted privacy. This era resulted in coined terms such as *avoidance rituals* (Radcliffe-Brown 1952), the rituals we have to ignore sounds we hear through walls, and *insulation from observability* (Coser 1961), the inability for children to model behavior of their parents when their parents are not in view.

Erving Goffman (1959) argues that our social arrangements restrict the symbolic nature of the wall as a communication barrier. It is okay, for example, to yell through the house that supper is ready, overcoming the communication barrier established by the walls. He coins the phrase *conventional situational closure* (Goffman 1963) to refer to the ways in which people acknowledge the division of space as complete barriers, despite it clearly not being so. Thus, they treat the room or space as a closed space, ignoring the sounds from the other sides. If you have ever ignored a fight or a conversation, or even a flushing toilet, from the other side of the wall, you have worked to help accomplish conventional situational closure to give more privacy than there actually is. Walls, then, come in and out of play as an element of social interaction (Peña-Alves 2020). Part of the reason we may ignore sounds from a shared wall is our belief that the home "should" be a sanctuary—an idea often tied to the middle classes.

Spatial Ecology within the Home

What does home mean to you? Home may not contain a nuclear family. Home may be someplace far away, for example for refugees or students. Home may contain harmful toxins, as in some mobile homes (Ore 2011), or in the case of mold. Kusenbach and Paulson (2013) argue that home is process; it is created through our interactions, ideologies, and practices. We work toward the ideal of home.

As we socially define the inside of a house as the private sphere of homeness, privacy can come to mean "confinement, captivity and isolation," particularly for women (Goldsack 1999). Statistically speaking, the home is, in fact, more dangerous than the public realm for women. The home is not a castle; it becomes a cage (Darke 1996). If, however, the public realm is unsafe, such as it has often been for LGBTQIA2S+, then home has the opposite meaning; that of safety (Darke 1996). The ideal home functions as a theme in contemporary society, "home as haven" (Moore 1984), however the true meaning of home is variable. It depends on gender, sexuality, ethnicity, one's relation to the outside world, and age, among other factors.

Home has different meanings for the different members of a household. Family members must constantly negotiate privacy along hierarchical lines. In the Western context, we assign a function to each room; however, these functions separate family members along gender and power lines. In the use of these rooms, *time zoning* can also separate (or not) individuals (Munro & Madigan 1999). In the daytime, the common area may serve parents and children alike, while in the nighttime only parents are allowed out of their bedrooms. The ideals of privacy, domesticity, and intimacy became the organizing rationale for the design and use of domestic space in the West (Rybczynski 1986). In Western ideology today, each child "should" have their own room where they sleep, play with friends, and hang out. This expresses the informality of multi-use for children, while the adult bedroom is still quite formal and not a place to spend leisure time or entertain guests.

Gender roles are constantly negotiated in light of the organization of the home. Although traditional gender roles are being challenged, and renegotiations of the use of space in the home can neutralize some gendered constructions (Mallett 2004), oftentimes gendered activities persist. The spatial structure and use of the home aid and encourage gendered roles. The house as a home away from the stress of the world applies more to men than women, who have to find their privacy within the family through time, rather than space (Madigan & Munro 1999).

Gender also plays a role in non-Western households, as with the Kabyle home which is spatially organized around notions of "male" and "female" (Bourdieu 1979). The Herero household exists only from the male point of view and consists of matrilineal hut clusters, while for women, this larger space does not represent a "household" per se, but rather their focus is on the more limited space within the larger hut clusters, a hearth with dependent children that is one small, spatially isolated subunit of what the male understands as his household (Harpending & Pennington 1990).

A house stands conceptually oriented toward the outside and stands for both shelter and privacy. John Brinckerhoff Jackson (1994) defines "house" as a

> space or a composition of spaces and walls and doors that makes certain relationships possible and impedes others. . . . Its role was to make visible how the inside world related to the outside . . . and how the hours of working with others were distinct from the private routine of the home. (57)

Since industrialization and the modern focus on the nuclear family, house and work have become separate zones, particularly for the middle class. As the design of houses has changed around the ideology of the home, public areas of the house, such as a parlour, have disappeared (Halle 1993). Now, there is rarely a back region, which means that the household is permanently on display, therefore standards of upkeep and tidiness now apply throughout the home (Madigan & Munro 1999).

In summary, there is a cultural code of behavior as one moves through the settings of a house (Frake 1975). In theorizing households, and therefore walls, one must consider that walls encompass and create a physical setting that reifies social relations and constitutes and reproduces social institutions (Saunders & Williams 1988, 82).

Between home and community stands the doorway, full of symbolic meaning. Doors may be contentious because they are thresholds, the point where the boundary of the wall may be crossed, from inside to outside, from family to community. They become a boundary between two worlds, or, as Pierre Bourdieu (1977, 130) calls it *worlds reversed*. Every time you go through a doorway, something becomes an opposite, be it the kitchen door, which food is not allowed to cross, a school-room door, which designates learning spaces, or a bedroom door, which defines lines of privacy.

Psychologists have also become interested in doors. They have investigated the phenomenon of going into another room and forgetting what you went there for. They determined that "moving through doorways, as opposed to moving an equal distance in the same room, caused forgetting" (Tamplin et al. 2013, 1111) as doorways are key in the memory's event horizon. We see, then, how crossing a boundary or threshold creates more mental distance than the same amount of space without a symbolic break or change in meaning. In the case of doors in and out of houses, these thresholds stand between home and community.

Community: Architecture and Buildings

We have long held architects as the pinnacle of designer and creator. We glorify structures, their histories, and their stories in urban sociology. Figures such as Edmund Bacon came to represent the development of Philadelphia, for example. With the turn to materiality, however, the role of architects has become problematized. Sociologists now view architecture as enacted power (Sudjic 2005), as colonial oppression (King 1984), and as a technological object developed apart from its users. Eileen Fairhurst (1999), for example, examines the architecture of nursing homes and finds that architects' work results from their *imaginings* of what older people want and need. Thus, the architecture takes form around assumptions, along with vague, abstract knowledge and stereotypical images of declining health and impending disaster at any moment. Peter Dawson (2008) terms culturally inappropriate structures, referring specifically to housing in Arviat, as *unfriendly architecture,* while Jackson (1994) writes of the *tyranny of incomprehensible architecture.* These are some of my favorite terms because they capture the struggle among power, bureaucrats, architects, and inhabitants.

Scholars theorize about buildings that make up a community in a simlar way to how they theorize about space and place. Buildings reveal things about the society from which they emerged and can, in a sense, be read like texts. Skyscrapers, for example, are demonstrations of power (Sudjic 2005). The architecture of the Hopi reflects the importance of repetition (Jackson 1994), and the Berber house echoes opposing notions of male and female (Bourdieu 1979). Buildings symbolize. They direct and stabilize social life, establishing and preserving behavior patterns (Gieryn 2002). They transform social meaning (Yaneva 2008). Buildings, however, also engage us in reciprocal, reflexive relationships. One can learn much by simply looking at a building; but once built, buildings also become agents of their own. We structure them and they structure us, back and forth.

Empirical studies focus on this recursive relationship. Thomas Gieryn's (2002) study follows the design, construction, and ultimate use of an academic research facility. He observes how, once built, the structure influenced the goals and plans of those using the space. The building stabilized social action. But he also notes how buildings, once constructed, conceal both what could have alternately been constructed and the politics and interests that were part of their design. The high cost of reconstruction and reimagining forces users to fall into technological somnambulism as they accept and begin to take for granted the structures around them. Buildings also, however, evoke narratives, often ones that were not intended. A. D. King (1984) has studied the history of the bungalow and finds that the built form connects to everything from culture, to political economy, to global urbanization. He argues for a multilayered, multidisciplinary approach to studying the built form. Brindley (1999) also points to power dimensions in his discussion of modern housing and how this style of architecture is used to socially exclude the poor. We see similar work in Dorries et al.'s (2019) edited work on Indigenous First Nations relations within and without the built form of the city.

Not all cultural or ethnic groups are living in architecture they developed, and thus this unfriendly architecture does not reflect their social or moral worlds, as in the case of Inuit. While there has been work done by architects to design culturally appropriate housing for some Indigenous groups (Stewart 2015), Inuit live within this unfriendly architecture. They will, inevitably, be affected by this architecture. Inhabitants of this architecture must, in turn, react to the mismatch of space and social practices and find ways to adapt the structures to their needs and social expressions.

Places, particularly conceptual places such as towns or boroughs, develop what Alkon and Traugot (2008) call *place narratives,* which allow people to conceptualize the meaning of place broadly. Using these narratives, people draw on whatever notions of types of places they have in their cultural toolkit. Cultural boundaries exist, and the physical environment reflects (and sometimes informs) these boundaries. Once established, people perform boundary work to maintain these social and cultural boundaries. Thomas Gieryn (1983, 2008) develops the concept of *settled* and *unsettled boundaries,* following Ann Swidler's (1986) lead of settled and unsettled times, to further the consideration of the places where realms of knowledge and identity meet at cultural boundaries. Fortin's (2022) work on *settler cities* resonates with this thinking. While those boundaries are not always physical ones, often they are.

Buildings and walls become *boundary objects* (Star & Griesemer 1989) through which cultural norms, values, or beliefs are negotiated, particularly when lived in or used by a knowledge community different from that which produced them. Because walls shape social practices (Gieryn 2008), they are implicated in this case study when Inuit confront daily, in the form of their built environment, a physical divide from their traditional lands, and a built form which imposes a Euro-Canadian culture and knowledge system upon them. The walls continue to face them every day as physical manifestations of cultural boundaries. Typically, however, the boundary work is performed at the design stage, and once a building is built, its form will settle the boundaries through its shaping of social practices.

The boundaries that buildings set include those between residents and outsiders to the community. That is, buildings, understood as a collective representation of culture, power, or knowledge systems, may be grouped together so as to imply the idea of a spatial community based on this built environment. Those experiencing homelessness will feel a lack of legitimacy among the buildings of a community or city. The built environment establishes their status as outsiders. For those displaced from the land into a community, such as a relocated Indigenous community, the town or community into which they are moved is the secondary experience. Thus, the town becomes *contra* the land in the place narratives of groups displaced from traditional lands, particularly those who did not previously live within permanent structures.

Architecture, then, as part of the built environment, creates a normative landscape (Cresswell 1996). These terrains can be disciplinary in nature. Think of the hostility architecture projects toward those experiencing homelessness (Rosenberger 2020; Starolis 2020). Benches have arms placed such that one cannot easily lie down, for example. Similarly, the architecture of buildings can create new practices or discourses. For some the built environment is a resource, for others a weapon that recategorizes people and groups and works to control them (King 1989; Starolis 2020).

To illustrate this, I digress for a moment to talk about walls in my field site. Permanent walls brought accelerated cultural change to the Inuit through imposition of a crash program of housing aimed to alter their behavior within a Euro-Canadian normative landscape (Thomas & Thompson 1972) leading to a culture crash. The Inuit bore many hardships and changes, but they retained many traditional cultural traits, such as gender roles. While struggling with inadequate housing and extreme overcrowding, Inuit "spatially graft their unique activities and cultural values onto the Euro-Canadian-style houses" (Gareau & Dawson 2004, 1). Field workers, myself included, have observed activities such as the butchering of animals in bathtubs or on kitchen floors. As Gieryn (2000) suggests, places are continuously made through interactions. By engaging in out-of-place activities, Inuit resist the normative architecture to perform Inuit identity, Inuitness, to themselves, each other, and the built environment of the community they occupy.

Walls are fundamental in establishing norms within the home, the creation of a built environment, and expressing social boundaries. By developing a sociology of walls to conceptualize various elements of the built environment, we can see boundaries and power relations, which we might not otherwise. We do more than simply read our built environment, we understand it as recursive. We move through our worlds attentive to the ways in which we succumb to and dominate over the ways we have boxed up space. Walls are a key component of the landscape of everyday lived experiences.

THEORIZING WALLS

One's walls surround one; protect one; specify where one is, and act as tools with which one defines who one is. The nature of walls, and our relationship with them, impacts us in myriad almost unfathomable ways, shaping the dance of our lives. Can one even accurately imagine a life without walls? I expand, from this case study and the dribs and drabs of attention to walls across disciplines, to an overall theory of a sociology of walls, which provides an important lens to many areas of sociological interest, particularly around identity, identity performance, and boundary work.

Walls construct our sense of place, define our relationship with nature and the outdoors, and guide our movements and interactions. Walls impede the flow of information while facilitating new kinds of ways of knowing and being, including how we engage with notions of public and private—especially relevant now in the age of the internet and television's transgressing previous conceptions of space and privacy. Walls are absolutely fundamental to the shaping of social, spatial, and symbolic dimensions of our lives. One may think of many colonized groups as having been *walled-in* by a colonizing force.

I argue that keeping walls in mind as technological objects (Bijker 1997), cultural objects (Griswold 2008), and boundary objects (Star & Griesemer 1989), as well as boundaries, helps one to conceptualize the built environment and its relationship to the surrounding land, to map the landscape of power at the point where it intersects most intensely with everyday life. Without walls, the built environment does not extend beyond the symbolic constellations of the land and nature. Walls intercede in life in the most mundane and profound ways possible.

Walls as Mundane Technological Objects

In 1948, Siegfried Giedion issued a call to historians to take up the study of anonymous history. He saw in the objects all around us artifacts which, due to their banality, are usually overlooked, a grievous error as this neglect results in much of history's eluding us. He writes:

> We shall deal here with humble things, things not usually granted earnest consideration, or at least not valued for their historical import. . . . In their aggregate, the humble objects of which we shall speak have shaken our mode

of living to its very roots. Modest things of daily life, they accumulate into forces acting upon whoever moves within the orbit of our civilization. ([1948] 1969, 3)

These "humble" objects of banality are a special kind of technology, *mundane technology*. While we may easily understand mundane technologies as having developed and changed over time, few stop to consider them as inventions in the first place. They lack the obvious innovative flair of the wheel, the lightbulb, or the automobile. They are, however, forms of technology so deeply rooted in our daily lives that they must be looked upon as obvious objects of study, rather than as mundane artifacts of little notice. Permanent walls slip in under the radar both theoretically and empirically.

Walls carve up space, creating a housing system (Marshall 2006). As meaning is given to these *spaces*, they become *places*. Several studies acknowledge the built environment, and thus walls, as technologies of control (Foucault 1977; Lawrence & Low 1990; Singh 2009). New users acquire knowledge and understanding of walls, ranging from their basic properties (i.e., walls are opaque and hard) to their complexities (i.e., walls contain interior space that houses electrical wires, insulation, pipes that can burst if the temperature is not regulated, and space that can fill with mold if there is water damage).

Sandra Marshall (2006) notes that Inuit who were newly introduced to houses are not limited by the same constellation of meaning as the architects. Inuit receive no training concerning their new housing[1] and are using their homes in surprising ways. Buildings, and thus walls, give context to social practices (Gieryn 2002). As the walls define space and establish a sense of place, *Arviammiut* adhere to many practices that Westerners might expect, while spurning others, establishing their own relationship with the walls, shaping their own practices and place-narratives. The back splash of a kitchen counter, for example, provides a convenient place for the storage of knives, not something I have ever seen Martha Stewart recommend.

Certain secondary adjustments may be employed by colonized groups, such as Inuit, as new users learn to negotiate a foreign system. For example, the placement of walls within the house may construct a certain room as a "bedroom," but users may reconstruct that space as a sewing room; however, a wall-defined washroom is always a washroom.

In short, walls constitute technological artifacts and have technological systems. The material culture of walls, that is the physically obdurate nature of walls combined with their existence as cultural residue, shapes our everyday lives in profound ways. Invisible technologies, as Mike Michael (2000) terms them, can have more ramifications in our daily lives than epochal technologies.

Mundane technology carries with it moral implications and is, therefore, important to study (Latour 1992). James Garvey (2007), for example, describes how the construction of low bridges on Long Island (inadvertently or not) impedes the passage of buses, thereby blocking access to Jones Beach for the poor. Walls are particularly important as a mundane technology that is almost always overlooked as it spreads material culture and reflects and enforces symbolic and power relations.

Arnold and DeWald (2011) maintain that colonizing regimes have less control over mundane technology than over epochal technology, and although this technology is still inflected with moral prescription, a study of everyday technologies exposes the researcher to a user-based, person-oriented level of analysis (Arnold & DeWald 2012, 1). One must study use. Mundane technologies in non-Western contexts, in particular, must be studied in that local context, on the ground. To study walls, one must be *with* the people, within and without their walls. This aligns with indigenous approaches to research.

The key, however, to theorizing and studying any technology, mundane or otherwise, in a non-Western context, is understanding that there is a pre-existing culture that will interact with the incoming technologies, ideas, and practices. While there are some ways in which a new technology will be deterministic, there are also ways in which local agency and preexisting cultures will determine use and meaning, its *technological frame* (Bijker 1997).

In this study, the issue of reflexivity emerged inductively as particularly salient in the relationship of Inuit to the mundane technology of their exogenous walls. Mundane technology does shape everyday lives and does carry moral prescriptions, but people also exercise agency. The literature has long recognized that technology is both constraining and enabling. Attention to reflexivity, however, is eclipsed in literature dealing with non-Western, and particularly colonized, locales. The attention the space and place literature devotes to recursiveness can benefit us here. Inuit are in the process of negotiating their relationship with walls; a social process, a back and forth process.

Interpretive flexibility (Bijker 1993) constitutes a key tool in arriving at a sociology of walls as technological artifacts. Various relevant social groups negotiate shared meaning or meanings for the technological artifact through use (Bijker 1997). While that meaning is negotiated, there is a great deal of flexibility in possible interpretations that may become dominant interpretations. When a technology develops its technological frame, the set of congealed meanings, uses, practices, and norms surrounding a technological object, it achieves closure, but not before previously existing schema, or ways of thinking, influence the technological frame.

I introduce here two different kinds of engagement between the social and the technical by focusing on technology's content and use; namely, *passive engagements* and *active engagements*. These terms are consciously anthropocentric. Although both passive and active engagements are operating at all times, one process might be more salient at any particular given moment. These engagements do not impose a dominant cultural model. They allow for a given society to "adopt the mode for which it has the cultural resources" (Taylor 1999, 164). In addition, this model accounts for the distribution of agency among human and non-human elements of our social world (Watts 2013). By conceptualizing passive and active engagements, not only can we investigate the technological frame in the full glory of its relative firmness and fluidity, but we can dig right into the reflexive process, sorting the sand from the waves while still viewing them as part of one social process.

Passive engagements *(1) are those in which individuals, at the micro level, and societies, at the macro level, are affected by the technology*; *(2) include unintended consequences*; and *(3) have homogenizing effects.* People are not unaware of passive engagements, or how technology has intruded into and changed their lives. They often raise concerns in reaction to the homogenizing effects of passive engagements. Rather than implying a technological determinism, this interaction illustrates the negotiation between passive and active engagements.

Active engagements *(1) involve some agentic movement or work on the part of the human component to engage with the technology*, either as an individual or a group, and can occur *(2) either consciously or unconsciously*; and *(3) entail diversifying effects.* When a new technological artifact is introduced, the preexisting cultural institutions combine with novel agency and innovative engagements with the object, producing a locally specific, socially constructed use of the technology. At the outset, there are a number of ways in which the object might be used—there is no innate meaning. Which of those uses will surface depends on the schema of the preexisting culture and its combination with this new technology. The concepts of passive and active engagements contribute to the understanding of technologies and ideologies, beyond walls (c.f. van den Scott and van den Scott 2019)

I will elaborate on passive and active engagements in the section on walls as technological objects. For now, let's move on to walls as cultural objects.

Walls as Cultural Objects

Walls constitute cultural objects. Wendy Griswold defines cultural objects as "shared significance embodied in form" (1987). Individuals and groups produce meaning for the object through interaction. The meaning that an object takes on is both an effect of the receivers of the cultural object but also has an impact on the social world. Walls, as with other material cultural objects, gain meaning and thus power from people's building a way of life around them, and yet they also have a cultural biography attached to them as a commodity produced and marketed in certain ways (Kopytoff 1986).

Different individuals and groups may not all share the same meaning of walls. As with all cultural objects, they are polysemic in nature (Schudson 2002). We saw above how walls can mean safety for some and danger for others, as an extreme example. Jackson (1994) exposes how the middle class defines space within their home walls very differently from some working-class groups who have multiple vernacular uses for their home spaces, interpreting the walls as creating space resources for them.

Just as school walls, office walls, and home walls have different meanings, so do prison walls, even among the inmates they house. Harré (2002) explicitly argues that walls are socially meaningful, using prison walls as an example. He points out that their meaning depends on the storyline of the prisoner. For those who are unjustly in jail, the walls are barriers to the outside, preventing them from leaving. For those who have become institutionalized, the walls create a place of refuge, holding back the outside world. Prison guards would also have their own meanings for prison walls. Thus, power is central to the spatial ecology within a living space, be it home or prison, and the meanings attached to structures influence how individuals and groups relate to the spaces which they move through in their daily lives.

The breaches in walls, called doors or windows, are part of the system of the wall. Doors and windows allow for movement within and outside of walled-in spaces. They allow for breaches in visibility and have their own etiquette and cultural meaning. Doors and windows are, then, both part of walls and not part of walls, and as such are important to consider how they impinge on the constraints of walls. Many cultures have superstitions around leaving by the same door one has entered, entering a new house for the first time through the front door (the back door will bring bad luck), or always stepping across a threshold with a particular foot (usually the right foot). There are also norms around the breaching of walls, such as the front door's being reserved for strangers, while friends understand through convention to come to the back door. Servants used to have their own side door.

Windows have their own cultural norms in how and when people attend to what they can see through them or not, the visual equivalent of accomplishing privacy. Windows provide a visual breach in a residence's private space. Most of the time, people try not to stare into others' windows. At the same time, they are aware that if their blinds or curtains are open, they should try to avoid inadvertently displaying private behavior, such as walking around nude. In 2009, a man in Virginia was convicted of indecent exposure for being naked at home in front of his picture window. He made the important point, however, that this result was gendered in that there might have been a different result had it been a woman inside and had he been looking in (Associated Press 2009).

Most observations of windows come from anthropologists studying non-Western cultures. When conducting an interview in West Africa among the Yoruba, Raymond Prince (1964) notes that some "old crones" kept chiming in through the window during his interview with other elders to add their opinion or to straighten out information. Other anthropologists have noted cultural proclivities toward windows that differ from Western ideas, such as the Dogon in West Africa who, in the 1980s, did not have windows in their houses and understood that as something white people do (Parin et al. 1986). Some groups, such as the Cherokee, express gratitude for technologies that allow for more windows (French & Hornbuckle 1981). For the Semai, a cultural group in Southeast Asia, closed windows in the morning indicated something was wrong and induced concern (Robarcheck 1978). Anthropologists also report local children and even adults staring through their windows in blatant curiosity (Dennis 1940; Strong 1981; Th Baigent 2004), reinforcing the idea that the othering of a stranger allows for norms to be breached.

Walls structure and are structured by preexisting social conditions. As such they impose certain behaviors upon us. However, we also have agency, which manifests in three ways. First, the intersection of so many multilayered structures creates unpredictable opportunities for creativity and changes in existing structures, and thus reproduction of meaning and behavior is not automatic (Sewell 1992). Second, walls are evocative objects that are used for meaning-making (Turkle 1995). We perform for and with our walls. Third, we construct strategies of action (Swidler 1986), particularly in unsettled times or when automatic cognition fails and we switch to a deliberative mode of thinking.

Identities and Sociology of the Home

Let's apply this thinking to identity, beginning with loss of identity and moving into expression of identity through the home.

Many groups experience *identity foreclosure*. Wives lose their husbands and become widows, the situation for which the term was first coined (van den Hoonaard, D. 1997). Groups become displaced. Migration exists as a global phenomenon. Immigration places individuals and groups into new landscapes of power with walls, which not only symbolize transitions but also impede or facilitate access to familiar ways of knowing and being. By extending studies of architecture, and space and power, and spending time with people within and without their walls, we learn about strategies that these individuals and groups develop to cope with various forms of identity foreclosure. For example, *Arviammiut* work to reclaim identity and reappropriate ownership of their images and traditional selves by photocopying or removing pages from older salvage anthropology textbooks, pages with photographs, and displaying them on their walls. This is one strategic approach to identity work in the face of identity foreclosure.

Walls structure beliefs and behavior around identity. The walls of a school foster comparison and competitiveness (Riesman 1950). Notions of the Great Wall of China were integrated into Chinese cognitive models of the cosmos and the development of "a medieval Chinese sense of identity" (Tackett 2008). As cultural objects that are also built forms, walls create a *normative landscape* or a *normative order* (Cresswell 1996), stabilizing and giving durability to normative ways of understanding the self and locating the self in a broader context.

Walls produce norms around attention and inattention and have meaning for those within and without. People use walls in their homes to express themselves. The most notable scholarly example is David Halle's (1993) study on art and the meaning art has for various New York City dwellers. He analyzes the shift from portraiture to family photographs in terms of the macro-processes at play, linking this shift to the idealization of the nuclear family. Families now have to *see* themselves "doing" family (Finch 2007); "doing" family has to be seen to be done (Dermott & Seymour 2011). Halle (1993) also discusses the meaning for residents of the increase in the popularity of artwork of de-populated landscapes, as well as abstract art and "primitive art." In sum, he argues that the materiality of the home has been drastically overlooked as sociologists search for patterns of meaning in everyday life. The use of walls for display involves meaning-making. When decorating one's walls, one invests that action with meaning, understanding it to be a way to express identity, be that the identity of an individual, family, ethnic group, and so on. By putting certain things on the walls, one aligns oneself with moral codes, beliefs, and norms. We may study the home as a symbol of the self. Objects on the walls become mnemonic devices, serving to construct, shape, manipulate, recall, or destroy memory (Kwint 1999; Kwint et al. 1999; Morton 2007). We interact with the things we live with in an ongoing negotiation of meaning.

The things we live with and the things we display are not only mnemonic devices, the residue of social life, and meaningful, but they are also linked to both the shaping and expressions of the self (Chapman 1999; Chevalier 1999; Clarke 2002; Finch 2007; Miller 2001). Aesthetics, which are primarily social rather than individual (Clarke 2002), help to determine what we choose to display. "Homes and possessions are seen here as active agents in the construction of taste and social relations" (Clarke 2002:131) that shape how we display objects as expressions of ourselves.

Many adopt a dramaturgical approach to study the things we live with. Sophie Chevalier (1999) extends Goffman's presentation of the self, emphasizing a "presentation of self through objects." She continues on arguing that objects link us to other individuals; they perform those connections in their materiality (Chevalier 1999). Thus, the expression and performance of identity is continually tied up in materiality and in relationships to others. Finch (2007) brings this point home in terms of expressing family with her definition of displaying families as "the process by which individuals and groups of individuals convey to each other and to relevant others that certain of their actions constitute 'doing family things' and thereby confirm that these relationships are 'family' relationships" (73). We express family on our walls, our location in our families, and other identities. I would argue that expressions of our marginal identities get priority on the walls, but this warrants further comparative empirical research among marginal and mainstream groups.

No matter one's social location, we often overlook the things we live with as part of our performance of self. We can interpret the home as a *social front* with which we project ourselves (Chapman 1999). The things we live with are deeply connected to our sense of self. As Chapman points out, burglaries would not otherwise cause "tremendous personal distress" (1999, 144). Home contains signifiers of the self, but a self that is a work-in-progress; a self that has a social location and develops through interaction (Clarke 2002) and negotiation with structural contingencies.

Kehily and Thomson (2011) attend to the presentation of self on our walls with their analysis of the dichotomy between displaying photos, which document a child's journey through life, and the display of bronzed baby shoes, which symbolically halt the child's journey. They contend that bronzed baby shoes suggest that parents can keep some part of their child a baby forever. These baby shoes represent truncated growth and immobilization of an idealized time—these boots will not be able to grow up and move away; they stay and keep a symbolic part of the child in idealized infancy with the parents.

One feature of the wall that has gained some limited attention is the mantel. Rachel Hurdley (2006) has studied mantlepieces and, along with Halle (1993), emphasizes the need to attend to materiality inside the home as a cultural residue of the home's inhabitants. She finds that

> by constructing narratives around visual productions in the apparently private space of the home, people participate in the ongoing accomplishment of social, moral identities. Thus, the practice of producing narratives around objects contributes to the personal work of autobiography and renders objects as meaningful participants in the social work of identity-building. (Hurdley 2006, 718)

As individuals and groups use walls as active agents, and as walls push back as active agents themselves, infused with power through our building our way of life around them, there is a messy ground (Miller 2001), in between structure and agency where both exist and interact with each other.

The section of this book on cultural objects will demonstrate how using this lens to analyze walls can offer fruitful analytic purchase.

Walls as Boundaries and Boundary Objects

Walls are the ultimate boundaries; impassable, often insurmountable, conveying literal and symbolic separation. Ursula Le Guin depicts this beautifully in *The Dispossessed*:

> There was a wall. It did not look important. . . . An adult could look right over it, and even a child could climb it . . . a line, an idea of a boundary. But the idea was real. It was important. For seven generations there had been nothing more important than that wall. . . . Like all walls it was ambiguous, two-faced. What was inside it and what was outside it depended upon which side of it you were on. (Le Guin 1974)

However, passage through walls, most often through doors, but occasionally in deviant ways, such as burglars through windows, happens constantly and is required for living our day-to-day lives. We must engage with walls, mostly through automatic cognition practices. We rarely note the fact that we are physically surrounded by walls, or else we are hyper-aware of them—walled-in—for example, claustrophobics' attempting to use elevators, or when doors are unexpectedly locked. Walls, however, through their virtue as physical boundaries, separate us from the outside, creating such a thing as "indoors," literally meaning being on the "in" side of the door. Walls create borders. I argue that walls are boundaries on two levels; physical and social symbolic, that is, boundaries between insider and outsider status. Let's first think about various kinds of walls as boundaries and then more directly about insider and outsider status.

Boundaries

There are different kinds of walls. I have theorized the walls of our homes and communities. There are also border walls, city walls, and even invisible walls. Walls, as symbolic of social boundaries, become metaphors for separation. For example, the trenches in World War I were a form of wall which helped to define the symbolic meaning of who is on what side. When, at Christmas, the soldiers from both sides came out to sing carols together, by coming out from behind their walls, they also symbolically, but temporarily, came out from behind the symbolic meaning of their walls, that is, that they were on opposite sides and no comradery was to emerge between those two sides.

War illustrates particularly well the use of walls to establish symbolic boundaries. Countries wage war with each other over invisible walls; the boundaries of their territory. When an army gains land during a war, the first act is to build forts, barracks, or trenches of some kind to establish a visible display of the invisible boundary of who now controls what. These walls politically reinforce the new spatial distribution of control.

The sociology of border walls is a subfield of its own which, while tangential to the sociology of the walls of permanent structures, my interest here, requires mention.[2] The field of border walls has exploded in popularity (e.g., Bikard 2011; Bissonnette and Vallet 2020; Kinberg 2008; Langerbein 2009; Linebarger and Braithwaite 2020; Wright 2020), particularly since the U.S.-Mexico border wall has gained notoriety and been the object of frequent study (Becker 2021; Heyman 2008; Tamez 2013; York & Schoon 2011; Wright 2020). International conferences have taken the theme of border walls, primarily focused on security, but with subsections on border walls and identity. As noted above, studies on the Great Wall of China point to it as a physical symbol of Chinese centrality, insularity, and identity (Chan 2008; Tackett 2008). The Berlin Wall also presents problems of meaning as an *interpretive resource* for Germans (Leuenberger 2006), as does the Israeli–Palestine Wall (Abulof 2014). The Berlin Wall, although demolished, still exists as an invisible wall in the psychological landscape of Germans (Leuenberger 2006). Its symbolic meaning is exemplified by how it was broken into pieces that are now on display all over the world. Hungary has recently built a wall to keep out migrants, echoing sentiments we see in the United States and other parts of the world. We are moving toward higher and higher tech border walls (Heyman 2008), even toward invisible walls patrolled by robot technology and sensors rather than actual walls (Marks 2010). Considering how these walls connect to identity has the potential to further deepen this field of study.

All kinds of walls represent some symbolic boundary, which can connect to studies in identity and boundary work as well. Ancient Greeks, particularly in the era of city-states, around the fifth and fourth centuries BC, fortified most of their cities (Hornblower 1991). Fortification created a boundary, which represented safety and strength. Although the walls followed the most easily defensible landscape, rather than the exact contours of the city (Wycherley 1976), the presence of the walls was a deeply entrenched cultural and psychological feature of Ancient Greek life. When the Persians retreated in 479 BC, the Athenians rebuilt their walls as quickly as possible. The Spartans did not have a walled city and tried to convince Athens not to build walls, but they failed and when the Athenians built their walls, the Spartans took it as an act of aggression (Hornblower 1991). The Athenians not only built walls around their city, but they built "long walls" to their harbor city Piraeus. In this way, communication and access to their naval fleet could not be cut off by land (Wycherley 1976). Walls often represent acts of aggression, from this complex political structural representation, to boys' building a tree house with the sign "girls keep out!"

Other symbolic boundaries, which walls aid in sustaining, are the separation of work and home post-industrialization, particularly in how we decorate walls in the two environments. We use the materiality of walls to make clear the differences in the place of work and the place of home. Walls are also economic boundaries in their creation of households and their circumscription of economic activities.

As key components of space and place, which are intimately connected, walls are linked to time as well. Walls help to define the time you are supposed to be within a particular enclosed space. For example, at school, children learn different conceptions of time than at home, and know when they are supposed to be in one or the other space. More formal business walls suggest more formal behavior which is, in turn, temporally structured and bound. Walls of the home, however, suggest a more relaxed backstage behavior, with fewer time constraints and more temporal flexibility.

Insider/Outsider Boundaries

As boundaries, walls demarcate spaces where one belongs, temporarily belongs, or does not belong. This idea applies differently to different groups and among different cultures. Police, across most cultures, technically need a warrant to enter a bounded space (although they may or may not observe that legality). Visitors, across most cultures, are granted a sense of temporary belonging, so long as they do not overstay their welcome. Activities are included in the demarcation of belonging and not belonging within walls (de Certeau 1984; Pile & Keith 1997). Sex is usually reserved for the bedroom, and we react to stories of sex outside the bedroom as particularly titillating, in part because of the defiance of the social norm.

The implications of walls for the world in which we live vary among groups according to their access to both "inside" and "outside." The exceptionally old (over 90), for example, may lack access to the outside, while the homeless seek, and are often denied, shelter inside. With the arrangement of walls putting most of the house on display for visitors, much of the house becomes a front stage, exposed to the judgment of the generalized other (Hunt 1989). Hospitality, while less formal now, still comes with an expectation of tidiness and cleanliness, which now includes most of the house. Exposure has gendered implications. Darke and Gurney (2000) find that by shifting much of the walled spaces of the home into the front stage, in the performance of hospitality, even if the work is shared, women bear the judgment of visitors.

Walls, as boundaries, aid in creating insider/outsider status, and hierarchical status within the membership of groups. Symbolic boundaries are created when individuals or groups ask, "Who is like me?" "Who is not?" (Lamont

2000). In their structural context, walls contribute in shaping the cultural repertoire available for these questions. You are defined as a factory worker, or manager depending on which walls encompass you. You are a member of this family or that, depending on which walls you sleep within. Walls lend legitimacy to claims of authority—having a corner office on the top floor of an office building bodes well for your claims of authority. Having access, via identity badge, fingerprint, or retinal scan to the inside of high-security areas designates you as an insider, and the more walls you can legitimately breach, the more important you are compared to others within the group of insiders.

While penetration of walls demonstrates legitimacy, authority, or power, janitors are an interesting exception as they can breach multiple levels of walls, and yet are quite powerless in the grand scheme of things. They, however, brandish impressive key rings, which display in symbolic terms their ability to legitimately breach walls and therefore make some symbolic claims to importance. In other cases, the ability to escape the confines of walls demonstrates legitimacy, such as when those institutionalized in mental hospitals, held by captors in war or kidnapping, or even children are confined to their rooms as punishment, can finally leave (or escape).

The arrangement of walls can be used to defy tendencies toward social borders and hierarchies, for example with open plan designs of office space (Attfield 1999). Walls facilitate the ideology of being at home by virtue of enclosure of that space (Chevalier 1999) and shape economic activity so that the household becomes the basic economic unit (Saunders & Williams 1988).

Walls, as boundaries, separate and control, thereby becoming a dominant mechanism of repression. As such, in Arviat, Nunavut, Inuit must constantly perform their Inuitness *to* their walls. In the performance of identity aimed *at* the walls, the walls can, through use, become boundary objects. Using the walls in particular ways can become strategies to bridge two worlds—Inuit and Western worlds. Through use of the walls, which brought with them anomie, Inuit can express an understanding of how to live and be in colonized spaces *as Inuit*. The use of the walls, therefore, can at times provide a bridge that facilitates the functioning of these two worlds together. Inuit are committed to being in and of today's global community, and walls as boundary objects can help, at times, to aid in their demonstration of global membership and participation.

The complex, layered social meanings and multiple and intersecting social processes surrounding walls parallel those surrounding the built environment as a whole, and its relationship to the land. Members of displaced groups with strong ties to undeveloped land engage with the boundaries of town/ land, inside/outside, and living within a foreign space while their knowledge is located elsewhere. Moving through a geography of knowledge and power involves the negotiation and experience of space and structures as symbolic relations and power relations.

Walls are part of the negotiation of identity and of boundary work. Because they can mediate a relationship between and among groups, they become boundary objects (Star & Griesemer 1989). By using walls in particular ways, a group not only resists, but also finds ways to come to terms with the new ways of living and being. For example, when Inuit perform Inuitness to their walls, they are interacting with walls that stand as synecdoche for their colonizers. Gradually, they learn to cope with being walled-in. As such, engagement with walls builds a bridge with the dominant group, allowing for coexistence, even though the power imbalance and atrocities cannot be erased.

While I get into more detail in the introduction of Part 1, specifically on boundary objects, for now let's move on to how symbolic relations and power underpin the built environment and cut across the three dimensions of walls (technological, cultural, and boundary-wise) when we analyze any relationship with walls. The built environment bears symbolic significance. It embodies power relations, both in form and practice.

SYMBOLIC AND POWER RELATIONS

Individuals and groups relate to the symbolic level of walls when walls can stand as representative, for example, of an ideology, such that it is an instance of synecdoche. Additionally, walls can be used as literary metaphors, ranging from metaphors of the everyday, to macro-structural power relations.

Synecdoche and the literary metaphor reside close together. The built environment is synecdochal when it represents an entire ideology, movement, or culture. For example, Duffles (2005) finds that the Japanese preserve traditional homes, *kyo machiya*, as symbols of traditional Japanese culture as a whole. Similarly, Silverstein (2004) extends Bourdieu's (1979) analysis of the structure of the Kabyle house, *akham*, to argue that the *akham* is a synecdoche for Kabyle tradition and cosmology. As such, where Japanese or Kabyle architecture erodes, the *akham* may be seen as congruent to the erosion of the traditional cultures for which it stands in.

Synecdoche is the representation of the whole by a part of the whole, whereas metaphors give us tropes and storytelling tools. Walls are common metaphors in literature, symbolic of separation and division. Not only do we find literary metaphors, such as Rapunzel in the tower (Harré 2002), but we find metaphors of the past. The Great Wall of China stands as a monument (and metaphor) of the greatness of its builders (Langerbein 2009). Walls can also undermine metaphors. The Statue of Liberty stands as a metaphor for the welcome and shelter to the poor, the weak, and the downtrodden. The U.S.-Mexico border wall, in contrast, is a metaphor for exclusion and mocks the metaphor presented of Liberty (Langerbein 2009). Acting as metaphor, the built environment gives impetus to thinking and reflecting about the aspects of one's everyday life.

We have seen above the many and varied ways in which walls involve power and power involves walls. Walls, structures, and buildings embody power relations as technologies of sedimentation and colonization through which those in power stabilize social structures and routines and impose their way of being on other groups. When a group's place is altered by others, or taken away, or relocated, the built environment is often directly implicated in the process. Indeed, the built environment can be a violent representation of power relations. Not only in homes, such as for Inuit, Bhotiyas, and Gujars (Collings 2005; Dangwal 2009; Dawson 2008; Duhaime et al. 2004; Thomas & Thompson 1972), but also in the relocation of peoples. Oppressive relocation has contributed to genocide of Jews and Native Americans (Kinberg 2008), nomads in Tibet, and many others. Colonizers articulate new expectations and cultural dominance through the built environment.

CONCLUSION

In summary, scholars have done a great deal of work on theorizing walls, but in diffuse and unconnected ways, like so many strands of an incomplete weaving. I pull these threads together to offer here a theoretical perspective that can bring richness to the ways in which we consider the spaces we study and the peoples therein.

Walls are mundane technologies, key facets of architecture that enable and constrain us. I suggest the concepts of *passive engagements* and *active engagements* as a means to conceptualize walls as technological objects without falling into technological determinism or extreme social constructionism. The technological frame of walls is malleable, even when they are fixed in form. By alternately considering walls through the lenses of passive and active engagements, we deepen our understanding of our relationship with new technologies.

Walls constitute cultural objects. Individuals and groups produce meaning for walls through interaction at the use level. As Wagner-Pacifici and Schwartz state, "it is the use made of it that brings it into the life of the society" (2002, 218). The meanings of walls vary for those contained within them (or kept without them) and have a *cultural biography* attached to them (Kopytoff 1986).

Walls are also the ultimate boundaries; impassable, often insurmountable, conveying literal and symbolic separation. It is through their physicality that walls create spaces and privacy. We value walls as physical boundaries. As boundaries, walls demarcate spaces where one belongs, temporarily belongs, or does not belong. Walls, as boundaries, aid in creating insider/outsider status, and hierarchical status within the membership of groups, as well as a front stage/backstage. Walls, as boundaries, can separate and control, thereby becoming a dominant mechanism of repression.

Walls then, are also boundary objects (Star & Griesemer 1989), key objects through which group relations are expressed and negotiated. By coming to terms with their walls, Inuit are, in a sense, interacting with physical representations of the dominant cultural group. Walls are a point of negotiation and interaction.

By considering walls as technological objects, as cultural objects, and as boundary objects, we have a theoretical framework with which we can approach walls. In doing so, we can account for the powerful symbolic nature of walls, as well as the ways in which they are implicated in power dynamics. I hope this book will serve as an example of the fruitfulness of this approach as I encounter and account for the lived experience of Inuit who were and are walled-in to colonial spaces.

NOTES

1. The government did create an educational brochure entitled *Living in the New Houses* in the 1960s. The educational programs, however, did not proceed as intended and this brochure was not made widely available. One thing that stands out from looking through this instructional brochure is that so many of the objects in the homes of Inuit were new to them—tables, plates and cutlery, shelving, and so on—and were foreign to them.

2. The subfield of graffiti may also be of interest to the reader, particularly the battle of graffiti as a battle over aesthetics of power and resistance (Ferrell 1993). See also Bushnell 1990, Gomez & St. Clair 2008, Lachmann 1988, Landry 2019, Macdonald 2001, Rahn 2002, and Snyder 2009.

Part I

WALLS AS BOUNDARY OBJECTS

IDENTITY-WORK ABOUNDS

Before I built a wall I'd ask to know
What I was walling in or walling out,
And to whom I was like to give offence.

—Robert Frost, *Mending Wall*

What is a *boundary object*? Star and Griesemer (1989) introduced this concept in the late 1980s, amid the turn to the material in cultural and science and technology studies. In short, boundary objects are those abstract or material things through which groups work out an understanding of each other and themselves. While engaging with these objects, a process of translation occurs. Star and Griesemer used the case of a zoology museum and the various groups, such as amateurs, scientists, and administrators, invested in the running of that museum to illustrate this concept. The museum acted as a boundary object between these groups; it translated viewpoints among them. It facilitated their relationship. It was the boundary point at which these groups met and developed an understanding of each other and themselves.

Scholars have used the concept of boundary objects to study the meeting point between and among groups through many kinds of objects. The literature on boundary objects includes analyses of a variety of things such as archaeological reports, an open-source code repository, sterile needles, hospital wards, traditional paper prescriptions, data, mental testing in Russia, accounting technologies, and even human remains.[1] All of these objects were located at the boundaries between and among groups who engaged with the relevant boundary objects in order to transcend, maintain, or come to terms with boundaries with other groups. This concept has even proved quite useful to the business literature on management (Sapsed & Salter 2016).

Walls also function as boundary objects. There is analytical benefit to approaching walls as boundary objects, to asking what constellation of groups is implicated, and to studying their social context from the ground up. Walls almost always naturally serve as boundaries between and among groups. In this sense, I argue that the social processes surrounding walls as boundary objects are generic social processes (Prus 1987), processes which happen again and again across different scenes. Rather than dismissing, I privilege local context. When analyzing walls as boundary objects, one must attend to the specific local context of the walls in question and examine the power relations implicit in the way that they are used in that instance. Nick Fox (2011) argues that Star and Griesemer eschewed any essentialist notions of boundary objects. I suggest, however, that the social processes around boundary objects, the ways groups, often agentically, use things at the intersections of their interactions (direct or indirect) with other groups to translate across social worlds, is a generic social process. By translate, I mean to decontextualize and then recontextualize the boundary object across social worlds (Delanoë 2015).

There are several elements that Star and Griesemer (1989) lay out in their definition of boundary objects. I will go through these elements as they apply to walls. First, boundary objects inhabit two or more intersecting social worlds. Walls are consistently located at the boundaries between groups; between designers and users, colonizers and the colonized, decorators and clients, girls and boys, and so on. When we take the time to consider walls as boundary objects, we gain analytical purchase which we might not otherwise gain.

Second, boundary objects have a fluid enough meaning and/or use that they can adapt to each local group implicated. Walls serve different roles and meanings for various groups depending on each local circumstance. Walls of prisons have a flexible meaning such that prisoners and guards have quite different relationships with them. The same walls mean constraint for one group and safety for another. Walls of homes are sites of expression and negotiation of family, the location of that family in the community, and the things that can happen behind closed doors that concern other groups such as social services and the police. Walls in offices enclose different groups at varying degrees of hierarchy within the organization and can mean different things to the members of each group, from power and success, to resentment and the gamut in between. The architecture of a courthouse, for example, can represent constitutional beliefs and define the relationship between law or state and citizen; what is public, what is private, and where each stands in relation to the other (Gieryn 2018).

It can be useful to keep in mind Benjamin Kelly's (2017) concept of *asymmetric boundary objects* with which he argues that boundary objects not only mean different things to different groups, but also serve the interests of one group much more than another. Boundary objects can adapt to each local group implicated, and yet this does not mean that these groups are necessarily on equal footing with each other or in relation to the boundary object.

Third, boundary objects must be "robust enough to maintain a common identity across sites" (Star & Griesemer 1989, 393). Walls have different meanings for groups, but they also have common ground across sites. Walls always structure the space and are part of the built environment. Walls are the ultimate boundaries; impassable, often insurmountable, conveying literal and symbolic separation. Walls can have different meanings, as illustrated above, but they are recognizable across social worlds. As recognizable things that also carry different meanings for various social groups, walls have a robust common identity across sites, and yet also function as objects through which social worlds are negotiated.

Expanding the role of walls as boundary objects, walls facilitate boundary work. Although Thomas Gieryn (1983) first introduced the concept of boundary work as a practical conceptual tool to analyze the rhetorical work done by communities of scientists to socially draw the boundaries of their field, the concept has had wide applicability in symbolic interactionism. It is not only scientists who feel they need to demarcate their professions, their groups (ethnic, interest-group, or otherwise), or their identities. Snow and Anderson (1987) focus on *identity-work* in their study of the homeless, also in the 1980s. Both the concepts of boundary work and identity work extend from the work and effort people exert to establish membership in a particular group or affiliation to a particular identity. Even when this identity is not directly connected to group membership, but rather a characteristic such as "good" or "funny," it implicates identity tropes (understandings of groups of certain kinds of people existing) as people work to define and align themselves in particular ways.

Walls become a part of boundary work and identity work, not only as physical things we use to display, but as boundaries, themselves. Maria Rentetzi (2008) demonstrates not only how the tobacco warehouse walls contribute to the insider/outsider status of the workers and the merchants, and play a social role in displaying the achievements of the merchants publicly, but these industrial buildings also serve to "subvert the boundaries between the city and the factory" (64). The warehouse walls act as a different kind of space which challeng and, to a certain extent, dismantle the dichotomy of "city" and "factory."

Cultural boundaries exist and boundary work is performed to make, blur, or maintain boundaries (Liu 2015). Gieryn (2008) develops the concept of *settled* and *unsettled boundaries*, following Ann Swidler's lead (1986). He asserts that "realms of knowledge meet at boundaries—cultural boundaries" (Gieryn 2008, 91). While those boundaries are not always physical ones, sometimes they are. Walls are boundary objects through which cultural norms, values, or beliefs are negotiated, particularly when lived in or used by a knowledge community different from that which produced the wall.

Because "the places people build shape the social practices inside" (Gieryn 2008, 99), walls are implicated, particularly when decisions are being made about how and where to put them, in the clash of unsettled boundaries. As Bugni and Smith (2002) demonstrate, constructing, knowing, and performing the self happens in relation to designed physical environments.

Inuit confront daily, in the form of their walls, a physical divide from their traditional lands and a built form which imposes a Euro-Canadian knowledge system upon them. Until they use the walls to resolve the anomie of their *culture crash*, redistributing agency throughout their world (Watts 2013), the walls continue to face them every day as physical manifestations of cultural boundaries. Walls, in this instance as representations of power, are an asymmetric boundary object. Typically, however, the boundary work is performed at the design stage, and once a building is built, its form will settle the boundaries through its shaping of social practices (Gieryn 2002). A building is, as Bruno Latour (1990) would say, "society made durable." As such, in Arviat, Inuit must constantly perform their Inuitness *to* their walls. In the performance of identity aimed *at* the walls, the walls, through use, become boundary objects.

In the first chapter of this part, I explore how using the walls in particular ways becomes a strategic and agentic approach to bridging two worlds—Inuit and *Qablunaaq* (Western culture from South of Churchill, Manitoba / Western people from South of Churchill Manitoba, usually white). Through use of the walls, which brought with them anomie, Inuit express an understanding of how to live and be in *Qablunaaq* spaces *as Inuit*. The use of the walls, therefore, can at times provide a bridge, which facilitates the functioning of these two worlds together, with varying success across class. Inuit are committed to being in and of today's global community and walls as boundary objects can help, at times, to aid in *Arviammiuts'* (citizens of Arviat) demonstration of this.

The second chapter of this part examines what it means to spend time inside the home and out "on the land," outside the perimeter of the hamlet's built environment. As Inuit knowledge is tied to place, this has implications for the learning and the transmission of knowledge. How Inuit traditionally learn does not work as well within the houses. This has gendered implications. In both chapters we can see how the walls mediate the relationship of Inuit to Western ways of being, and between Inuit and Western knowledge and ways of knowing.

NOTE

1. For examples see: Byford 2014; Cooper 2011; Delanoë 2015; Meier 2015; Owens 2015.

Chapter 2

Ujjirusuttiarniq amma Isumatunikkut Tukisiniarniq [Having an Awareness and Seeking to Understand]

Anomie and Geographies of Knowledge

Each of the chapter titles, going forward, anchors on an *Inuit Qaujimajatuqangit* *(IQ)* principle. Loosely translated, this means the knowledge that Inuit have always known, or "traditional knowledge and practices." For many of us, our identities are rooted across a variety of spectrums. *Arviammiut* (citizens of Arviat) closely link knowledge, including *IQ* principles, and identity. Spatially, Inuit knowledge is deeply tied into the land, while Western or *Qablunaaq* (Southern) knowledge is tied into the hamlet. Walled-in to *Qablunaaq* spaces, however, Inuit must negotiate their identities and the meaning of Inuit and Western knowledges in creative and resourceful ways through their relationships with their walls as boundary objects. This includes making sense of their world through *ujjirusuttiarniq amma isumatunikkut tukisiniarniq* (having an awareness and seeking to understand).

Emile Durkheim's concept of *anomie* has particular resonance when talking about Inuit. Durkheim introduced this term in 1893 to make tangible a specific sense of despair. Each individual typically has their own sense of the norms in their social context. When a social context gets rearranged, or changes in some dramatic way, there is suddenly a mismatch between how the individual understands appropriate behavior and what the actual expectations around appropriate behavior are. The norms have changed, and the individual (or group) in that new changed environment is unsure how to act, what to do, how to be. Even those who win the lottery are often hit with a sense of confusion and depression that can be attributed to anomie. If you do not know how the world around you operates, and your role in that world, it means you find yourself in a situation with opaque norms, a sense of normlessness—even if there are social norms, you are not sure what they are. This means it is hard to grasp ambition and comfort in ritual or norms. What follows is a

49

sense of disorientation tinged with despair. When Inuit in the Kivalliq region were relocated, by force, into what is now Arviat, and their new houses, their norms and knowledge no longer applied in this new social context. They were disoriented and unsure how to adapt, and although many have exercised tremendous agency in adapting, a sense of anomie pervades Arviat.

Walls are deeply implicated in the performance of identity and the linkage of identity and knowledge as *Arviammiut* are separated from the locus of their traditional knowledge by walls that represent their colonization. This makes *ujjirusuttiarniq amma isumatunikkut tukisiniarniq* (having an awareness and seeking to understand) difficult. Along with that colonization, comes the anomie of Inuit relocation to within walls. *Arviammiut*, therefore visit the place of their knowledge and identity while living within colonized spaces, seeking knowledge and connection with identity. Although in many places, the urban and non-urban present a false dichotomy (Dorries et al. 2019), in Arviat, people view their walls as *Qablunaaq* constructions and as representative of *Qablunaaq* eyes. *Arviammiut* perform Inuitness to those eyes, to their walls, and engage with those walls as boundary objects to relieve their anomie.

This chapter takes an ecological approach to power relations. That is, buildings, as a collective representation of culture, power, and knowledge systems, may be grouped together so as to communicate the idea of a spatial community. Problems of meaning juxtapose the concepts of "before" and "after," of "nature" and "community," with the physical boundary of inside and outside of town. For those displaced from the land (the term *Arviammiut* use to describe outside of the hamlet) into a community, the town or community into which they are moved is the secondary experience. Thus, where city dwellers usually understand the countryside as *contra* the town, for *Arviammiut* the town becomes *contra* the land. Power knowledge systems (Mukerji 1994) map onto the town and the land. The town acts as a disciplinary terrain, a normative landscape (Cresswell 1996), which induces new practices and discourses (King 1989), in addition to spurring resistance (Dorries et al. 2019). It is within this context that *Arviammiut* work on *ujjirusuttiarniq amma isumatunikkut tukisiniarniq* (having an awareness and seeking to understand), creating meaning out of anomie within their walls.

I turn first to the concept of walls as symbolic of anomie and the ways in which *Arviammiut* engage with their walls as a means of overcoming that anomie and establishing Inuit identity within *Qablunaaq* spaces. Our journey thus begins inside the home with *Arviammiut* who stare at the walls, and the walls that stare at *Arviammiut* as they navigate the landscape of their everyday lives, taking into account the heterogeneous experiences across class. This chapter then moves outside the homes and examines the experience across class of the grouping of homes and buildings in Arviat as it relates to boundary work, identity work, and a geography of knowledge and power. As

Dorries et al. (2019) point out, cities (or in this case hamlets) are traditionally places where people perform resistance to colonial violence. The analytic consideration of walls as boundary objects furthers our insight into this moral geography of colonial contestation.

ANOMIE INSTANTIATED IN AND BY WALLS

Any built-up structure, whether fixed or mobile, vividly represents a system of knowledge. The Inuit confront daily, in the form of their built environment, a physical divide from their traditional lands; a built form which imposes a Euro-Canadian knowledge system upon them. Until they use the walls to resolve the anomie of their *culture crash*, the walls continue to face them every day as physical manifestations of cultural boundaries.

Lily's Wall

From the start of my time in Arviat, I noticed that the ways in which *Arviam-miut* treated their walls varied tremendously. The spark that pushed my socio-logical imagination to the fore was Lily's wall (see figures 2.1 and 2.2). She had viscerally taken control of the built environment, enacting the *IQ* principle of *ujjirusuttiarniq amma isumatunikkut tukisiniarniq* (having an aware-ness and seeking to understand). Lily and her husband, Brennan, collected rocks from areas where her family used to roam nomadically. Using these

Figure 2.1 Lily's Wall (1).

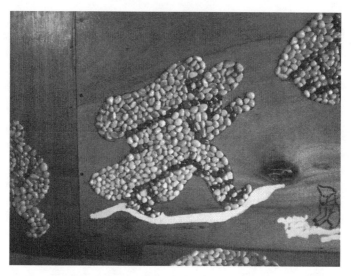

Figure 2.2   Lily's Wall (2).

rocks, Lily carved traditional scenes into her wall and created an impressive mosaic. She engaged with her built environment and used it to express her Inuit identity. Her home particularly stood out because many other homes I went into had completely bare walls, while still others had a collage of family photographs, attached with tape or push pins, and other paraphernalia cover-ing their walls in a chaotic scrapbook of their lives. Lily's home was remark-able to other *Arviammiut* as well. In fact, so many participants mentioned her wall that it became its own topic when I was reading for themes.

Lily's wall was the most overt and successful example of how *Arviammiut* found peace and attained awareness and understanding with the expanse of white walls enclosing them into *Qablunaaq* spaces. Not only had she and her husband, who helped finalize Lily's vision, created an impressive piece of artwork around themselves, but they transformed the space into one expres-sive of and welcoming to Inuit culture. Faced with a symbolic representation of anomie, the *Qablunaaq* walls' constantly watching her and her family, Lily engaged directly with that object, her walls, to negotiate a new way of being, a new sense of feeling grounded, and a space conducive to Inuit norms and *IQ* principles. Others in the community admired her walls and felt comfortable in the space she had created.

In the mosaic itself, figures accomplish mundane and routine activities from life on the tundra. Men fish and drum dance, children play, and women prepare food and walk while *amak*-ing (carrying a child on their back in the hood of their *amoutik,* an Inuit-style outer garment). The figures are all in action. They are doing. In point of fact, they are "doing" Inuitness onto the wall. The images of *iglus* and lakes are imposing an Inuit landscape onto the wall. These images speak *to* the walls, as a boundary object, and rework how the walls speak to those in the space.

Variation across Class

Arviammiut, as a heterogeneous group, have varying degrees of success in coming to an understanding of their walls by practicing *ujjirusuttiarniq amma isumatunikkut tukisiniarniq*. This resolution of anomie correlates with social class. While Lily has successfully negotiated a partial resolution of anomie by engaging with her walls, others in the community have been more and less successful in practicing *ujjirusuttiarniq amma isumatunikkut tukisiniarniq* in and to *Qablunaaq* spaces.

I quickly realized that the literature on class, even class among other Indigenous groups, did not apply in this context. The following account of class emerged over my time in Arviat and participants confirmed this interpretation. Arviat is roughly divided into three social classes, which I present here as ideal types. Of course, many live on the margins of one definition or another, and class manifests itself as a continuum. There are, however, three notable groupings along that continuum; the *walkers*, the *riders* who drive ATVs, and the *drivers* who are primarily power elites who drive enclosed vehicles, mostly trucks. *Arviammiut* establish, perform, and judge class by forms of physical mobility. With the historical nomadic past, where the size of dog team, for example, would indicate status, it is perhaps not surprising that mode of transportation defines class today. Status "before" the relocation certainly plays into a family's current standing in the community.

Walkers

This group is the lowest on the socioeconomic scale and cannot afford ATVs and the like. For walkers, it is not only that walking is their mode of transportation, but there is also a constant restlessness. This directionless wandering or visiting of others may be endemic to their lack of structured time, tasks to perform, and lack of a general need to do very much. They experience anomie comparable to that of Newfoundland fishermen after the fisheries collapsed and when, in 1994, the cod moratorium was extended indefinitely from the initial two years (Davis 2008; Harris 1998). Demoralization, lack of direction, and anomie are prevalent (Arms 2004). Just as Newfoundlanders tried to agentically adjust (Steele et al. 1992), so do the Inuit. However, the restlessness that pervades the walking class in Arviat persists as they seek to understand and build awareness.

As I walked or drove around the community myself, I would often see groups out walking, most notably groups of children and mothers or female caretakers with children trailing behind or ahead of them.

> On the way home, we passed a number of people out walking despite the cold rain and the chilly wind. Most look pretty miserable and bedraggled. Several were young women walking with children meandering after them. Getting everyone out of the house. I thought about what home must have contained for them to be out in this weather, meandering aimlessly. A pair of girls passed, about late middle-school age. Three bedraggled children between 4–7, a girl alone, maybe 7/8. The dreariness of the day seemed to imprint on them. Most were just outside to be outside. There was no walking with purpose. It was a slow shuffle, particularly for the women with all the children (3–4 kids each). (Field notes, May 10, 2012)

This scene describes the street life in Arviat on almost any day of the year, in almost any weather. Some of this has to do with the overcrowding of houses, which is extremely common among the walking class. One woman I interviewed had had 22 people living in a four-bedroom house at one point. They were down to 19 people at the time of the interview. Alberto Gasparini (1973) finds that having a ratio of more than two people per room in a house leads to high levels of what he terms *quarrelsomeness* and that families with higher levels of quarrelsomeness spend more time outside. Abuse, air quality, and drugs were often "indoor" problems that walkers in Arviat sought to escape.

Inuit, whom the government settled into this area by force, primarily consist of two groups, *Ahiarmiut* and *Padlirmiut*. *Ahiarmiut* lived far inland and had delayed contact with colonizing society. *Padlirmiut*, on the other hand, lived closer to the shores and had earlier and more sustained contact with their colonizers. As a result, government workers and traders used *Padlirmiut* as guides and gave them the first jobs and job training. *Ahiarmiut* became known for their traditional knowledge, but also bear stigma as being poorer and more often a part of the walking class, while *Padlirmiut* tend to have more material wealth. While fading, these divisions remain today and when disagreements break out, an association with *Ahiarmiut* will surface and be used as an insult. Many of the people I would encounter walking the streets would be from an *Ahiarmiut* background.

Restless walkers often have a loose route they routinely follow. Thus, while the meandering and visiting others may seem rather aimless, it also develops into a routinized path which they then take without realizing or thinking about it very much. In her interview, Bethany tells me the order in which she tends to visit people, noticing for the first time that she has an order. She also tells me whom she visits more often or for longer. She cycles back to Lucia's house several times throughout the course of the day. Lucia is in the driving class and spends most of her time at home. She always has coffee on the go for visitors to help themselves. Walkers sometimes patronize the homes of the driving class to partake in resources—such as checking e-mail or having coffee.

The restlessness, however, plays an important role, as I noticed when I stayed with a family who are members of the walking class. They were six people living in a two-bedroom house, although there was only one large, queen-size mattress and they all slept there together—sometimes taking turns sleeping. They faced the problem of *killing time*, as Nels Anderson (1923) describes in his study of the hobo.

> And I just enjoy it, like, I walk, I love walking. Walk, I wanna walk, I wanna walk. (Samuel)

> Watching them, I feel restless, too. With unstructured days, the urge to wander, to do something, is persistent. . . . From talking to Bethany, it sounds like the adults spend longer times visiting than the youth, but there is still this restless and constant movement. (Field notes, May 16, 2012)

Four participants, all members of the walking class, referred in interviews to the walking around that Inuit had to do in the past as nomadic people. Also, when Lily describes the traditional scenes on her wall, she uses action verbs. The mosaic of a woman with a child is not described as standing, but as walking; "the lady walking with the baby" and "a child walking towards the hunter." All the upright figures, in fact, are described as "walking." Walking, it seems, was a key component to *ujjirusuttiarniq amma isumatunikkut tukisiniarniq* (having an awareness and seeking to understand), in addition to the restlessness all groups face during times of anomie.

At the same time, walkers refer to the nomadic past as further in the past than riders or drivers do; "long ago" even if, as for Bethany, her parents lived "on the land." Walkers are largely limited to the community, unable to access the tundra around the hamlet easily. Their lives are contained in roaming around a very small patch of land, especially as compared with the vastness of the tundra. Thus, they feel further from the land, and, at the same time, disconnected from the *Qablunaaq* institutions. This makes coming to terms with anomie through seeking awareness and understanding difficult. A walking pattern winds primarily through the residences, perhaps passing along an aspect of the perimeter of the *Qablunaaq* center, but rarely venturing in among those buildings—other than the grocery store and post office—highly social places for all. The spatial existence of the walking class lies within what one might think of as a path between the source of *Qablunaaq* knowledge and the land as a source of Inuit knowledge, yet this is still a dominantly *Qablunaaq* space, reflected in the built environment of permanent, fixed, structures.

There are a few, however, in the walking class who mostly stay at home because they have been the object of bullying, backbiting, have burned too many bridges, or became fed up with the drama of small-town life. Brittany, along with two others, tells me in informal conversation, "I'm mostly at home now" (Field notes, May 17, 2012). Walkers are the largest group, and one which absorbs many of the negative effects of forced settlement.

Those in the walking class tend to have engaged less with their walls and been less successful in coming to terms with the anomie that accompanied colonization. The walls of the walking class are often quite bare. Those who have engaged with the walls have typically done so in minimal ways. There are some walkers who have done more to come to terms with their walls; however, the anomie is most acutely felt in this group and the walls communicate clearly how a particular family is coping in that regard. Some families place a large mattress in the center of the largest room of the home and sleep there together as a family, huddled as far away from the walls as they can get. Depending on the family, this mattress may or may not stay there throughout the day.

Riders

The *riders* consist, roughly, of a grouping in between the most poor and the most wealthy. There are some who struggle, and yet manage to maintain an ATV (colloquially called a "Honda" in Arviat) or a snowmobile (called a skidoo or simply "machine"). Then there are those in the riding class who have a little more wealth and some more family resources. Riders also often take to the streets, but riding around on their Hondas and/or machines rather than walking. Again, this restless movement may connect to the *IQ* principle of *ujjirusuttiarniq amma isumatunikkut tukisiniarniq* (having an awareness and seeking to understand).

Most of the riding class engage in fairly mundane activities when they are out and about, going to and from the grocery store, or simply cruising around. People drive around and engage in a street life that consists more of waves than of hellos. They exist in the same space as the walkers, but yet higher and faster, symbolically and explicitly expressing higher status by sitting on their vehicles. Riders, by virtue of having resources which allow them to own machines, have better access to the land. They often have the resources to engage in traditional activities such as hunting.

Members of the riding class engage with their walls in a variety of ways. Some have little on their walls, but many have a hodgepodge of wall artifacts that create vibrant and cluttered appearances (see figure 2.3). Their walls are in transition, undergoing a process of formation and transformation, as the people are themselves. Faced with the standard factory-white *Qablunaaq* walls, the riding class responds by pushing back with a variety of items that

Figure 2.3   Cluttered Wall.

are symbolic of Inuit identity. Family photos demonstrate the Inuit value of interconnectedness and locate each family within larger family groups. Hunting items, such as knives, animal parts, or toy guns exhibit the role of hunting and food in Inuit society. Families reclaim old photographs taken by anthropologists, sometimes photocopied or even taken out of books, and place these on the walls. When describing to me what is on their walls, they often use the term "in" their walls. They are placing these values straight into the walls and negotiating the meaning of their Inuit identity in the time of colonization through their engagements with the walls.

Drivers

Drivers consist almost exclusively of people who have government jobs. They own ATVs and snowmobiles and do spend weekends and vacations on the land when they can, but around town they primarily use trucks. This seats them even higher in space than the riders, although slower in speed on the bumpy dirt roads. They also engage in street life, more with nods than waves or hellos—but, as with riders, if they see someone with whom they feel like stopping and chatting, they will—despite class lines. While there exists the prejudice against the walkers, class is less restrictive for interactions in a community of only a few thousand. There are, of course, a few outsiders, as in all groups, but for the most part, it is not unusual to see members of different classes (and families) stopping to talk on the street.

> As we were walking, [a friend] pulls up with her jeep/truck behind me and gives a holler, making me jump. We both laugh. (May 11, 2012)

However, in terms of visual interaction, the walkers say hi to the walkers, the riders wave (or nod) at each other, and the drivers travel the roads almost in a world apart with nods here and there to others. Drivers have heat in their trucks and, although driving outside, they are still somewhat symbolically inside, in bubbles of space passing through the air and weather without feeling their caress or their bite.

Driving-class Inuit have often had a longer affiliation with *Qablunaaq* ways of being. They are often from families who were consulted by initial forays by the government and missionaries. They have had long-standing working relationships with *Qablunaaqs* and have traveled much more extensively. They have had more resources to address anomie by *ujjirusuttiarniq amma isumatunikkut tukisiniarniq* (having an awareness and seeking to understand). This group engages with their walls to perform Inuit identity in ways that are more familiar to outside eyes. For example, they may have Inuit art on display, which is fairly uncommon in other households. They organize the pictures on their walls, still of family, in ways that match a more *Qablunaaq* aesthetic, with frames and alignment.

For all three classes, engaging with the walls addresses feelings of anomie. As a physical manifestation of symbolic cultural boundaries, they become the nexus of boundary and identity work in the home as *Arviammiut* struggle to show their walls, to perform to their walls, and hence to the South, what it means to be Inuk today.

Engagements with walls are the processual manifestation of the interaction of power knowledge systems where cultural meanings and boundaries are negotiated and contested. I follow the power knowledge system through a geography of knowledge and find that the boundary between community and land is highly salient in the everyday lives of those inhabiting the community. When a colonial power separates, or walls in a community or group from its traditional lands, "the loss of place [the separation from the land], it follows, must have devastating implications for individual and collective identity, memory, and history—and for psychological well-being" (Gieryn 2000, 482). This separation from land inhibits *ujjirusuttiarniq amma isumatunikkut tukisiniarniq* (having an awareness and seeking to understand), the most useful cultural tool in overcoming anomie.

GEOGRAPHIES OF KNOWLEDGE AND IDENTITY ACROSS CLASS

A geography of knowledge and identity emerges from the spatial layout of a place and the constellations of meanings ascribed to the built environment of the community and the built-in-meaning environment of the land. I first lay out the spatial arrangement of Arviat, reflecting on the meanings and influence of the central buildings, the role of elders as co-opted by *Qablunaaq* institutions, and shared spaces. I then address "traditional" as a sensitizing concept and the varying and surprising responses to the question "How traditional do you consider yourself to be?" I am not interrogating the term or the definition of "traditional," but rather addressing it as a sensitizing concept, a concept that emerges from the regular use of the term by *Arviammiut*, and attending to what it means in that context for them at that time, given that "traditional," in practice, has an ever-evolving definition. The geography of knowledge and identity through which *Arviammiut* move emerges through this analysis.

The Relational Ecology of Arviat: The Hamlet

Arviat resembles a long rectangle. Embedded in the tundra, Arviat consists of a small clutch of houses, relatively closely packed together. Churchill lies 260 kilometers (160 miles) to the south. East is the Hudson Bay, and west is seemingly unending tundra.

When considering the geographic space of Arviat, consider not only the physical structure of the built environment, but also its symbolic nature. The built environment demonstrates power structures within Arviat, as anywhere, and reflects a colonial history (Dorries et al. 2019). By considering the placement and symbolic presence of various structures in town, one can understand more about the sway which these institutions hold in establishing a sense of anomie at the community level.

Central Buildings as Representative of Qablunaaq Knowledge

When looking at a map of Arviat, the central location of the schools jumps out. This central area is dedicated to the dissemination of *Qablunaaq* knowledge for all ages. The schools serve to spatially orient the community toward its center, helped by a slight hill that raises the middle and elementary schools aloft. There are playgrounds outside in the center of the schools, and teachers and students alike can often be seen scampering across from school to school, coat thrown on quickly, half-zipped, and mitts and hat in hand as they brave the brief blast of cold (Field notes, 2008). This in itself is revealing. Although there are other structures located equally close, it is unusual not to dress fully and completely when running in between other buildings. The unity of purpose of these buildings serves to create a symbolically connected space, which helps to lessen the meaning of the physical distance between the buildings.

With over half the population of Arviat's 2,500 residents under the age of 15, these schools not only structure the orientation of the community, but also engage each family in town. Through centrality, proximity, and unity of purpose, the buildings impose a substantial presence. Together they represent the seat of *Qablunaaq* knowledge within Arviat.

Just north of the schools are the two grocery stores, both operated by *Qablunaaq* imports. Other buildings include the post office, government offices, the small office of the parliamentary representative of the region, as well as the Hamlet Office, where community members come to pay their local water, sewage, and garbage pick-up bills. There are also convenience stores south of the schools, which opened relatively recently.

These buildings represent *Qablunaaq* institutions. Money is necessary for legitimate presence in these buildings. Exchanges of money are routine and purposeful. Where norms around traditional food include a strong ethos of sharing (Uluadluak 2017), within these buildings, individuals can only access food through financial transactions. The symbolic status and power of the *Qablunaaq* ethos around capitalism and finance are enacted both by and within the stores. These stores, including the post office, represent the seat of knowledge about (and enactment of) *Qablunaaq* transactions and perspectives in town.

To the west of the central core of town stands the Health Center on the other slight hill in town. While not as centrally located, the hill helps to foreground the building as a landmark. In addition to emergency services, the Health Center works to disseminate *Qablunaaq* understandings of health and well-being to the community.

Being thrust into these spatial arrangements created anomie. *Qablunaaqs* also imposed a bureaucratic structure which entirely rearranged Inuit society. Grouping Inuit together made "them" easier to deal with (Scott 1998), particularly in dispensing support and health care (Thomas & Thompson 1972); note the othering process. With the good hunting grounds far away and the Hudson's Bay Company setting up shop, economic forces, by means of colonization, created the concept of *job*. Inuit in this area were introduced to a capitalist society with little economic lead-up. While a great deal of subsistence hunting still occurs, it is costly with the new snowmobiles, gas, guns, and bullets. To eat, Inuit now had to go sit in an office from nine to five for no apparent reason, producing things far removed from their past experiences. Alienation accompanied the *culture crash* and anomie of these unsettled times. In this disorientation, it is not surprising various classes had different resources to enact *ujjirusuttiarniq amma isumatunikkut tukisiniarniq* (having an awareness and seeking to understand).

Fading Institutions and Shared Spaces

Churches had previously been located at the center of the hamlet, but they are now spread relatively evenly across the most used streets in town. When giving directions, one can always use the churches as reference points, particularly because there are no street names. Since this study, street names have been put in place, but due to the political nature of naming the built environment, the names are all numerical and rarely used. Which families would street names honor? Would they be Inuktitut names or *Qablunaaq* words? In the end, numbers were affixed to corner houses, but *Arviammiut*, when they refer to roads at all, primarily refer to them by their function—such as "dump road" being the road that leads out of town toward the dump.

In the southwest corner of the community is the John Ollie Complex Community Hall and Arena. The arena, which until recently had only naturally frozen ice, rather than artificially cooled ice, nearly always remains a skating rink, but the schools, the hamlet, or other groups may take possession of the shared community hall space by reserving times. The hall is a flexible space often used for convening court, weddings, meetings, community feasts, dances, music festivals, and other group activities. The space, then, becomes alternately used for religious, hamlet, government, and recreational activities.

This space, itself, can become symbolic of a Southern presence, the enthusiasm of youth, a political space, the church, and colonial institutions, among other things. The location of the community hall on the fringes of town serves to further enable it as a flexible space. It is close enough to occupy a Western or Southern presence in the minds of *Arviammiut*, but far enough that it can be connected to the land and traditional practices and a source for practicing *ujjirusuttiarniq amma isumatunikkut tukisiniarniq* (having an awareness and seeking to understand). In front of the hall, police enter with defendants, children play in the Southern-style playground, and ATVs come and go. In the back, which looks out over the land, women cook over fires with massive pots for community feasts, young men engage in feats of daring trying to hydroplane their snowmobiles over a small body of water, the bear patrol drives slowly by, ready with their banger shots to scare the polar bears from town, and teenagers (and elders) steal secret kisses.

Flexible space is a hallmark of how *Arviammiut* maintain their homes. In most homes, although not all, furniture in the main room is minimal, consisting of a couch, small wooden kitchen table (about the size of a card table), and a few wooden chairs. Whatever the furniture, *Arviammiut* almost always push it up against the wall, creating a large central space. For the television, there will often be a small stand, but this depends on the socioeconomic situation of the family. Often the floors are linoleum. The main rooms are fairly large, usually encompassing the kitchen and living room in one.

Peter Dawson (2008) notes that the Western categories of rooms are rarely adhered to by *Arviammiut*. From hanging out watching television, to sitting on the floor around some frozen meat on a piece of cardboard, to butchering meat, to laying out patterns and fabric to cut for sewing, to large gatherings for drum dances or birthday parties with games, the space can be and is used in many ways. Mainstream Western people like to have spaces designated for particular uses and establish much less flexibility both by the heavier furniture they choose and by how much of it they choose. The Government of Canada advocated such use with their publication *Living in the New Houses* (Needham 1968), which was intended to "educate" Inuit on the use of space.

The constant negotiation of space in Arviat reflects a constant negotiation and struggle with the structure of the home and the spaces the unfriendly architecture creates as *Arviammiut* work to perform their Inuitness to the walls (as a manifestation of *Qablunaaq* ways of knowing and being), each other, and themselves. Gareau and Dawson note that *Arviammiut* "spatially graft their unique activities and cultural values onto the Euro-Canadian-style houses" (Gareau & Dawson 2004), echoing the theme of flexibility in the use of space.

For Inuit, their emplacement on the land is central to their knowledge. By understanding Arviat through an ecological lens, a geography of identity and knowledge emerges. Western, or Southern, knowledge is located at the center of town, while "traditional" knowledge is located on the land. The physical centrality of *Qablunaaq* institutions brings normative messages which are mismatched with Inuit practices. Seeking to know and understand are not embodied in Western systems which teach through memorization and discipline.

TRADITIONAL KNOWLEDGE AND BEING TRADITIONAL

One of the most prevalent sensitizing concepts (Blumer 1969; van den Hoonaard, W. 1997) that emerges from time spent in an Inuit hamlet is the notion of *traditional knowledge*. This phrase is bandied about constantly. People talk about traditional food, clothing, and practices at every turn. The radio in Arviat has at least three periods during the day, of several hours each, when *Arviammiut* can call in to the radio station and speak relatively freely over the airwaves (one cannot, however, slander individuals or businesses).

There is also a wide CB radio system in place. It is common for the word "traditional" to come up frequently when individuals are talking over these instruments of group communication. When one visits people's homes, talks about traditional practices and skills can be practically non-stop. This may increase when I am present because I am a *Qablunaaq*, but after having lived there for so long, I expect this effect would have waned, and I was witnessing something near a normal backstage level of talk about traditionality.

Tradition carries malleable elements which are used for political ends—but it is somehow more than that in its appeal, its resonance, and its symbolic nature. Tradition is, strictly defined, "anything transmitted or handed down from past to present . . . that which has exemplars or custodians" (Shils 1981:12–13). In order to define the idea of tradition, however, we must define it *against* something else. Traditional acts are laden with symbolic meaning. Tradition works to ally individuals and groups with an imagined sense of the past through guiding patterns (which may have changed dramatically through time, whether people realize it or not). It is for this reason that the name of a society is so important to its members, particularly when interacting with other, more dominant, societies.

What does being traditional mean to *Arviammiut*, as a sensitizing concept? I should pause here to remind the reader of my positionality as a non-Inuk person in the scene. One advantage to this was that *Arviammiut* taught me about traditionality quite overtly, educating me as a newcomer to the community. What I present here is what emerged through the data as traditional for them, from their perspective, not mine. For them, being traditional involves having traditional knowledge, particularly having skills which come from and have context on the land. Certain things are irrelevant to certain places. The hamlet is both a *Qablunaaq* and a colonial place, whereas the land is an Inuk place, although persistent resistance in the messy context of colonial contestation works to undermine that (Dorries et al. 2019). Irrelevant to the land are things such as bureaucracy, formal schooling, and air travel. The practice of traditional knowledge is not imperative to the hamlet, however *Arviammiut* bring the rhetoric of traditional skills into the community and practice or adapt it whenever possible, to leverage status, identity, political power, and to preserve their culture.

Many institutions, albeit colonial-inspired in format and symbolic of Southern presence and knowledge, try to connect with people at the grassroots level by employing terminology such as "traditional." For example, the Inuit-led Department of Education, discussed above, maintains a rhetoric centered on traditional knowledge and practices. As Inuit assert their own agency and identity through these Southern-imported institutions, they turn to this rhetoric as a way to make the institutions their own.

The *IQ* Principles, briefly introduced above, are the clearest example of this process. The Department of Education, as well as the territorial government, espouse the *IQ* Principles as guiding beacons for all activity (at least in rhetoric). The Nunavut Government defines *IQ* Principles under the Inuit belief system as follows, "*Inuit Qaujimajatuqangit* is traditional Inuit Knowledge" (Dept. of Human Resources, Nunavut 2013), while Mark Kalluak, who is *Arviammiut*, defines it as "what Inuit have known all along" (Kalluak 2017, 41). You will see some of the *IQ* principles in the titles of this book's chapters. *IQ* distinctly bring Inuit values forward as principles that have importance in any contemporary setting (Akittiq & Karetak 2017; Ayalik 2017; Karetak, Tester, and Tagalik 2017) such that practicing *IQ* principle, that is, Inuit knowledge, is a way of being, not only a collection of traditional skills. *Inuit Tapiriit Kanatami* (ITK) is an organization that applies *IQ* principles to improve the well-being and health of Inuit.

"HOW TRADITIONAL DO YOU CONSIDER YOURSELF TO BE?"

From the institutional level to the grassroots level, the term "traditional" is leveraged to perform identity work. I (incorrectly, despite living there for five years) assumed that by using this term in an interview question, a term which had emerged from my field sites and participants themselves, I would be asking an "easy" question. I asked, "how traditional do you consider yourself?" This question turned out to be anything but simple and provided a puzzle about space and place, power, knowledge, and its relationship to identity, revealing the symbolic meaning of the built environment.

Many participants meeting their *own* requirements for being traditional and whom I had considered very traditional, based on their behavior and their own narratives, responded that they were not traditional at all, and vice versa. The answers I was getting were not what I expected and, therefore, confusing. What I had assumed would be a simple question was far from it. I had forgotten my own positionality, and am grateful for the gentleness with which participants showed me this was a loaded question.

Taking a space-based approach, the geography of identity and knowledge, the spatial arrangements, emerge as an explanation for the surprising (to me) answers. Take a look at the map of Arviat in figure 2.4. Western knowledge is located at the center of town, while traditional knowledge is located on the land (Takano 2005). For *Arviammiut*, being traditional is connected to place. I was, essentially, asking how close participants are to the land. They agentically reflected on the situation and answered by evaluating how far from the center they are, not how far from the edges. My question implied that there

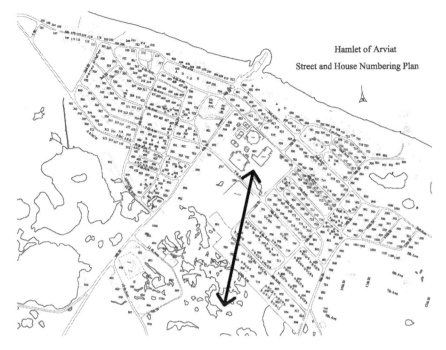

Figure 2.4   Street Map of Arviat, with Highlights and Continuum of Traditionality.

was one scale between the center of town and the land. In this frame, it was more important to them to show me, as an outsider, their close relationship to the center of town, that they were *Qablunaaq-fluent*, than to show me their traditionality. *Qablunaaq* fluency is the ability to engage smoothly (fluently) in *Qablunaaq* ways of being when necessary. In order to demonstrate this fluency to me, they had to place themselves further away from the land, distancing themselves from traditionality in order to appear more *Qablunaaq-fluent*. *While I was inadvertently asking "how close or far from the land are you?" they were answering, "how close or far from the centre are you?"* This reflects the power of the *Qablunaaq* institutions and how power ties in with the built environment and problems of meaning, particularly in this colonial context.

By locating themselves on the sliding scale between the land and the center of town, *Arviammiut* conceptualize of themselves both as being in close proximity to one location (i.e., one kind of knowledge and way of knowing), but also farther from the other location (i.e., the other kind of knowledge and way of knowing). In actuality, there are two continua, and strength in traditional knowledge is correlated with being *Qablunaaq*-fluent. The negotiation of meanings around traditional and *Qablunaaq* fluency occurs spatially, with walls acting as boundary objects, both at the level of the home, as with facing anomie, and at the level of the built environment of the hamlet, as with facing my question of how traditional one is. In addition, in line with the *IQ* principle of *ujjirusuttiarniq amma isumatunikkut tukisiniarniq* (having an awareness and seeking to understand), participants sought to demonstrate successfully having an awareness and seeking to understand *Qablunaaq* ways of doing and being, despite this being a mismatch.

Participants come across as relatively traditional or not according to their *behavior* and how that behavior either aligns or does not align with *their own definitions of traditional practices*. If, however, a participant can make any claims to being *Qablunaaq*-fluent—either from being so, *or by not being traditional*, they usually do. Most participants are both traditional and *Qablunaaq* fluent, or neither traditional nor *Qablunaaq*-fluent. This is correlated with social class: those who are both more traditional and more *Qablunaaq*-fluent are in the higher classes.

Fluent in Two Worldviews

When interviewing people whose behavior the community views as both traditional and *Qablunaaq*-fluent, I was constantly amazed at the response to "how traditional do you consider yourself?" Drivers, by and large, answered that they were not traditional. At the same time, as Nadia responded that she does not think of herself as traditional, she was eating seal intestines and dipping them in *igunak* (aged, raw meat). Lauren, a teacher, also known for teaching sewing in the community and participating in and promoting drum dancing and throat singing, answered "Mm, not really."

This trend was apparent most of the time for participants who exist in both worlds. Often the lack of specific skills or, conversely, the presence of certain routine practices would be cited to justify the answer:

> Not traditional like my parents. Like I don't have country food here. We go to my parents to have country food and go have tea and bannock and stuff like that, but not so traditional here. We speak a lot of Inuktitut, but not as traditional as my parents. (Abigail)

Abigail justifies her answer by tallying for me her participation in certain skilled practices, such as the preparation and consumption of country food. I should stress that the consumption of traditional foods can indeed be a skilled activity, just as the consumption of *Qablunaaq* foods can be.

Meanwhile, Carmel takes the opposite approach. She stresses to me the *Qablunaaq* behaviors that she, and others, engage in as justification for her response:

Today, nowadays, it looks different. But, um, compared to long time ago, but I don't, *illa* [I mean], [pause]. . . . I was not born in 50s. So I don't know [about a] long time ago, but nowadays. . . . We got school and we have to be clean, *illa*, our body. And health, we have to be healthy. *Ii* [Yeah]. (Carmel)

She clearly vacillates about how to answer the question, but after her slight pause, she decides to emphasize how the community as a whole should be seen as *Qablunaaq*-fluent, as participating in certain behavior which minimizes stigma that she might encounter from *Qablunaaqs* about education, cleanliness, and health.

Only participants in the driving class and who are generally considered by the community to be both traditional and *Qablunaaq*-fluent made references to the idea that normalcy, today, consisted of not being traditional. Carmel, attuned to both sets of knowledge, ways of knowing, and worldviews, most clearly articulated the relationship between knowledge and geography when she asserted that "normal" means living in town and *not* being traditional, being more *Qablunaaq*-like. In addition, these participants realize that, having defined the community as rather more *Qablunaaq* than not; making claims to normalcy affords the participants, personally, some further claim to being *Qablunaaq*-fluent.

Some are explicit in their alignment with ideas of normalcy:

Well, um, I'm just more like, *qanu* [how can I say it?]. Just like being a mom, trying to be, *I'm not like a real Inuk*, but I never graduated and all that stuff, cause I was abused here. Yeah. *So I'm just, like, normal.* [Author's emphasis] (Amber)

Amiu [I don't know]. Maybe, *like all the other people* now. [shrugs] [Author's emphasis] (Nina)

Amber and Nina both succinctly align themselves with normalcy and also define normalcy *in opposition* to being traditional. By doing so, Amber and Nina, among others, are agentically communicating that they are well and truly "located" close to the *Qablunaaq* institutions which dominate the center of the hamlet and which exert power over *Arviammiut*. They are performing both identity work and reputation work. The institutions' location at the center of the hamlet emphasizes the value of being *Qablunaaq-fluent*, conveying to *Arviammiut* how they should position themselves when given opportunities to present themselves to and do reputation work for a *Qablunaaq* researcher, forestalling judgment on my part, as a *Qablunaaq*. The word "normal" is a powerful word.

Participants chose, more often than not, to represent themselves as *Qablunaaq*-fluent over traditional. When one considers *Arviammiut* knowledge to be geographically situated, with traditional knowledge on the land, and *Qablunaaq* knowledge at the center of the hamlet, that is, when considered from the Inuit worldview, these answers make sense. While I imagined my question to be seeking a determination of how close or far they are from the land, participants determine how close or far they are from the center in response. My position as a white researcher and the interactional effect on participants was never quite as stark as when I reviewed the responses to this question. Stuck within the confines of my question, participants resort to telling me that they are not traditional, even though, by their own standards, they would be considered traditional.

One participant stood out from the others in this category, Samuel. Although he has some community college education and is *Qablunaaq*-fluent, he now wraps himself in his Inuktitut identity, having felt extreme frustration with the nepotism in town, his inability to get a job, and the government's treatment of him and his family. When I asked Samuel how traditional he considers his family to be, he responded:

> We're very traditional, *tia'na* [for sure]. For example, like, right now social assistance and *hunaikkua, nutaqanu,* [how do I say it? Child something] child tax, our main *kiinaujak* [money], money, *kihiani* [but] today we just had, we just had our child tax and my children would be very happy to have sour chewy things. Good. And at the same time, if I catch seal, caribou, fish, bring it in, they would stop eating what they're eating and then they would go for fresh blood right away. . . . Now I wish my children to keep them in mind at least you, you feed [them] fresh blood, fresh blood, fresh blood. Best of my ability, fresh blood, fresh blood.

Here, Samuel not only appeals to a particular activity to align himself with traditionality, but he refers to the specific activity for which the Inuit are most harshly judged, eating raw meat. Samuel invokes this powerfully with his repetition of the words "fresh blood." Samuel has *Qablunaaq* fluency, but has routinely been denied an identity which includes that fluency, such as when he is consistently denied jobs because he has no important family connections. In the face of this denial, he turns to traditionality for strength of identity, even while telling me about his plans for further education.

Fluency in Inuit Worldviews

Most of those in the riding group have more access to resources to practice traditions than the walkers through an ability to afford to be out on the land. They may not have, however, access to training which makes them *Qablunaaq-fluent*. When participants have no way to make a clear claim on *Qablunaaq* fluency, but are traditional, they unanimously say that they are indeed traditional. Again, behavior becomes a reference point for the participant to justify their answer. Beatrice, for example, expands her answer to include the family, giving the family a collective traditional identity.

> *Ii* [yes]. From one, I know these girls, they're usually making something, like *Inuk*'s [an Inuit person's] picture or iglu or dog team or *kamutik* [traditional dog-team and snow mobile sled], something like that.

Beatrice lists her children's demonstration of their connection to traditional iconography as a way to explain her answer in the context of physical separation from the land and traditional knowledge. Gabriella, on the other hand, cites her family's inability to behave in ways that she considers expected and appropriate to *Qablunaaq* ways of being:

> *LJ:* How traditional do you consider yourself?
>
> *Gabriella:* We live our lives the way we do, like Inuit style. Sometimes we can't, *illa* [I mean], we can't do how *Qablunaaq* do, we don't know how, so it's our Inuit way of doing, you sleep there, you sleep there, so we can fit in each other.

In both cases, riding class members who are traditional and not as *Qablunaaq*-fluent not only lay claim to a traditional identity, but also respond to direct questions about themselves with answers that encompass the whole family. This is representative of their responses throughout the interview. This not only speaks to the ways in which individuals relate to their own identity but also the ways in which knowledge is considered as valid only when it emerges organically from a group through consultation. It is not what you or I know, but what we come to agree to together. It is not that Gabriella or Beatrice is traditional or not, but what their behavior looks like within the entire family. If Beatrice's children are drawing pictures of *qamutik*, she is implicated in the process because they are a family. Others, such as Brandon, however, could not formulate a response to the question;

> I don't know. I haven't really thought about it. I, *amiu* [I don't know]. Never really thought about it, actually.

This answer was surprising because of how constantly and consistently the community mobilizes the rhetoric around the sensitizing concept of *traditional*. Brandon reveals how *Arviammiut* sometimes struggle with engaging conceptions of the self in the formal interview. Brandon does think about and talk about traditionality within the community. When pressed, however, to verbalize a connection between his conceptions of himself as external to and comparative to the community, he responds that he has not thought about it.

Fluency in *Qablunaaq* Worldviews

A minority in the riding class, on the fringes between riding and walking, identified as not traditional but was fluent in *Qablunaaq* worldviews. Of these participants, one did not answer this question, one prevaricated, and the other two, the only two who clearly addressed the question, asserted that they were not traditional.

Valerie emphasizes the value she places on traditional culture but admits that she falls short when it comes to acting traditional:

> *LJ:* So how important do you think it is to maintain traditional skills?
>
> *Valerie:* It's important. Really, like, I, like my mother taught me most of the stuff, and I feel it's important for us who learn from our parents, like we need to give that knowledge before we lose them. So, us new parents who were not giving any knowledge to our younger ones, like, we're just being quiet. We're not sharing or we're not, I think it's important to teach and share the knowledge that we got from our parents.
>
> *LJ:* So do you guys work hard to do that?
>
> *Valerie:* Not really. No. We're busy with today's society, I guess.

She admits to having learned traditional knowledge from her parents, but aside from some modern sewing, she does not typically engage in traditional activities. It is the knowledge of and participation in activities, or not, which establishes the participants, according to their own definitions, as traditional or not. Because Valerie is too busy with "today's society," which is located physically in the hamlet and implies *Qablunaaq* society, she neither passes on her traditional knowledge nor engages in these activities herself. This affects her identity as Inuk, and that of her family and children.

Uncertainty about Fluency

Most members of the walking class struggle for access to the land but also lack legitimacy in the center areas of town—in *Qablunaaq* institutions of education and finance. These participants were ambivalent in their responses, often vacillating or avoiding committing. In making claims around traditional practices, young women refer to behavior and activities that they engage in with their families. Jasmine stood out as a walker who answered the question with relative confidence. She does not partake in traditional activities regularly, such as sewing or drum dances, so she references speaking Inuktitut:

> *LJ:* How traditional a family do you consider yourself?

Jasmine: We're very traditional.

LJ: Can you say more about that?

Jasmine: We mostly talk in Inuktitut to our kids. First it was English, then I wanted my girls to know Inuktitut more than English, so. So, we talk to them more in Inuktitut.

In all, this segment of the population, the majority of whom suffer greatly materially and socially within the community, finds itself in a morass, and my appearance on the scene is more confusing than anything else. Because I had spent many years developing friendships with these participants, they were willing to talk to me and were quite open in their interviews—insisting I take pictures of the worst of their living conditions, willing to talk to me at length about the items on their walls, and eager to help me in my schooling.

However willing they were to allow me to see inside their daily lives, they seem lost in the suffering around them. Brittany hardly goes out. Her husband is addicted to drugs and occasionally becomes violent. She has appeared at my house to say goodbye before being flown by social services back to her mother in the next town North, only to return shortly thereafter and resume vigil over her children in that household. Melissa, as another example, shared with me during our interview, stories of family abuse, rape, and both emotional and physical violence she has experienced from her family. Of course, not all in this category suffer from internal family violence. Alice, for example, has a very happy home and has adopted many children. All in this category, however, do suffer material poverty, often quite acutely.

This poverty prevents these women from participating fully in the life of the greater community, as well as from acquiring the socialization necessary to be able to engage with me in quite the same way that others in the community could. In addition, they lack the material resources to afford access to the land (snowmobiles, ATVs, gas, and so on). This cuts them off from access to traditional knowledge and presents a challenge for their identity as "real" traditional Inuit—they are "more inside now" (Brittany), associating the internal space inside their walls as a *Qablunaaq* space, with different cultural practices attached to it. They lack resources for *ujjirusuttiarniq amma isuma-tunikkut tukisiniarniq* (having an awareness and seeking to understand). This group also has engaged far less agentically with their walls (and their ano-mie), many of which are simply blank, despite the successful ways that other groups agentically use their walls to express Inuit values such as intercon-nectedness (*aktuaturaunniqarniq*), and bring those values inside the walls.

Elders

Being an elder is a *master status* (Hughes [1945] 1984), which directly con-
notes strength in traditional practices. They represent a time that was. Several
elders alive today were in their early twenties or late teens when the relocation
into houses happened. By that age, they would have had their own children.
Other elders remember living in tents near the settlement before all the houses
were shipped up, or in one of the earlier houses, such as the matchbox houses.

Evelyn, for example, remembers living in a house when there was only a
handful of houses in town. Her daughter translates:

LJ: Do you remember the first time you came into a house?

Evelyn's Daughter: She wants to show you a picture. . . . She can't remember
because they already had a house, or there was already a house before they
were born. Even before . . . they had a house that was their house. Arviat had
only five houses, buildings, that, um. Anglican Church, the Roman Catholic
Church, RCMP, Northern Store and their house, and my dad's house.

LJ: And how come you got to be one of the first to go into houses?

Evelyn's Daughter: Her father was rich because, um, he had caught a lot of,
um, he caught a lot of foxes. That's how he had a lot of, she considered him
rich. Even had a boat. Her dad was very *ajungi* [able]. Very rich. He had many
dogs.

Evelyn grew up in a privileged family, but still trades on her mastery of traditional ways of being as an elder by continuing on to talk about spending
time in tents in the summer and the difference of sewing indoors and outdoors, remarking that sewing inside a house with traditional skins is difficult
because of the dry air. Tori and Oliver, however, do remember living on the
land before houses.

Tori's translator: During summer, they would go boating to Padlei. Her father
would go by kayak by river. And, the rest of the family would go to Maguse
River from Akuq by walking on the side of the river when Tori was a child.
When they reach their destination at Padlei, they would spend the winter there.
End of October, they would start living in iglus. During the summer they lived
in *tupiks*, tents. And, they stayed in tents all summer. When it gets cold, her
mother would sew caribou clothing. While they are still living in iglus during
winter, her father would hunt and trap foxes.

Oliver's Translator: Yeah, whenever he sees old pictures on the wall, he gets
happy because he gets reminded from the old days.

LJ: Did you live in an iglu when you were a child?

Oliver's Translator: Ii [Yes]. Yeah, he makes iglus and he knows the land.

LJ: So how is an iglu different from this kind of house?

Oliver's Translator: The house is more warmer than the iglus.

LJ: Do you remember the first time that you saw a building?

Oliver's Translator: Yeah, he first saw a building, he remembers first seeing a building at Padlei.

LJ: What did he notice first about it?

Oliver's Translator: The first building he saw was a get-together building at Padlei. They would have a feast or dinner or supper get-together.

Tori then says she started making *kamiks* [boots] at the age of 13 and continues on about where in the iglu activities would happen and how the sleeping shelf was maintained. Oliver continues on to talk about the changes in expectations around privacy, as well as the difference in temperature in the contemporary indoors and how that has altered how and when people wear clothing.

As elders, they are expected to routinely tell stories about Inuit culture "before." They are valued members of the community because they embody symbolic links to what makes Inuit, to the core of Inuit identity. They have lived on the land, whether in tents or iglus, located at the heart of Inuit knowledge. They know. They are definitively Inuk. Elders come, in essence and in fact, *from* the land. In some sense, they are long-term visitors to the hamlet and are regarded as symbolic connections to the land and the knowledge located thereon. Their identity is completely tied up in their knowledge which they bring from the land, and their role is to create a symbolic presence of the land-ways-of-knowing-and-being within the walls. Evelyn returns to this theme several times during her interview, for example:

Evelyn's Daughter: Back in her day Inuit, from living on the land and off the land, and now to living in today, and she enjoys putting stuff to show, like, for everyone to see or . . .

When she started, like, when she was on the land, she didn't even know that there, other things would have existed. She, from nothing to something. She felt she's a capable person, *ajungi* [able], because of that experience. She's seen two, Inuit way and *Qablunaaq* way. Her parents were, uh, very able people. Very able. And, um, they helped her when she was a child and now she, because they're no longer around, she's now living in modern world. Modern today.

Evelyn conceptualizes herself as not only coming from the past but as part of the past. That was "her day." Note that she also demonstrates the prioritization of *Qablunaaq* over Inuit ways of being, saying she went from nothing to something as she gestures to the house around her. Of course, she did gain substantially in material possessions.

She also sees herself as a being from that past and living in the "modern world." She brings with her knowledge from the land into the space of the walls. This is her master status. She remarks to me casually as I tell her about my challenges when sewing seal-skin *kamiks*:

> *Evelyn's Daughter:* You didn't grow up with it. It'll be hard. And herself too, she didn't grow up in the Western world, so she'll find other things difficult too. Just the same.

She did not grow up in the Western world. By definition, she, and the other elders, are traditional and most of them have not developed the skills of *Qablunaaq* fluency because they are rewarded for their master status as icons of traditionality. Although separated from the land, they have the awareness and understanding to resolve their anomie in unique ways.

Note that three participants stood out from the overall pattern, all of whom were both respected in the community for their traditional knowledge and practices and also known for their *Qablunaaq* fluency, and by all members of the driving class. They each also earn their livings as cultural representatives of Inuit traditions to *Qablunaaq* institutions or people. I should note that selling traditionality may sound coarse to our *Qablunaaq* ears, however, for *Arviammiut* it carries a different meaning. *Arviammiut* have observed the introduction of Southern money. Money is used to purchase things of worth. Therefore, if a *Qablunaaq* is willing to pay for something, it is a marker that the object of purchase has worth. Following this logic through, if a *Qablunaaq* pays for traditional knowledge or behavior, they are showing, from the perspective of the Inuk, a respect and acknowledgment that traditions have worth to them. *Arviammiut* have come to expect, and even demand at times, that *Qablunaaqs* pay for traditional knowledge and activities as a way to elicit demonstrations from *Qablunaaq* that Inuit traditionality is worth paying for, that is, valuable, in a *Qablunaaq* world. The resulting problem is that some institutions, as I mentioned above, will then hire or pay for elders only as token representatives.

Nevertheless, those who make their living as representatives of traditionality need to maintain that traditional identity as their most salient identity at all times. This accounts for these three participants' breaking the pattern. All three show themselves through their own activities and according to their own definitions to be both traditional and *Qablunaaq*-fluent, however, all three answered that they are traditional.

Felix, for example, works for a *Qablunaaq* institution as a "young elder." He represents, for that institution and the people who work there, a source of traditional knowledge and practices. He talks about how traditional he considers himself:

> Like each group has their preferences, and because we prefer so many varieties, our family has a wide range which makes it a lot more work. . . . We're, you know, we're trying new things that we're aware of that we like to have and it takes an organized crew to produce a volume [of traditional food]. And I think, *because I was brought up with the program* where I was every day living that style, *I can maybe manage it.* . . . But it is, and always has been, Inuit tradition to, soon as people visit from other places, or anybody from your family gets in and the, um, to offer them something to eat. . . . And so I think it's still part of a natural, cultural event. But I think you have to have been influenced by the program, I think. Cause there's a lot of people who grew up without it already and it's pretty hard even when you know how, so of course it's way harder if you don't. It's not that you don't like to. You just don't know how to process it or use it. . . . So even a simple product like bannock is, people don't make that anymore. I mean, everything else is so easy to get. We just have to open a package, I mean. So I think that's partly why I think a lot of them will be traditional when they visit somebody. [Author's emphasis]

In this brief excerpt alone, Felix provides much insight. He reveals a very Western understanding of cultural systems, in this quotation and elsewhere in his interview, referring to them as "programs," but at the same time, he refers to practicing traditionality as practicing certain skills, which one learns from growing up in the "program." Felix reveals his master status as a representative of traditionality both in his content and form. His traditionality and how he can sell that to *Qablunaaqs* have become a large part of his identity in town and within his family.

All three of these anomalies demonstrate experience with selling their traditional knowledge in particular ways to a Southern audience or Southern-style organizations and are, therefore, both well-versed in presenting themselves as Inuit who are strong in traditional cultures, as well as invested in maintaining this identity as highly traditional. They are also, of all participants, the ones who have had to field questions like this before, but in very specific situations and almost always for pay as representatives of tradition. They have all, therefore, developed a particular *signature story* (Kenyon & Randall 1997) about their traditionality.

SCALES OF KNOWLEDGE: CONTINUA OF INUIT AND *QABLUNAAQ* FLUENCY

Throughout all the interviews, across groups, participants mobilized skills and behaviors to make claims on traditionality and/or *Qablunaaq* fluency. What, exactly, does traditionality mean to *Arviammiut* and what does *Qablunaaq* fluency mean? As figure 2.4 (above) demonstrated, my question revealed an understanding from the Western perspective of one continuum from traditional to *Qablunaaq*-fluent. However, these are, of course, better considered from an Inuit perspective on two scales of knowledge; one measuring proximity to traditional knowledge and one measuring proximity to *Qablunaaq* knowledge. It is to these two scales I now turn.

As I constructed these scales, I relied heavily on my fieldnotes and ethnographic experience, in addition to my interviews. In considering the nature of these scales of knowledge, the continuous nature emerges as salient. It is not simply a matter of what is traditional knowledge and what is not. These forms of knowledge are experienced as continua (see figure 2.5). Sewing, for example, is a form of traditional knowledge for which Arviat is particularly renowned in the North. One can be proficient at sewing traditional items with traditional materials, primarily animal skins. One can also sew traditional items, such as parkas, with modern materials and a sewing machine. One may have learned to sew by watching elders or parents, or may have been taught at school. Or, one may not be able to sew at all. These are not binary categories of ability or non-ability, of having-knowledge or not-having-knowledge.

I have placed an (S) or a (B) after each of the items on the list. These stand for Skill (S) or Behavior (B). I am *not* arguing that any of these elements constitutes a skill or a behavior, and, if pressed, I would argue that they are all different forms of knowledge and enactment of knowledge. These denote, rather, whether people, themselves, consider each element to be a skill or a behavior.

What becomes notable when taking this into account is that the majority of the elements which comprise "traditional," according to participants' own definitions, are considered to be skills. Skills, according to the understanding of participants, can be taught and learned. Most are eager to teach and pleased when Southerners show an interest in learning Inuit skills (i.e., learning about Inuit traditionality and how to participate in it, practicing having an awareness and seeking to understand). *Qablunaaq* fluency, however, requires one to practice behaviors which, according to the understanding of many people, are not learned but innate. There is a *kind of person* who is on time or not. Broadly, people believe it is not learned. Carmel says that *Ariviammiut* know they "should" be clean now, but *Arviammiut* and *Qablunaaqs* alike consider that to be a personality trait that is hard to learn.

Traditional Knowledge

More:	Less:
Traditional Sewing Ability . . . Modern Sewing Ability . . . Learned at School . . . Cannot Sew (S)	
Speaking Inuktitut (S)	Speaks "Baby" or "Lazy" Inuktitut
Is an Elder/Spends Time with Elders (S/B)	Does not Listen to Elders
Prepares/Eats Country Food (S)	Eats Only Store-Bought Food
Hunting Ability/Time "On the Land" (S)	Does not go "On the Land"
Endures the Cold Well (S/B)	Does not Emphasize Cold
Religious (B)	Not Religious
Informal Behavior (B)	Formal Behavior
Dog Sledding/Transportation (S)	Relatively Sedentary
Engages in Community Life/CB Radio (S/B)	Stays Mainly at Home/Quiet

Qablunaaq Competency

More:	Less:
Speaking English (S)	Limited English
Willing to be Disciplined by Bureaucracy (B)	Ignores Bureaucracy
Attends School (B)	Does not Attend School
Explains with Linear Thinking (S/B)	Explains Things with Stories
Cooking Ability/ Cooks Meals (S/B)	Does not Use Recipes/Cook
Clean House (B)	Messy House
Formal/Polite (B)	Never Knocking
Travel "South" (other than Medical) (B)	Travel North/No Travel
Not Spitting (B)	Willing to Spit, even Indoors
Belief in Rules/Structured Time (B)	Eating/Sleeping Anytime

Figure 2.5   Continua of Traditionality and *Qablunaaq* Fluency.

In short, people feel that one can learn traditional knowledge (and therefore fluency), but one cannot learn *Qablunaaq* fluency in the same way. Therefore, if one is not traditional, one is simply lacking the knowledge to practice authentic Inuit identity. But if one is not *Qablunaaq*-fluent, then they are considered to have innate problems. It becomes obvious, now, how stereotypes develop and perpetuate. Revealing a generic social process around the formation of stereotypes is my only goal in presenting this table. The process of laissez-faire racism reproduces a sense of group inferiority and superiority along colonial lines (Denis 2015). I hope this adds to our understanding of how stereotypes form. By understanding, we, all together, can dismantle.

CONCLUSION

Walls act as boundary objects both at the level of the home and at the level of the community. The walls of the home come to represent *Qablunaaq* eyes and

Inuit perform identity work at those walls as they work to bring their culture indoors and turn these colonized spaces into Inuit spaces. The walls become symbolic of Inuit experiences of *anomie*. As *Arviammiut* interact with their walls, they work toward overcoming anomie as they discipline their walls into Inuit objects. In doing so, they are negotiating and defining their relationship with the power relations of the built environment as well as their relationship with their colonizers. They do this with varying success across class groupings, namely the walkers, the riders, and the drivers, depending on their ability for *ujjirusuttiarniq amma isumatunikkut tukisiniarniq* (having an awareness and seeking to understand).

In addition, the community works to define and navigate its relationship with Western (Southern) knowledge and power relations through the built environment of Arviat. Overall, an ecological view of the community helps one understand the responses across categories to the question of how traditional participants consider themselves and their families. The *Qablunaaq* institutions are located at the center of town, which represents *Qablunaaq* power and is the locus of *Qablunaaq* knowledge. Traditional knowledge is located on the land. This makes it hard to seek awareness and understanding of Inuit knowledge and identity from within town.

Socioeconomic class influences how *Arviammiut* move through these spaces and access traditional knowledge and identity. *Walkers* roam restlessly through the liminal spaces between the center (*Qablunaaq* knowledge and ways of being) and the periphery (traditional knowledge and ways of being), accessing neither completely successfully. *Riders* move through these same spaces higher in space and status. They are able to access *Qablunaaq* and Inuit spaces more successfully. *Drivers* travel these same routes, from an even higher perspective, enclosed in bubbles of space. They have more decision-making power in the community and fully access *Qablunaaq* spaces and they, other than the few *Qablunaaq* power elites, also can afford time on the land and easier access to traditional knowledge.

The spatial arrangements of Arviat place *Arviammiut* in *Qablunaaq* spaces, walled-off from their traditional knowledge. Performance of traditional skills, as opposed to what they perceive of as behavior, entwines with the performance of identity as Inuit. Knowledge is key. The walls act as boundary objects through which the cultural boundaries between Inuit and *Qablunaaq* ways of knowing and ways of being are enacted, negotiated, and contested.

Chapter 3

Pilimmaksarniq [Skills and Knowledge Acquisition]

Transmission of Knowledge and Sewing

Because of the deep association between the land and traditional knowledge, Takano (2005) argues that time on the land, outside of the walls of homes and hamlet, is equivalent to traditionality. This chapter explores the meaning of time on the land, and how, through rhetoric and dramaturgy, *Arviammiut* strive to reconcile accessing traditional knowledge on the land while living within *Qablunaaq* structures.

Knowledge, in the past, was transmitted by watching and doing, visually and by hand (Ayalik 2017; Uluadluak 2017). Walls create insulation from observability (Coser 1961), which is a problem when learning through observation is the primary way in which knowledge is transmitted through generations. Telling people what to do and how to do it, a model which Western educational practices embody, is not only incongruent with Inuit educational practices of *pilimmaksarniq* (skills and knowledge acquisition), but is diametrically opposed to them. Inuit allow people to make mistakes, believing that this is the only way to learn what are good and bad mistakes, rather than telling someone what to do, including when this involves danger (Uluadluak 2017). In addition, Inuit associate telling someone when and what to learn, and how to do things, with the Canadian South. Thus, if they were to embrace this approach, it would undermine their ability to perform Inuitness.

In short, Inuit learning practices do not work as well in houses, and the specific ways in which they would need to adapt go against their cultural practices in ways that would assimilate them into the ways of being of their colonizers. The transmission of knowledge suffers. Additionally, gendered knowledge suffers in different ways, with women's knowledge at a greater risk of being lost. First, I discuss learning on the land, and then move to learning within walls. Following that, I use the example of sewing to demonstrate the gendered impact.

LEARNING ON THE LAND

Due to the close relationship of the land and traditional knowledge, *Arviam-miut* place a high degree of importance on going out on the land for the sake of learning (Takano 2005). There is a sacred relationship with place (Watts 2013). The land and the hamlet represent "two worlds" (Evelyn). While I wonder in my field notes if "before" seems less salient to walkers and "less time on the land, less connection [with the past]?" (Field notes, May 16, 2012), many participants draw direct links to the importance of being on the land with their own learning about both the past and traditional activities. When telling me about time on the land, they referred to things they had learned from parents or elders, such as Melissa who tells me that her grandparents taught her to fish. Time on the land was also considered part of my education as an outsider (Field notes, September 2, 2004).

In considering the education of their children, the land becomes even more prominent. Lily, for example, plans on taking her granddaughter Emily on the land because she is getting older and it is time to "teach her how the elders used to live" (Field notes, July 20, 2010). Gemma talks about the importance of time on the land for her children:

> Big difference. It's more free in here [on the land]. And back home, like for kids, like they can go out where there's no traffic or kids fighting kids. That's why, since what? April, they've been not going to school every day cause we're back here and forth. Just to know how it is. *Illa* [I mean], I want them to learn their education, but part of my other thing is how to be out in the land. . . . Like, helping my mother, their grandmother. And she teach my younger kids what they are. . . . And the caribou skins. From cooking, to make *nipku* [dried meat], how to cut up *tuktu* [caribou], and from little, *hunaiqua* [what are they called]? Worms, bugs. (Gemma)

Lucia shares this sentiment as well, explaining that she considers it important to go daily to the land "just to be there all day and just be with our grandchildren. Let them play outside and whatever." While Gemma and her mother are continuously articulating to the children what they are doing, for Lucia merely being on the land is enough for them to learn and grow, as well as to connect to traditional knowledge, gaining *IQ* principles (Akittiq & Karetak 2017; Ayalik 2017). In either case, the importance of the land in learning is highlighted. Lily tells me of her hopes:

> If they teach [traditional skills] in the school, maybe they would learn. Or if an elder would talk in front of the students. Students are good learners, but some, they would just listen. So for the good learners they would survive and learn and remember, *if they go to a land trip*. [Author's emphasis]

Lily sees the learning as incomplete and ineffective if it is not solidified with actual time on the land for *pilimmaksarniq* (skills and knowledge acquisition), beyond the *Qablunaaq* built environment of the hamlet. *Arviammiut* term this a *land trip*.

Participants often come back from land trips with found items. Ruby, for example, tells me that the new baleen on her wall was something they found on the land "from before" during a land trip near Repulse Bay. They were able to roll it up to bring it home with them (Field notes, May 10, 2012). Abigail also displays found items on her wall, listing a grouping of found items as the best thing she has ever seen on a wall, explaining:

> My dad gave it to me. His brother, my late uncle, made it back in the 80s, early 80s. And it's a collection of things that he found on the land. Uh, even there's, um, a binocular, very old one, like that [holds up imaginary scope]. (Abigail)

Lily, however, has the most significant collection of found items in her home. She and her husband have constructed a display case for those items alone, with a secondary display location near the entrance of the home (see figures 3.1 and 3.2). She tells me that when they go out on the land:

> When we have nothing to do, we would take a garbage bag and see if we could find something that we could take back home. So I only picked the [tins] that had the words. The one we could see. (Lily)

These items provide a symbolic token of the land and all that came before on the land, a link to the land from within their homes. They also take the form of mementos through which memory of time on the land can be triggered. In the reengagement of artifacts, such as a door and door handle Lily brought back from the old trading post, artifacts serve to remind those who had lived on the land about their past, as well as to create links to the next generation as they can appreciate the relationship of these found objects to the land and therefore to their own history and Inuitness.

While the meaning of the land has many common threads within the community, practices can be quite varied. Brandon and Bethany, both members of the walking class, do not go out on the land at all, while Oliver spends most of his time on the land, through a good part of the year, and Lucia and her family are back and forth to the land from the moment it begins to warm up through the end of the summer. These variations are largely class-based.

Land Trips and Land Values

Today, participants who regularly go out on the land try to take advantage of every opportunity. Almost all regular land-goers have cabins. There is

Figure 3.1   Lily and Brennan's Found Items (1).

a dirt road leading out of town to the West. It stretches along for many kilometers before petering out to nothing. This road is maintained by the hamlet to provide easier access to hunting grounds. One can zoom out this road on an ATV and be rid of the community quickly. Stretched along this road are cabins, often grouped along off-shoots from this road. *Arviammiut* may spend their time on the land hunting or may go to their cabins and relax. Day trips are also made to picnic at the end of the road, or to have tea and go swimming in the icy waters of inland rivers, streams, or lakes. Carrying a gun is of the utmost importance in all cases, however, as polar bears may appear at any time of the year. While land trips are exponentially more frequent from June through September, winter land trips are also quite common, although with less emphasis on time at the cabin. In the winter, trips, beyond hunting trips, are often made to specific locations, such as sledding at Wolf Esker or tea at Sentry Island. Wherever travelers stop to rest, they tip over their *kamutiks* (sleds pulled behind the snowmobiles) and bring the

Figure 3.2   Lily and Brennan's Found Items (2).

snowmobiles into a semicircle to create an area somewhat protected from the wind.

Spring, however, is when land trips flourish. Time at the cabins is spent relaxing or preparing *nipku* (dried caribou) or other traditional foods and drinking tea. Participants who frequent cabins report going out on daily trips more frequently than overnight trips, often staying the entire day. If work prohibits them, they will go out to cabins for a few hours in the evenings, and all day on the weekends. These patterns are common for Sandra, Gemma, Lucia, Abigail, Gabriella, and their families. Abigail prefers not to sleep on the land, even in a cabin, because it is "too cold," but tells me that her parents regularly sleep out at the cabin. There is a smaller group of the population who regularly sleep at their cabins, and an even smaller group (two families that I am aware of) who spend several weeks at a time on the land, with one of those families preferring to live at their cabin (which has most of the amenities of houses) for the entire summer. Cabins are usually roughly built with scrap wood, often from sea-barge crates, with little to no insulation, often no windows, and no internal division of space. There may be chairs, but more usually there are sleeping platforms with old matrasses where people sit around while they drink tea, nap, socialize, or rest.

Time out in the fresh air for so long can be exhausting. Those returning from the land usually rush to either wash or sleep upon return.

We go to visit Kim. When we get there and go in, Kim is at the table rolling tobacco. I pop my head in before taking off my parka and ask if they have time for a visit, since she looks rather guilty. She looks at the tobacco and says "busted" and laughs. I laugh too. We come in. Her mother sits up from the couch and looks half-asleep. She says she was sleeping because she just got in from being on the land all weekend. (Field notes, May 28, 2012)

While on the land, there is a code of welcome and hospitality which pervades interactions even more than in town; an emphasis on kindness (Ayalik 2017). Once in a while, someone would mention to me that now cabins should be locked because of thieving. Phoebe, Felix, and Elise's husband all expressed concern to me that young Inuit would not be able to survive on the land because they have lost the Inuit values, the *Inuit Qaujimajatuqangit* (*IQ*), associated with survival in that context.

We weren't scared of anything. Like, we were free, in the tent. Nothing to scare you away, like no drugs, no sex, no big animals coming your way, creeping up on you. Um, right now, living in the tent, even, especially when you're out in the land, it's hard to spend a night cause there would be big game, *illa* [I mean], big animals, polar bears, grizzlies, and maybe close down there would just take away some things that you had left in the tent, somebody would just take them. It's, it changed a lot, since I remember, my first recollection of being in a tent. There would be no polar bears and no grizzlies and no drugs or somebody would respect each other's things and not take them, just take them. But nowadays we have lots of bears and grizzlies and it's kind of hard to leave your hunting gear in a tent and leave them outside of town. You always have to try and take your things now instead of just leaving them there. Yeah. (Phoebe)

As a rough estimate, about three-quarters of cabins are locked when not in use, although there is an understanding that in an emergency one should break in. Some of these locked cabins, however, are efforts to keep bears out, not thieves.

While many refer to the peace and calm of time on the land and at the cabin, such as Amber, Sandra, Gemma, and Lucia, they also, among others, express concern for values connected to the land which are being lost. Melanie, an elder who grew up on the land and who works as a janitor now, was upfront about the difference as her daughter translates for her:

She was saying that it was regular life out there and that she finds this style of living really different. And then I tried to elaborate more, like, what your question was, and then she said it, you know, as a kid she saw it change and change and change and that now, um, she's sort of just adapted to this life. She's just seen. [Melanie interrupts and keeps talking, as elders are wont to do] She's saying that there, on, *when they lived on the land, there was a lot more harmony within people*. Now that they've come here, there's like, *revenge and stuff and not helping out* . . . and then she said that, um, [she starts talking again] She said about, like, *drinking and smoking and suicide and stuff, that like it wasn't regular before and that now she sees a lot of it.* [although Melanie's voice had not changed, the translator's gets quiet for this last sentence]. [Author's emphasis]

For Melanie, it is not simply that these problems came with the built environment of the community, but that there was a loss of harmony associated with the land. *IQ* principles such as respect, openness about troubles, and trustworthiness are linked to the land. These are also, however, for Arviammiut, skills and knowledge acquired from the land (*pilimmaksarniq*). Removal from the land is removal from these values, this knowledge, and *Arviammiut* struggle to connect to these values given their spatial ecology.

Amber also notes these shifts in behavior, particularly behavior associated with interconnectedness:

> Um, mostly teenagers, younger than me, are married now. They have lots of houses. To me it's a big difference that they don't get to visit their, um, like, grandparents or their parents a lot now. They're mostly spending time at hall. Doing different things now. I see the big difference and I used to be with my mom and my older brother, spending time with them. Now these days I'm just at home, being busy with my kids. It's a big difference. And they don't gather anymore like they used to gather, on the land or at their place, like just having a family dinner or talking. (Amber)

While Inuit are successful in various ways in bringing the key values of their culture inside the walls, they also connect the dramatic culture shock with a loss of connection with the land.

When individuals seem particularly misguided, or when teenagers seem on the wrong track, they are often guided into programs which provide opportunities to go out on the land, to learn skills to survive on the land. The high school has a land skills course that works to get teens, who might not normally have had the opportunity, out on the land. These programs are based on the premise that as they reconnect with the land, healing occurs, and these values are imbibed from the very air of the tundra (Takano 2005). Indeed, when lives are on the line, one must learn to listen and have respect. Despite the connection of the land with values, however, the values themselves are more connected to conversations and rhetoric about before and after, rather than directly to conversations around traditionality—which consistently comes back to performance of skills and knowledge through activities.

Danger and Skill

The dangers of the land are also a necessary part of the rhetoric to show that surviving on the land required great skill. In the past, Jade's mother, for example, told me that she gave birth to 13 children and lost all but 3 of them either in labor or in infancy. Life was also difficult, requiring heavy physical labor. Even tying knots with bare hands in −40 degree weather is an experience that is shocking to witness as someone from my positionality, despite its being a relatively minor task. Today, however, the dangers are still present, though mediated by various technologies. The harsh cold, the presence of polar bears and other dangerous animals, and the sometimes unpredictable nature of the ice or snow you are walking on are but a few of the dangers of the land. Novices will get sunburn and snow blindness in April, or get turned around, not realizing the peaks of snowbanks always point in the same direction, make the wrong decision when a snowmobile breaks down, or fall prey to swarms of blackflies in the summer. Indeed, despite my carefully going out on the land only with very experienced people whom I trusted, I had no fewer than four instances when my life was tangibly on the line. This is a regular occurrence for those who frequent the land. Had I not been with experienced people, this book would not exist.

As it stands, it happens quite regularly that people are lost on the land, sometimes permanently. Oliver, for example, shows me a certificate that he got for rescuing someone from the land. Through Facebook and community radio, one hears with regularity (even weekly or daily at times) of people lost on the land. Family members ask for prayers and Search and Rescue, comprised of accomplished hunters for the most part, takes to the land in droves, fanning out and looking for the lost individual(s). Roughly once every two years while I lived there, one or a pair of people out together would die in a blizzard or if their snowmobile broke down. One youth made it on foot to within a mile of the community before succumbing. In white-out conditions, going outside even within the community poses great danger. In fact, recently, someone died trying to walk to the grocery store in town during a white-out blizzard. He got disoriented and wandered out onto the tundra without realizing it. My husband and I nearly made the same mistake one year. We lost track of how many lampposts we had passed and were not sure if we had already made the turn we were supposed to make. One direction would take us out into the tundra, and the other home. A few steps away from the lamppost, nothing was visible, and we would not know whether we had made the right decision until it was too late. Fortunately, we made the right decision, but our former student did not. When people are found, the news is posted on Facebook and announced on the CB, such as this post from Facebook:

> So Happy that my dad is ok, finally heard his voice this afternoon *quvianaq* [I'm so happy] now just waiting for him to come home. (Field notes, June 7, 2012).

Some have remarkable stories of survival. Lily tells me Brennen's and her story:

LJ: What's the longest you've been on the land before?

Lily: Three weeks [was the plan], [but it was] six weeks. Without anything. Because a pilot forgot to pick us up. Cause somebody that brought us there to Hennik Lake, we told him that we need to be pick[ed up] at this date. But a different pilot started working and no, he didn't tell anyone. So when the last pilot, when we stayed there, six weeks later we went to the pilot and asked "can you please bring us back home? Somebody forgot to take us back home." And he said, "how did you get here?" And instead of answering him [we asked], "can we use your phone if you have a phone?" And he said yes, so we phoned Lumber [the business which owns the helicopter] and told him "can you please tell this pilot that we're stuck here and we need to get home?" So they talk with him and, cause we already paid our return, so six weeks later we got home. A good thing we had fish and caribou and lots of tea and other dry goods. . . . [laughter] Cause the pilot thought that we were ghosts. Cause nobody's there, for a long time. . . . We tried waving, but nobody ever saw us. [much laughter]

LJ: You must have scared that pilot so much!

Lily: Imaa [yes]. . . . [laughs] But [afterward] we never told anyone in Arviat that we were stuck. In case they don't want to go [with us on the land]. [laughter]

LJ: So when you got back to your house, what's the first thing you did?

Lily: So release. So comfort. Cause they, my grandchildren didn't know who to call when they noticed that we're so late going back home. Three weeks later. [laughs]

While telling this story, Lily at times can hardly get the words out through her laughter. She now delights in this story. She and Brennan survived, and giving the unsuspecting pilot a fright plays well into the Inuit sense of humor. She also minimizes the hardships of that time in the story, saying merely that they are lucky they had dry goods. By minimizing how difficult it must have been, she shows that she is an Inuk who is connected with the land and accomplished at traditional skills.

Another friend does the same thing in a radio interview after his more dramatic rescue. He and his son became stuck on a piece of ice near the floe edge while they were out seal-hunting. After being out for three days in −56 Celsius (−69 Fahrenheit), separated from the bulk of their supplies, a helicopter came to rescue them. The helicopter landed, but the ice at that end was thinner than the pilot expected and it broke off. The helicopter plunged into the water and began to sink. The pilot could not free himself quickly enough, so my friend dove into the water, even after having been out in the cold for so long, to rescue the pilot, which he did successfully. They had to wait another few hours for another helicopter before they were finally rescued. After this, the CBC interviewed him about his ordeal (As It Happens 2013).

The reporter had clearly not been fully briefed on the situation. She was doing a routine interview, but when she asked him what temperature it was, and he told her, she completely lost her composure and said, "oh my God!" As the story unfolded, she was more and more amazed while my friend became more and more nonchalant about it. The more shocked she became, the greater the performance of Inuk identity was made possible by his treatment of these temperatures and situations as par for the course. Which, indeed, they often are. When she asked him if he would ever go hunting again, akin to asking someone if they will go to the store again after having had a car accident, he treated the question as it was; ridiculous and culturally ignorant. At the same time, this question highlighted the cultural difference and provided an opportunity for him to perform how resilient, resourceful, and impervious to cold the Inuit can be.

The connection Inuit feel with the land runs deep, and going out on land trips is a way to show traditional practices (Takano 2005). Priority is given to time on the land, along with status. Learning is also a key component of time on the land as the locus of Inuit knowledge and values. Each course at the Arctic College, in fact, spends a day or two on the land, regarding that experience as invaluable, even when learning *Qablunaaq* sciences, to reinforce the *IQ* principle of *pilimmaksarniq* (skills and knowledge acquisition) as land-based.

LEARNING WITHIN WALLS: TRANSMISSION OF KNOWLEDGE

When knowledge and knowledge-enactment become so intimately linked with identity, questions about the transmission of knowledge arise. Being walled-in has a profound effect on the transmission of knowledge. For *Arviammiut*, the differences between learning on the land and learning within walls emphasizes the importance of learning on the land. The effect of the built environment on learning and socialization manifests as *contra* learning on the land, therefore *Arviammiut* understand the two approaches as both linked to place and defined relationally.

The built environment of the house affects the transmission of family and Inuit knowledge in two ways. First, walls inhibit traditional ways of disciplining children. The root of the word "discipline" is from the Latin *docere,* "to teach," and its derivatives. However, Western frames of discipline are not culturally appropriate. Shaping how children behave, how to orient their behavior toward the community and around a moral compass, presents a challenge for the community. Like many Western adults (they would say Southern, indicating South of Churchill, Manitoba), *Arviammiut* adults complain about the behavior of unchecked and uncontrolled children. Second, walls change the transmission of skilled knowledge in gendered ways.

Transmission of Behavior Norms

Shame and learning from failure were the two most common ways that behavior was curtailed and shaped in childhood. An Arviat elder is quoted in Bennett and Rowley as describing how children learn to behave:

> Baby birds follow their parents all over the place for some time before they are able to do things themselves. When they are able, the parents leave them alone. Then, even when the parent bird is nowhere to be seen, the young birds have exactly the same ways that their parents had – they follow the examples that have been set before them, just the same way that our parents do for us. The ways of good parents can be followed in order to live a good life, to be able-bodied and wise. (2004, 11)

Children would follow their parents around and were encouraged to mimic them when playing. Donald Uluadluak recalls that he "started being aware" that his grandfather was teaching him (Uluadluak 2017, 150). Children learned what and what not to attend to as parents "cultivated in their children the fine sense of discretion that allowed people to live closely together and yet maintain a degree of privacy" (Bennet & Rowley 2004, 15). Adults shaped this, and other behavior, through shaming children if they acted inappropriately and refraining from giving them verbal guidance on what the boundaries of behavior were, allowing them to learn by overstepping (Ayalik 2017; Uluadluak 2017). Bennett and Rowley (2004) include, in their discussion of family, a story where some boys recklessly took a boat out and feared for their lives. They were rescued in silence, and the raconteur says that later they found out that the adults had known where they were the whole time but had let them behave in such a way to teach them a lesson.

Today, adults find it challenging to administer discipline. With divided spaces, culturally appropriate shaming becomes more challenging, as does teaching by example, since parents and children are out of each others' view (Ayalik 2017; Dawson 2003, 2004). In addition, some adults may be nervous about practicing shaming which might seem overly harsh in front of *Qablunaaqs* or in *Qablunaaq* spaces. Additionally, although strong self-discipline was required for survival on the land, harsh admonitions by adults to youngsters via yelling, explaining, or seeming strict may come too close to formality and strictness of rules that are associated with the Canadian South. Inuit discipline in the past has only been experienced by the elders. Today, many struggle to teach and discipline because they have not experienced traditional forms of acceptable shaming, nor by allowing failure (Uluadluak 2017). However, these forms of discipline are not as effective in their current community setting, nor are Western ways of teaching and disciplining appropriate.

> Our first year here, we found out that a polar bear was being skinned up the road from us. We went there. There was a circle around what turned out to be two bears. A mother and a cub. They cleared room for us at the front of the circle since we were *Qablunaaq*. The hunter was busily skinning the mother. The carcass of the cub was off to the side, already skinned. Kids were painting themselves with the blood and playing with the carcass, kicking at it and jumping back and forth over it. A few of the adults looked embarrassed by the behaviour, but no one stepped in to correct the kids, nor did they shame them, or make fun of them (a traditional way of disciplining). Those who looked uncomfortable mostly ignored them, but not enough to make a point. If a kid with a blood-painted face talked to them, they would talk back, rather than make a show of ignoring them and their behaviour (another traditional way of disciplining). There were no elders there. (Field notes, May 24, 2012)

The behavior of these children was appalling to both us and Inuit. It showed extreme disrespect for the polar bears, something which could bring bad luck and undermine the cosmology of Inuit.

Clued by Peter Dawson (2003, 2004) into the idea that having eyes on each other was culturally significant for *Arviammiut*, I asked participants about what it meant to them to be in divided spaces where they could not always see each other. Several participants drew a straight line between this and the lack of good behavior.

> There's a lot less communication in a house. But you can do a lot a' teaching or interacting in a *tupik* or *iglu*. You feel more closer to your child. (Jane)

> *Kihiani, mannali?* [But, now?]; we used to watch our grandpa working. Nowadays, in modern days, TV screen replaces our grandpa working. And we used to hear so many advice from our grandma. And the speaker replaces our grandma, in modern days. And it changes and affects it, affects the majority, community. *Ii* [yes]. And I believe that has shaped the, *qaniurimna?* [what is it?], [the] community standard. It has changed a lot since 1980, the difference I see. *Ii* [yeah]. (Samuel)

You can't really tell what your children are doing if you're not looking at them constantly, when you're not in the same, like, iglu or *tupik* all the time. Cause I have to constantly watch what my boys are doing on the internet or watching on TV. Have some more tea. (Nadia)

The walls create a visual barrier between parent and child, non-existent on the land, making it difficult for the adult to teach simply by example, or even to know when a child is behaving badly in order to discipline him or her. Bethany emphasizes the impact of children's watching behavior when she reacts to my question about what you can tell from someone's walls by saying:

I always say "*maaaai* [sound indicating something bad, in this context], clean your wall. Wash it! That's not the way it is. *Maaaii.* Use your brain. *Your kids watching. They're gonna copy,* eagh!!" *Ii* [yeah]. [Author's emphasis] (Bethany)

Here Bethany stresses the importance of learned behavior through copying and watching, as would happen on the land. Shaming, however, happens less and less. Alice Ayalik (2017) writes about the importance of not showing anger to your children as they watch and learn.

Shaming was also used to control adult behavior. Shamans imposed strict behavioral restrictions, called *tirigusiit* (Merkur 1992). In rituals performed with everyone present, shamans "would pick individuals who had problems or had done something wrong and mimic them, and they would confess and bring out all the bad feelings or wrong-doings" (Bennet & Rowley 2004, 406–407). Shaming was a regular part of the social discipline of the group.

Today, other bad behavior, such as stories of abuse and rape that Melissa and Amber shared, are common among certain people who struggle. I include this as an example of bad behavior that would have been constrained and curtailed in the past, but this category is by no means an Inuit problem; it is a patriarchy problem and Inuit were not really a patriarchy in this sense. Bethany tells me that her son drinks a lot and that the holes in her walls are mostly from his punching them. During my time living in Arviat, twice I had women come to my home seeking safety immediately after having been beaten. In one case, the woman told me that her parents-in-law were in the next room and that she knew they could hear it happening. She wished that her brother-in-law had been home because he would have intervened (Field notes 2007). The general opinion is that domestic violence has increased dramatically since the introduction of housing, not only because of the over-crowding and alcohol, but because such behavior can now happen behind closed doors. The opportunity for controlling behavior through shaming is minimal. Lucia sums it up when I ask her how things have changed since the move to houses:

> It changed everything. In good ways and some bad ways. Both, good and bad. But it's good to sleep in your bedroom, put the door closed, with nobody watching you sleep, but then it's not good for some people who might want to do something bad. You know. Like, anything bad. Like, we never know what's to happen, *illa* [I mean], it's, it's good and bad to have walls. (Lucia)

Lucia prevaricates because there are many benefits to the homes, but they also protect those engaged in bad behavior. *Arviammiut* already had high levels of practiced inattention from living in one space, and walls serve to reinforce that something happening out of view should not be attended to. Shaming practices weaken and more *Qablunaaq*-space appropriate forms of discipline have not emerged, although some in the upper classes have made some adjustments to *Qablunaaq* ways within walls, using more Western techniques to socialize and control behavior.

Transmission of Skilled Knowledge

One of the *IQ* principles is *pilimmaksarniq*, the title of this chapter, which translates as skills and knowledge acquisition. Knowledge was a family resource, even a commodity, before settlement. The introduction of housing and hence divided spaces has affected the transmission of family knowledge in profound ways.

Learning used to be through watching. *Arviammiut* are not accustomed to telling their children that they have to learn something. Previously, children were a captive audience. They would follow along and learn by watching and practicing (and failing). Multiple female elder participants in Bennett and Rowley (2004) remember watching their mothers as they worked, learning by practicing, by making smaller-scale clothing for their dolls and then smaller-scale items such as mittens. Male elders reported similar training. They would watch their fathers and start by making toys, copying the methods of their fathers. Gradually, these toys would progress to usable instruments for hunting, and then the boys would accompany their fathers on hunting trips, learning by apprenticeship (Bennett & Rowley 2004:30ff).

My elder participants gave me similar stories about how they learned skills from their parents on the land.

> They learned from the grandmother and then the mother and if you had an older sister, they would teach you and if you had a younger sister, you would watch and because *watching you can do, you would follow everything your mother or grandmother is doing*. Because when you're talking, she said, if they had asked

you, you wouldn't know how to do it because you couldn't see it or whatever. Or you know what I mean. You couldn't, I wanna say you couldn't, this is like. You can't imagine, like, if you're on the phone, "where, how do I sew it?" "This is how you sew it." You know. *You have to be able to see it to actually sew.* [Author's emphasis] (Melanie's Translator)

The emphasis here is on watching, learning by doing and seeing and trying, rather than by being told. This form of learning, associated with the land, connects individuals to the land symbolically when practiced or talked about within the hamlet. Emily, a young woman starting out her family, refers to Inuit ways of learning versus *Qablunaaq* ways of learning as "learning by hand or by mouth." Knowledge, for *Arviammiut*, has to be experienced first-hand in order to be had, as illustrated above. Certainly, when I was learning how to make seal-skin *kamiks* (boots), it was a long process of watching the elder work on hers and trying to copy her. The elder would allow us to make mistakes, and then take our work and rip it out and tell us to do it again. When I would ask if I should do something this way or that way, she would tell me to do it however I wanted. This way I would learn what worked, and what did not, through my own frustration and failure. First-hand experience gained through watching, doing, and failing led to situated knowledge which ultimately made me a better, more successful sewer, as well as connecting me to the land while located within the walls.

Those without first-hand experience were often unwilling to speculate. Other than laughing that she would fail if she tried to survive on the land, Jasmine offers little beyond her own experience when I ask her about what it was like for Inuit living on the land before colonization, "I've never lived in an *iglu* or a *tupik* [tent], so I don't know" (Jasmine).

When does one have knowledge? Can only have knowledge here from experience. Even though she may have ideas about it, she does not consider herself to have knowledge because it was not experienced first hand. (Field notes, Jasmine's Interview)

One must see and do to learn traditional skills. One must have traditional skills to lay claim to Inuitness.

Housing, however, interrupts the process of culturally specific Inuit transmission of knowledge. Where children were a captive audience before community life, parents did not have to tell their children to start learning. Many whom I interviewed said that they would wait until their children asked before teaching them. Only a few, those who had had longer exposure to *Qablunaaq* ways of being and learning, said that they would make their kids learn traditional skills. Most, however, were like Brittany who said, "It is

important for them to learn traditional culture, but I will wait until they ask."
The children, however, are not asking.

Because those who are more *Qablunaaq*-fluent are more willing to adopt
new ways of teaching, more able to conceive of *telling* their child they have
to learn something, they are, therefore, ironically, more successful in passing along traditional skills. This may be one reason that being *Qablunaaq*-
fluent and being traditional are highly correlated. Transmission of knowledge
within the family cannot happen in the same way it used to once settlement
occurs and walls divide.

Many feel that the elders are the only ones left who are able to teach traditional skills. Elders are asked by the schools to come in and teach sewing, or
butchering, or other traditional activities. They go to the schools and essentially perform the task, expecting the children to learn by watching and doing
at the same time. This has varying degrees of success.

> [*Arviammiut*] need houses nowadays because they do not know how to make
> actual caribou tent with the actual threading, stitches that they need. *Qaujimang-*
> *nita* [they don't know how], they lost it. *Kihiani* [but], only few elders can teach
> it. For those young people who are willing and have understanding without
> being judgmental, an elder can recognize that kind of young person. So the more
> open the young person is, an elder would share more advice and things to do and
> how to do it. *Ii* [yeah]. (Samuel)

Some elders are only teaching when paid by the schools. Their own families
are rarely apprenticing. One way in which the elementary school compen-
sates is to hire a few elders to build an iglu on the outskirts of town. For the
week of the "iglu project," the school buses classes back and forth all day
while elders sit in the iglu receiving them, drinking tea with them, and telling
them stories from the past. For a few walkers, this was the only time they had
been in an iglu.

> When it's winter, the school always teaches kids traditional . . . they go see what
> they, long time ago they used to do. In the school. In the iglu. They always do
> that. It's different now and it's good now. They teach, elders teach how to sew
> or to seal or . . . dogsledding. That's good. (Bethany)

It is more that children are being exposed to ideas about what is traditional,
than that they are actually learning skills or acquiring resources to be able to
align themselves with traditionality. Going out on the land at all, however,
removes the children from the *Qablunaaq* built environment and, by merely
being on the land, they are connecting to their own Inuit identities.

SEWING

I now turn to the example of sewing as a skill which stems from land knowledge and which requires negotiation of the spatial ecology of Arviat. *Arviammiut* consider sewing extremely important to their cultural identity. In 2004, as a facilitator for a project bringing together elders and youth (youth being broadly defined as roughly over 18 and under 35), I aided in the video interviewing of elders by youth. The last question on the guide for the semi-structured interviews had the youth asking what the elders thought was the most important thing that the youth should be learning from the elders. Almost unanimously, the elders, male and female, answered traditional sewing. Ayalik (2017) writes that instructors struggle when they teach alone.

Traditional sewing primarily involves the creation of *pualu* (mitts), *jappa* (parka), and *kamik* (boots), but also can include snow pants, although those have become less common as a need, and as an expression of traditional sewing. *Arviammiut* primarily use seal and caribou skins to create this clothing. *Pualu* often are made from rabbit or fox, as well as seal or caribou, and fox fur is often attached to the hoods of parkas. Truly traditional sewing would have been done with a bone-needle and sinew for thread. Today, even the most traditional sewers use contemporary, imported needles. For thread, *Arviammiut* often take pleasure in expressing adaptability and ingenuity by using dental floss, which, with its waxy texture, feels and acts very much like sinew.

The first task in sewing is obtaining animal skins. In the past, a hunter was always not only seeking meat, but skins for clothing.

> When it gets cold, her mother would sew caribou clothing. While they are still living in iglus during winter, her father would hunt and trap foxes. At Qamaniq, her mother would always sew, and her father would go out hunting on the land for food and clothing or the furs. Seal skins or caribou skins. (Tori's Translator)

Animal skins continue to be supplied, in most cases, by a male relative. If, however, your family has no accomplished hunter, or cannot afford the material goods required to hunt, you can go on air, on the local radio station, and ask for anyone with extra skins to get in touch. These skins are usually bought or traded, rather than shared such as the meat might be. They are difficult to collect, and not all hunters can successfully skin their kills to produce large pieces to work with. Bullet holes can be sewn, however, and are less a concern. There is a small proportion of women in town who are capable of sewing traditional product entirely on their own. For those who are able, they become known for certain articles of clothing and the demand on them for this clothing will exceed that of their family and friends, such that they are in constant need of more animal skins.

Jennifer, for example, was known for her seal-skin *kamiks*. When I was learning to make *kamiks*, along with three others, my friend, with whom I was learning, told me that Jennifer had a waiting list of several years. Because she was also known for this, people would often bring her their extra seal skin to buy. Since Jennifer was an elder, she was also gifted seal skin on a regular basis. This would, however, be understood as a gift, rather than an instance of sharing.

Kamiks are often made from two different kinds of seal, bearded seal and harp or harbor seal. Bearded seal are much larger and harder to find. The skin is much tougher and is commonly used for the sole of the boot. When we were looking for bearded seal, one of the group negotiated a price over CB radio with Jennifer. When we went to purchase the materials, she handed each of us two large pre-cut oval pieces of bearded seal. It was not softened, but it had been stretched (see figures 3.3 and 3.4) and cleaned. The harbor seal we had bought from a neighbor of mine had been stretched. We cleaned it and softened it by putting a cord through the holes the stretching had created and pulling it like a drawstring to make a bag-like shape with the skin and then dancing on it and working it with our hands. Bearded seal required systematic chewing, however, in order to soften the leather—roughly 8 hours per sole. (Caribou skin requires scrapping rather than chewing or softening.)

Jill and I had also learned how to make *kamiks* together. She had [only] one tooth [left] on top at that time. We were all chewing the seal skin; forever we chewed! 8 hours per foot. She was chewing along and then made an

Figure 3.3 Caribou Skins Being Stretched.

Figure 3.4   Seal Skins Being Stretched.

exclamation of pain. We all stopped and looked at her, worried that she had lost her one tooth. We held our breath as she wiggled her one tooth, ensuring it was still firmly in place. Smiled at us and nodded, and we all, went back to our work, quite relieved. After that point we all thought it best for her to use a grinder from the Arctic College to soften her seal skin. (Field notes, May 11, 2012)

If the chewing proves to be too much, one can borrow the grinder from Nunavut Arctic College; however, there are few grinders in town.

Her mother sits down and starts to fold up her seal-skin *kamiks* she is making, one leg of which was sitting on the floor. I comment on it and she tells me about taking a course at the Arctic College to learn how to sew. . . . She says that she learned to measure, it is one hand-width across and two long, and make it a curve around that measurement. I wish I had known that when I was making them! . . . She gets up and goes to the TV. . . . Underneath there is some storage. She pulls some things out and shows me her grinder. It is quite large and really very impressive. She paid $150 for it and it looks great. It is made of wood and looks rather like a press. . . . When you lift it, on the inside are metal teeth on the bottom and on the top (the part that lifts). I would not want to get a finger caught in there! On the top are some metal circles, which I am not sure if they are decorative or integral. She demonstrates it a few times. After I admire it for a few minutes, she puts it away. (Field notes, May 10, 2012)

Pilimmaksarniq (skills and knowledge acquisition) is specific and contextual and generally obtained in action.

As the above demonstrates, traditional sewing requires great skill. This skill, however, is difficult to transmit within the heated *Qablunaaq* spaces. The greatest contemporary challenge for traditional sewing is the dry air inside.

> Ladies notice a big difference. Like, they used to skin their own, *illa* [I mean], scrape their own skins, like caribou and seal. In a iglu and *tupik* [tent] it used to be the perfect, perfect scraping. But in a house, it's different, cause they never get soft as nicely as they used to in a iglu and a tent. In a house it's very stiff and dry and hard to sew. (Lily)

> But when she sews out on the land, it's, like, it's very, it's nicer because sewing inside, sewing *tuktu* [caribou] and stuff inside is very dry. . . . When it's inside it's too hot and it makes it really dry. (Melanie's translator)

Melanie experienced the transition to living inside and finds that the air inside *Qablunaaq* space encumbers her traditional sewing. Phoebe echoed this experience. Animal skins must be kept moist and soft while being sewn. The heating is either electric baseboard or forced air. In either case, the warm and dry climate indoors makes the animal skins dry and difficult to work with.

In the past, being "inside" a tent provided the perfect conditions. With no extra heating, the warmth and moisture of body heat, trapped by the skins of the tent, created the perfect environment for traditional sewing. Ellen points out that taking the skins outside of the *tupik* [tent] was inadvisable "cause they could quickly dry out."

> When they would stop working on the sewing stuff, materials, they would put them under the caribou bed inside the tent so it won't dry out. (Tori's translator)

In order to navigate the spatial ecology of Arviat and access and perform the traditional knowledge of the land, *Arviammiut* develop certain strategies. One technique is to leave the skins in the unheated "cold porch" when they are not being worked on.

> What she does is she'll work on it and then put it outside in the porch, cold porch, and then when she has to sew it she'll sew it, and when she's done, she'll put it back in the cold porch and then take it back and then start again. Yup. (Evelyn's translator)

And while many still try to work outside as much as possible, others resort to techniques such as a bowl of water, or a constant moistening and softening of the skin with saliva, administered via spitting or chewing.

LJ: I saw some people sew with water nearby to keep it moist. Do they do that?

Evelyn (through translator): They have different ways of sewing, so what she does is she just wets the skin on her mouth, lips, and then sews again.

Traditional sewing produces clothing that is both striking and functional. When I would wear the boots I had made, everyone would ask me who made them. This reflects how my boots did not have the distinctive style of a known sewer.

Knowing how to admire traditional sewing, in itself, is a learned skill that is key to performing traditional knowledge within *Qablunaaq* spaces.

> She also asks if we sew. I bring out my cross stitch to show her, which she really likes and takes some time admiring. She touches the front and seems like she is not sure it is really hand made. I turn it over for her and she sees from the back that it is. She turns it back over and looks over at the bees on the side and sees my needle there. She takes the needles out of the cloth and holds it lightly. It is attached by black thread. She puts it back and gives it back to me. . . . [She] shows us *kamiks* that she made. They have beautiful beading done on the top of the foot. I admire it and examine it closely, including the inside where the seal skin is stitched so that she knows that I know how to admire it properly. (Field notes, May 14, 2012)

Proper admiration indicated to the woman I was visiting that I have some knowledge of traditional sewing and made my appreciation of her work more meaningful, particularly given my background and positionality.

Admiration can also come in the form of deference from a place of no knowledge, particularly from men.

> We start chatting with Kim . . . she retrieves string and pauses at the pin cushion on the wall to select a needle. She pulls one out, decides on a different one, pushes the first pin pack in and deftly removes the other one as she turns to head back to the couch. I see that the string she is using is a fake sinew-like material. It is bright yellow. Jeff and I ooh and aah over it and [her father] says it's probably man-made. Her father also says that he doesn't know how ladies do it, making parka. They just cut the pattern and then make it into a parka and he doesn't know how they do it. [Meanwhile] Kim folds the fur in half, then puts the needle through the middle point. She then folds the hood in half and puts the needle through its mid-point, drawing the two together. She sews them together from there. (Field notes, May 28, 2012)

Here, Kim's father gives her the highest praise possible. He cannot comment directly on her work, or brag about her and single her out as accomplished, which would be culturally inappropriate. He can, however, talk about the category of "ladies" and their abilities while she is sewing. Her mother, in another visit, does tell us more directly that Kim's sewing is now in Cambridge Bay, Rankin, Repulse, in addition to Arviat (Field notes, May 10, 2012). Kim looks very uncomfortable through this, but her mother is establishing for the *Qablunaaq* visitors that her daughter is an accomplished Inuk.

Claims on sewing skills extend Inuit identity. Jane, for example, tells me:

> No one told me "you have to sew." No. It was, being an Inuk woman, you have to be able to sew so your husband and children will not go cold. That's the mentality. Mm hm.

For a woman, sewing is an inherent part of being Inuk. This extends from using skins to fabrics. Any participation in sewing aligns oneself to some degree with Inuit identity. My translator, half Inuk and half *Qablunaaq*, found herself constantly trying to reaffirm her Inuit identity for status in the community. I was amazed as I walked around town with her, how many people exchange a few words with her in Inuktitut and then told her (either in English or Inuktitut) how good her language skills were and that she was a "real Inuk." She bore this with a remarkable level of patience, but she also did have to constantly express Inuit identity to maintain a claim on it.

> She has told me how desperately she wants kids and *how she wants to sew for them.* She is currently making a parka for a child. (Field notes, May 11, 2012)

Amber also demonstrates an affinity for sewing, as well as some knowledge about traditional treatment of *amoutik*s, through which she expresses her Inuit identity.

> I love materials. I love sewing. [She shows me how to fold an *amoutik*, I take a picture of it rolled up. (See figure 3.5)] My mother taught me how to do that. I don't know why she taught me how to do that, but, cause I never heard anything like that before, but she told me how to. Cause she told me that back in the old days they used to put up their *amoutik* like that then use it as a pillow or for sitting. (Amber)

Amber refers specifically to knowing how it was done in the past to strengthen her own Inuit identity.

There is an understanding that sewing was a dominant part of life on the land before houses, and that practicing these skills today connects the doer to a less diluted Inuit identity. Status is associated with that. An ability to sew

Figure 3.5 *Amoutik* **Folding into a Pillow.**

with traditional materials, in particular, can be leveraged for status as *ajungi* (capable, smart, and talented).

LJ: I remember I made *kamik*s with Jill.

Bethany: And she made *pualu* [mitts] now. *Aiungitut* [she's so capable]. Jill'*jua* [that Jill].

Many, however, felt that they could no longer make claims to Inuitness through traditional sewing.

They were good, the Elders. *Ii* [yes]. We can't sew caribou skin or, they used to wear caribou skin a lot. We can't sew anything like that anymore cause they're into commanders [a popular contemporary fabric] and stuff. (Gabriella)

Choice of material can also demonstrate affiliation with *Ahiarmiut* or *Padlirmiut.*

The whole time that we were sewing, she would be making gagging noises because she is from an *Ahiarmiut* family (from inland, caribou hunters) and wanted to indicate her distaste of seal skin. *Ahiarmiut* are considered to be more rustic than *Padlirmiut.* Mostly these tensions are dormant now, but at times, such as when a fight erupts at school, the final insult to fling will be about what tribe you are from. (Field notes, May 11, 2012)

Evelyn says that several tribes were brought together here and that "*Ahiarmiut* is the lowest one." She says that not many are actually from the Arviat area, but that she is, and her husband [i.e. they are *Padlirmiut*]. I ask if *Ahiarmiut*, coming in as the lowest before are now the ones that are in the walking class or if it was mixed up. She says mixed up, but then continues that Ahiarmiut are the ones that maybe don't want to work as much, are happy just to take welfare and not do anything. (Field notes, June 3, 2012)

Although both have equal claims to Inuitness, *Ahiarmiut* carry the complex and contradictory statuses of being both more rustic and "primitive," a negative, but also therefore more purely traditional, a positive.

Traditional sewing, however, is only the far end of the spectrum of sewing. By working with animal skins, one automatically invests oneself with a strong Inuit identity. The more traditional the sewing, the more status is associated with it. Samuel tells me that his wife "doesn't want to use, *hunai'na* [what is it], sewing machine. Only her hands." His emphasis on skins over fabrics is heightened by his not having the word "sewing machine" at the ready, despite being an excellent English speaker. Phoebe also reveals the hierarchy of status around sewing when I ask her whether she sews. She answers, "Yeah. I can make *kamik*s, parka, caribou stuff, seal skin, fabric, but not as good as everyone else." She first lists traditional kinds of clothing, then the materials with which to make the clothing, first citing caribou, which is connected to the *Ahiarmiut* and is thus more purely traditional, then secondly seal, connected to *Padlirmiut* people, then, lastly, fabric. Emma also reveals the hierarchy when she answers my question about whether she sews with "*only* with sewing machine" [Author's emphasis].

Arviammiut distinguish between spectrums using the terms *traditional* and *modern*. Carmel is clear about the difference.

LJ: How important do you think sewing is for Arviat today?

Carmel: There's lot of ladies and young ladies. They sew a lot, cause they're into sewing. *Modern, sewing modern.* Nice colors.

LJ: II. So what's the difference between modern sewing and traditional sewing?

Carmel: They're difference, the *traditional clothing is like caribou hide, seal skin and modern, right now the materials are really good. They're big difference.* [Author's emphasis]

Kathy, meanwhile, connects sewing directly to making claims on traditionality as I ask her about her traditionality.

LJ: Do you feel like you're a traditional person?

Kathy: Both. Yes and no. Yes. *Ii* [yes].

LJ: Which way is yes and which way is the other way, the both?

Kathy: Traditional, keeping Inuktitut language and advisors. *Ii* [yes]. Sewing all the stuff. Mm. . . .

LJ: When you sew, do you use both modern and traditional?

Kathy: Traditional.

LJ: With skins?

Kathy: Ii [yes]. *Illa* [I mean], material. I'm really slow with skins. Very slow. They gonna take me a year. . . . It's hard. I cannot really do anything so I've been using the material. *Ii* [yes].

Kathy's sister: I'm the only one who don't know how.

LJ: For skins?

Kathy's sister: Yeah.

LJ: Do you do material?

Kathy's sister: Yeah.

As we go on, Kathy reveals that she sews parkas with materials the most frequently. She, therefore, has more claim on traditionality than her sister, who uses traditional materials, but sews traditional clothing far less frequently. There is, along the middle of the spectrum of sewing, a liminal area where the term traditionality is applied to the kind of clothing (i.e., parka), but not to the style of sewing, which can cause some confusion, as it did with Kathy and me. When I asked her if she does both modern and traditional, she took that to refer to *what* she sews, rather than *with* what.

Madison also talks about this liminal zone of traditional clothing made out of non-traditional fabrics.

LJ: How important do you feel it is to pass on those sewing skills?

Madison: It's very important because winter-time it gets really cold and we need to make our own home-made parkas. I'm not really into traditional sewing. I wish I got those skills from my mom, but, um, it's hard work and she said if I want to learn I can learn on my own. . . . I don't really want to put my teeth through, uh, it's, I wanna keep my teeth as long as I'm around. [laughs] There's lots of chewing.

Home-made parkas do count as traditional, as something for which *Arviammiut* are known; however, in the context of a discussion about the mechanics of sewing, the materials have more status as traditional and linguistic deference is made.

Figure 3.6 Modern parka.

Sewing then, runs along the scale of; traditional clothing with traditional materials (animal skins); traditional clothing with modern materials, such as *amoutik*s; clothing for the winter, particularly contemporary Arviat-style parkas with box hoods and a longer, curved backing made from fabric (see figure 3.6); and other forms of fabric sewing, such as bags. Sewing arose in my field site incessantly as a traditional everyday activity. Housing brings dry air, but also large flat surfaces for cutting materials. This, along with sewing machines and contemporary fabric, has impacted the forms of sewing and has, therefore, emphasized the ability of a woman who sews to make claims on traditionality by aligning herself with this activity.

GENDER AND THE TRANSMISSION OF KNOWLEDGE

Houses have strong gendered implications in terms of transmission of skilled knowledge. When allocating space in the new houses, "woman's work" was honored and given space in the back bedrooms, despite overcrowding. While many women haul their sewing machines into the main rooms to sew, daughters are often not even at home, or are in their bedrooms, or in the same room but watching television, not their mothers. Traditional skins are hard to work with. In terms of learning, daughters much more rarely learn by watching or apprenticing with their mothers. A few will, as they become young adults, come to their mothers and ask to learn how to sew, but most do not. Even when they do ask, often modern sewing is the starting point, rather than animal skins.

"Men's work," however, happens outside in front of the house. The unintended consequence of the spatial arrangement is that women's work is not being passed on to the daughters in the same way men's work is being passed on to the sons. Boys linger outside in front of the houses. When they are bored, they start to watch their fathers. When they get their own machines and ATVs, they set them up outside next to their fathers' and learn how to maintain them through watching and doing. The men do not have to hope their sons ask to learn, unable to figure out how to tell them due to their cultural practices. They may be similarly constrained as the women in their ability to tell their sons to learn something, but there is less need. Tinkering with machines passes time for young men. Then, since they have developed a shoulder-to-shoulder connection with their fathers, falling in with the apprenticeship model, they naturally begin to accompany their fathers on hunting trips (if the family has the resources for this).

In short, the effectiveness of transmitting family knowledge and for gaining *pilimmaksarniq* (skills and knowledge acquisition) is not only unequally distributed along class lines, but it is also gendered—an unintended consequence of the unfriendly architecture of the hamlet and houses.

CONCLUSION

The land is the locus of Inuit ways of knowing and being. *Arviammiut*, however, live within *Qablunaaq* walls and must visit the land. Time spent on the land represents time accessing, learning, and practicing traditionality, making time on the land deeply meaningful. While on the land, knowledge is passed on through watching and doing.

Knowledge within walls, however, cannot easily be transmitted by watching and doing due to the interior division of spaces. Teaching by mouth, telling and instructing, represents an adoption of *Qablunaaq* ways and undermines their ability to perform Inuit identity. Knowledge transmission, therefore, is weakened by living in the houses, as the above example of sewing demonstrates. One unintended consequence of the walls is that successful transmission of knowledge is unequally distributed across genders. As Inuit navigate their time within and without walls, as boundary objects, they navigate their relationship with *Qablunaaq* ways of knowing and learning.

Part II

WALLS AS CULTURAL OBJECTS

CULTURE IN MATERIAL FORM

I am hitting my head against the walls,
But the walls are giving way.

—Gustav Mahler

The previous part explored how walls act as boundary objects and the resulting analytic purchase one gains by conceptualizing walls this way. As walls mediate the boundaries between groups, they are also cultural objects.

A typical definition of culture speaks to the norms, values, beliefs, and practices within a given society, or other culturally cohesive group.[1] Every object one uses, touches, or sees during the course of a day is embedded in a cultural setting. Wendy Griswold (2008) defines cultural objects as having "shared significance embodied in form" (21). Something as mundane as a bedroom door operates as a cultural object. All of those in the same culture *share an understanding* of what a bedroom door looks like, appropriate use of the bedroom door, and so on. If someone walked into a home and saw a front door on a bedroom, they would notice immediately that this was out of place. We *understand together* that bedroom doors are for privacy and we, therefore, keep most of our intimate moments with others hidden behind these doors. Parents work to keep their children's privacy at a minimum when they insist that the bedroom door stay open when the children have friends over—especially once puberty hits. We all share the significance of the door. That shared significance is embodied in the material form of the door. That door is a cultural object.

Scholars have to study cultural objects within their context because meaning changes across place and time, and may not have any meaning among some groups. The traditional Inuit cultural context did not have people separated out into bedrooms. Pre-colonization, Inuit homes in this area were primarily iglus and tents, with no internal divisions or bedroom doors. The family would sleep together at the back of the iglu on a sleeping platform (Kershaw, Scott, & Welch 1996; Lee & Reinhardt 2003).

Various groups within the same cultural context may also carry different meanings for a cultural object. This often reflects differing socioeconomic participation or status within the larger group. In contrast to Inuit, traditional Herero homes, a Bantu ethnic group in Southern Africa, consist of matrilineal hut clusters. The entryway to each of these huts represents different things to the women and the patriarch of the family. For the women, the hut encompasses their family or household. Crossing the threshold is crossing into her realm. For the patriarch, that threshold represents a spatially isolated subunit of his household (Harpending & Pennington 1990).

Cultural objects are material representation and residue of culture (Mukerji 1994). Because one cultural object can have more than one meaning, they are polysemic in nature (Schudson 2002). The meanings of cultural objects are flexible and change through use. As with the example of doors above, walls can mean different things for different people, even within the same culture, depending on one's location within that culture. The walls of prisons mean different things to prisoners and guards. For guards, the walls represent their work environment and safety. They come and go to work. The walls separate them from prisoners whom they perceive as dangerous. For prisoners, the walls represent various degrees of confinement, based on the time they serve. A short sentence sets the walls up to represent a barrier to freedom. A "lifer" who has become institutionalized may see the walls as a different kind of

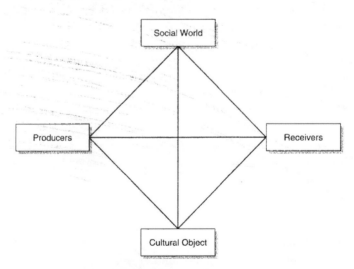

Figure B.1   Wendy Griswold's Cultural Diamond.

safety; a familiarity that protects the inmate from having to reintegrate with outside society. Walls often carry different meanings for the groups within them; school and hospital walls are two other poignant examples. The meanings of cultural objects are flexible and change through use.

Wendy Griswold (2008) offers a way for researchers to think about cultural objects when studying culture, cultural practices, and the role of materiality. She terms this the *cultural diamond* (see figure B.1). Cultural objects are produced somewhere, with a meaning and use in mind. Consumers receive cultural objects and may or may not use them exactly as intended. By framing cultural objects in this way, one gains analytic purchase, as illustrated in the following two chapters.

Just as boundaries are negotiated through boundary objects, discussed in the previous part, so is cultural meaning negotiated through cultural objects. We produce meaning for an object through interaction with others and with the object itself. Walls, as cultural objects, gain meaning and power from people's building a way of life around them. They also, however, are commodities that are produced and marketed. There is an entire industry and tradition around piping and wiring inside walls, dry wall, paint, and so on. We attach cultural value to our consumption of these products. Imagine, for example, a concrete wall inside a home, or a brick wall. It has a different feeling (i.e., meaning) than a regular (i.e., socially defined as normal) wall. Wallpaper is passé. Accent walls are in.

In terms of resistance, people use objects in ways that are normal according to their cultural socialization. When someone uses the object in a novel way, perhaps they are rebelling or resisting something. In that case, this action, especially, needs to be embedded in a particular culture so that others can understand that the rebel is breaking a norm to make a point. Otherwise, your use of the object would not stand out as rebellious. Think, for example, of a child slamming their bedroom door. It is precisely the norms of not slamming doors that make slamming the door such a forceful way to express rebelliousness and frustration with others.

RECIPROCAL RELATIONSHIP OF WALLS

Preexisting social conditions, norms, and beliefs shape the form, look, and placement of walls. In this way, walls impose behaviors on us. Walls profoundly shape how we move through the world and conceive notions such as what is public and private. This stands out when we consider walls developed by one cultural group and imposed on another group, such as the walls in Arviat. Mainstream Western culture informed the construction of the walls in Arviat, and they do not match their current cultural context. The producers and the receivers are located in adjacent cultural diamonds. The walls communicate Western beliefs and practices around privacy, such as with the shape, size, and placement of bedrooms and bedroom doors, to *Arviammiut*, who traditionally did not have walled-off bedrooms. Walls equally impact thinking in mainstream culture; however, our social history means that, while impacted, there is little change. The walls fit with how we are socialized already. Not so in Arviat. It is through the introduction of new and different walls to Arviat that we can see the truly constraining and influential nature of walls in communicating and enforcing cultural norms.

As walls constrain and shape their users, we also have agency. This means that we have the ability to make decisions about our interactions with cultural objects. We adjust our behavior. We adapt. This is exactly what Inuit in Arviat have had to do. They have displayed a remarkable degree of agency in their creative solutions for navigating life inside culturally inappropriate, architecturally hostile, walls.

The result is a reciprocal relationship between walls and those who interact with those walls. *Arviammiut* react to their walls and find ways to agentically bring their culture indoors. In Southern Canada, the backsplash of the kitchen wall behind the counter may have a decorated or stylistic side, but in purpose primarily serves as a backsplash. In some Arviat homes, I saw people using the backsplash as a convenient place to store knives (see figure B.2). Through use, they are giving an extended meaning to the backsplash—one which expresses the Inuit value *Qanuqtuurunnarniq* (being resourceful to solve problems) (DoE 2007, 34). The walls push back as active agents themselves (Miller 2001). The shape and form of the walls limit their repurposing and some previous practices. *Arviammiut* negotiate, manage, and interact with walls to exercise their agency, changing the meaning, uses, and symbolic

Figure B.2   Knife Storage.

meaning of the walls, with varying degrees of success across classes. Structure and agency balance and are in tension with each other.

The built environment carries symbolism and embodies power relations. Individuals and groups relate to the symbolic level of the built environment in four ways. Walls can stand as representative, for example, of ideology, such that it is an instance of synecdoche (one thing standing in for the whole). The Berlin Wall, and its fall, often stands symbolically for communism. Second, walls can be literary metaphors, such as in the case of Rapunzel. Rapunzel is locked away, high in a tower, and the walls of that tower represent the protection of her virginity and purity. Third, walls inspire meaning-making as evocative objects (Turkle 1995). We think about who we are when we decide how to decorate our walls, for instance. Fourth, walls become symbols of personal and social identities when we display ourselves on our walls. These four levels of symbolic relations apply to the built environment and the land, and the boundaries in between.

The built environment embodies power relations and becomes a tool for the powerful and the not-so-powerful. The built environment embodies power relations as technologies of cultural control and colonization. Chetan Singh (2009) notes that as pastoralists fell into the care of the government, those in power needed control of them. The built environment, particularly housing and communities, is one means of influencing and controlling. Settling nomadic populations is a way for the state to count, control, and give aid to people (Scott 1998). Because the built environment stabilizes social structures and routines, those in power impose their way of being on groups who are being colonized through the built environment, the houses, and the community ecology of buildings and space with devastating consequences for identity, memory, and history (Gieryn 2000). One may view the built environment as embodied forms of power and technologies of colonization and oppression, as well as sites of resistance (Dorries et al. 2019). It is worth taking the time to study how individuals and groups relate to the built environment as power systems; conceptualizing of walls as cultural objects works to that end.

The first chapter in this part discusses the family photographs and mementos *Arviammiut* display on their walls. By conceptualizing walls as cultural objects, they become tools to enact Inuitness through the display of wall artifacts. Not only does this "spatially graft" (Dawson 2008) Inuit culture onto the *Qablunaaq* walls, but it also contributes to the relocation of memory. In addition, they accomplish *spatial fusion* by using gifts to construct multiple, distinct spaces as part of the same place, meaning families are living in extended families in one "home" spread across several houses.

The second chapter in this part discusses contemporary food consumption. I examine how Inuit redistribute norms around content, preparation knowledge, and eating practices across both traditional foods and *Qablunaaq* food, resulting in cultural hybridity. *Arviammiut* navigate food consumption of both traditional and *Qablunaaq* food in ways that agentically maximize their performance of Inuitness to their walls from within *Qablunaaq* spaces. In this way, hybridity works as a mechanism of resistance. Again, Inuit spatially graft their culture indoors using walls as cultural objects.

NOTE

1. See Wendy Griswold (2008) for a healthy discussion on the definition of culture and cultures in the social sciences. The above suffices for the purposes of this book.

Chapter 4

Aktuaturaunniqarniq amma Inuuqatigiitsiarniq [Interconnectedness and Interpersonal Relationships]

Family, Connected Spaces, and Memory

Walls, as cultural objects, become a cultural and social resource for Inuit to bring their culture, literally, indoors. They do this by enacting *aktuaturaunniqarniq amma inuuqatigiitsiarniq* (interconnectedness and interpersonal relationships). This chapter explores items on the walls, in particular, photographs of family, mementos, and gifts. Displaying family photos is important for expressing and highlighting interpersonal relationships. While in Western culture people turn to walls for clues as to a person's identity, interests, and so on, Inuit turn to walls to determine family location. In addition, photos and mutually exchanged gifts on the walls work together to create symbolically connected interior spaces, what I call *spatial fusion,* where the common areas of various homes become one extended home system. Photos, along with mementos, are also part of a relocation of collective memory from oral practices, to material, mnemonic triggers.

DOING FAMILY

"Doing family" (Morgan 1996) involves performing family connectedness by engaging in practices that people associate with healthy and happy families, whether the families are actually healthy and happy or not. David Halle (1993) notes that the kinds of family photographs that people display have shifted from portraiture to contemporary action shots of the family enacting, or doing, "happy family." He argues this is because the nuclear family bears so much pressure, despite—or because of—being fragile in today's day and age. Many pin all their hopes and dreams on having the perfect family. Social media only heightens this sense as a platform where people regularly post pictures of family-in-action to demonstrate their success and confidence in their nuclear family. Janet Finch's (2007) work argues that displaying family is a key component of doing family. This display conveys to others that the family acts as, and therefore supposedly is, a healthy and happy family. This is key in an era of unrealistic expectations and stresses on the nuclear family.

Arviammiut, those who live in Arviat, have experienced similar increases in the imperative to display family as a component of doing family; however, they also work to perform Inuitness, to enact it onto their walls to overcome anomie (see chapter 2). Having previously traveled in extended family groups, Inuit now must negotiate and perform family connections across and within Arviat. While rhetoric around Indigenous groups sometimes paints them as having a homogenous culture focused on community, in actuality, Indigenous groups are incredibly diverse and *Arviammiut* are more family-oriented than community-oriented. In Arviat, it is extremely important in framing one's identity to communicate to which family one belongs.

Family locatedness, that is, placing oneself in a family, is paramount. This is a form of enacting *aktuaturaunniqarniq amma inuuqatigiitsiarniq* (interconnectedness and interpersonal relationships). When I met anyone new, they did not ask me what I did for a living, where I worked, or what my interests were—that could all come later. The most important thing was to learn about where I am located in my family, to demonstrate my interconnectedness and interpersonal relationships. How many brothers and sisters do I have? Who is older or younger? What are their names? Parents? So on and so forth. Getting to know each other involves getting to know where we stand, respectively, in our families. This knowledge creates a mental map of the world from which I came, of how that world now connects to their world.

Conversation during visits also demonstrated the importance of one's place in one's family. During my fieldwork, I spent hours talking with friends and participants about who was related to whom. Not only did this practice reflect the roots in oral culture, but it drove home the vast knowledge *Arviammiut* possess about how each person is interconnected.

I realized how I cannot overstate this phenomenon when I decided to ask participants to draw me a mental map of the community. It did not take long to realize that this was an impossible task. All the interconnectedness of all the families and individuals to each other would have had to go on that map! I certainly showed my Western thinking and positionality at that moment. Thanks to the flexibility of qualitative work and the importance of letting the data be the guide, I was able to adjust my approach as I went along. I did learn, however, that the spatial layout of families within the hamlet is a key component of the spatial knowledge of *Arviammiut*. The two knowledges are inseparable.

Given the importance of family to Inuit culture and personal identity, the walls present a perfect opportunity to perform and display family connection. Family pictures on the walls also serve other purposes—*Arviammiut* delight in their loved ones' faces as much as any group. These photographs serve several purposes in the webs of meaning they weave. Displaying family brings joy not only because one sees their loved ones' faces, but also because these displays reassure one that their family is as they know it to be, and Inuit values are as they know them to be. That is, it provides ontological security. One feels comfort in seeing that they are part of a family; that the images display a healthy and happy family. That their mental map of their world, based on the interconnectedness of those who populate that world, is as they understand it to be.

Where David Halle (1993) and Janet Finch (2007) find that families have shifted to displaying families doing family things, I found that *Arviammiut* present a mix of activities and faces in their photographs. When they do display activities, they are most often connected to their role in the family *as well as* a performance of Inuitness. Madison, for example, shows me a picture of her husband as he skins a caribou and pauses to smile for the camera. In this photo, he performs the role of a good provider to the family, and a good Inuk hunter at the same time. Lauren shows me a picture she describes as "the boys and their uncle out hunting." When an adult individual is alone in a photo, other than in the case of elders, it is often a male accomplishing Inuitness, such as receiving recognition for his participation in dog team races. Pictures of children are equally spread across brothers and sisters, typically including graduation photos, from kindergarten graduations on up.

Most often, however, a mix of smiling faces greets me as I enter most homes. This is particularly common for members of the riding class, the largest class group. This may come across in a hodgepodge of photographs, or in a framed collage. There is a proliferation of candid smiles decorating clocks, under glass tabletops, framed, and tacked to walls. Residents and visitors to the house can immediately see the family and its location in the community and their relationship with other families.

This displaying, or performance, of family is one agentic way Inuit bring their culture indoors. *Inuuqatigiitsiarniq* (interpersonal connections) form a bedrock of the Inuit value system. In the past, family would have been performed in a variety of ways. In homes, walls become a tool for this performance. *Arviammiut* engage with their walls, overcoming the anomic discussed in chapter 2, and spatially graft their cultural values onto the walls of their "Euro-Canadian-style" houses (Gareau & Dawson 2004). The importance of communicating family and other interpersonal connections becomes immediately apparent during interviews. When I would start by asking for a tour of their walls, most participants began by listing the social location in the family of those depicted in photographs on the walls. Beatrice, for example, ignores other things on her walls when I ask for the tour and goes directly to a photograph of her and her husband. She then proceeds to other pictures of family; her children and their spouses, her grandchildren, and some people from another hamlet to whom they are related. She also tells me who brought her the photograph from the other hamlet. The collages of photographs are one way in which *Arviammiut* act out their values on their walls (Sizemore 1986).

Being what Lauren calls a "family person" reflects well among Inuit. Carmel tells me that walls "tell you more about a person's family than their personality." Where mainstream Western culture would turn to walls for clues as to a person's identity, interests, and so on, Inuit turn to walls to determine family location and connection. Family displays, then, become markers of who is included and excluded in the family and extended family connections (Heaphy 2011). Because these family displays include extended family, they indicate to visitors and residents alike the location of the family within the broader community. The nature of walls and displays foster comparison (Riesman 1950) and, in Arviat, these comparisons result in socially situating individuals and family in relation to each other.

This finding is, perhaps, not surprising since previous studies have found that the need to display family as part of doing family becomes more intense for mixed-race couples and LGBTQIA2S+ couples (Haynes & Dermott 2011). These displays push back against heteronormative and white mainstream narratives of a "good family." Being part of a minority group sweeps up relations to the dominant culture in their displaying of family. Indigenous groups face continuous threats to their culture from foreign peoples (Alfred & Corntassel 2005), pushing them into a position of needing to express Inuitness and resist dominant narratives imported from mainstream Southern Canada. Inuit, then, enact Inuitness on their walls and with their walls as they display family and spatially graft the cultural values of *aktuaturaunniqarniq amma inuuqatigiitsiarniq* (interconnectedness and interpersonal relationships) into house spaces. This can also situate spaces in relation to each other, to which I now turn.

SPATIAL FUSION

I introduce here the concept of *spatial fusion*. Spatial fusion occurs when two or more spaces, physically distant from one another, become symbolically connected and conceived of as components of the same place. In Arviat, spatial fusion occurs when the public areas of a house, such as the living room and kitchen, become symbolically linked with public areas of other houses, usually the houses of close relatives. Residents of these houses then consider the public areas of each house as components of the same *home*. This happens through a performance of *aktuaturaunniqarniq amma inuuqatigiitsiarniq* (interconnectedness and interpersonal relationships), which shows how *Arviammiut* agentically bring their cultural practices into unfriendly architecture.

For *Arviammiut*, spatial fusion is in part a result of negotiating homes built for nuclear families while they traditionally lived within extended families. They accomplish spatial fusion through family photography, extensive gift-giving practices, and visiting practices. Family photographs locate people within families and act as a display of family practices and Inuit values around interconnectedness by connecting uncles, aunts, grandparents, and in-laws to their families. Gifts augment this process and contribute to spatial fusion.

Gifts and mementos proliferate on Arviat's walls. In nearly every interview, participants showed me an impressive number of gifts on display from extended family members.

And I got that little statue on the wall, I got it from my sister-in-law. (Carmel)

My brother-in-law . . . made me a knife one day, so I just. [indicates where knife is hanging on a nail on the wall] (Felix) (See figure 4.1.)

A lot of the things that are on the wall, they are gifts from family or friends and this [clock] is from her daughter, Janet. . . . A lot of her children, us, we buy her stuff and that [puzzle] was one of the gifts that she put together. (Evelyn's Translator, also her Daughter)

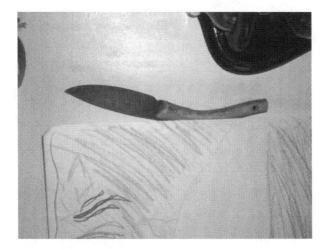

Figure 4.1   Gifted Knife on Wall.

These are representative of the kinds of gestures toward gifts that participants would routinely make during the tour of their walls.

During my time in Arviat, it became clear that these gifts closely matched visiting patterns. Kim and her mother Tori exemplify these patterns, and I was privileged to interview them both. While I was in Kim's home, she showed me gifts from her mother on her walls. When I was in her mother Tori's home, her mother showed me gifts from her daughter. The following quotes from Kim were spread throughout the first 20 minutes of the interview:

> [laughter] This one I got it from my mom. . . . And I got this from my brother. . . . And there's my mom. I got it from my mom and she got a copy from Mikilaaq Centre. Lynn's brother laminated it and gave it to my mom, when she was pregnant. 15 years ago. . . . I got it from my mom. [laughter] . . . This, I think I got it from my sister. Yea. . . . And my mom bought these from a house sale. . . . And these small stuff I got from my mom. (See figure 4.2.)

In total, Kim points out 17 items that are from her mother, sister, or brother (all of whom live together in another house). This includes her mother's spoon collection:

> *Kim:* My mom was collecting [spoons]. Whenever I go out [of town], I used to collect glass and spoons for my mom.
>
> *LJ:* And now it's here.
>
> *Kim:* Yeah. So I got them off my mom. (See figure 4.3.)

Figure 4.2   Kim's Gifts from Her Mother.

Figure 4.3 Kim's Mother's Spoon Collection.

The spoon collection has not transferred from the mother to the daughter. Rather, the mother stores it at her daughter's house, on display in that space as if it were on display in her own home.

When I interviewed Tori, she not only mentioned a few gifts from her daughter but also noted how many of her display items were located at Kim's house.

> *LJ:* So, can you tell me about, just what the different pictures you have on the wall, the different things you have on the wall? Take me on a tour of the walls.
>
> *Tori:* Some of them were brought to Kim's place.

From the moment we start the interview and I ask Tori to take me on a tour of her walls, she starts off by letting me know that many of the things on her walls are at Kim's house. As we continue, she points out a foreign currency tucked into the corner of a frame, and says, "and the one-dollar bill is with Kim now." She also points out gifts from Kim, "that one with the Inukshuk was a gift from Kim." At one point, Tori's family moved into a smaller home and she tells me,

> Yeah, we would have more stuff, more decorations over at our old place because we had higher walls. But since it's very small for us here, I gave the pictures to my daughters, to Kim and Janelle.

Tori and Kim are decorating each other's walls through gift-giving, which contributes to the sense that the family home is spread across multiple houses, symbolically connecting these interior spaces, enacting spatial fusion. In considering their behavior, their visiting patterns speak to their comfort in each other's spaces and how, in fact, they treat these spaces as if they were at home in either space. Kim's sister routinely ends up sleeping at Kim's house. Kim often eats at her parents' house. When I ask Kim how her sister's visits changed her sense of privacy, she seemed confused and told me that since her sister is younger, there is no change in her privacy. Aside from the interesting age-related comments, Kim and Tori *act* as if the public areas of each other's houses are part of the same home. There has been mutual accommodation of families and walls (Miller 2001). The meanings of the two spaces have co-mingled into one place. Thus, although the homes do not permit extended family living, *Arviammiut* enact traditional living patterns within unfriendly architecture by accomplishing spatial fusion by enacting *aktuaturaunniqarniq amma inuuqatigiitsiarniq* (interconnectedness and interpersonal relationships).

RELOCATION OF MEMORY: ORAL TRANSMISSION TO MEMENTOS ON DISPLAY

Part of locating the self in one's family and town and spatial fusion is the collective remembering *Arviammiut* accomplish on their walls. In mainstream Canada, family memories live through storytelling, but often also have a locus. Photograph albums may serve as triggers, mementos may contain active memories, and souvenirs may recall special times. In the past, Inuit memories found their locus on drum-dancing songs and storytelling (van den Scott 2017). Today, while drum dancing and storytelling persist in an altered format, primarily as a performance-based art form, families have come to rely on physical memorabilia, which they can both store and display on their walls. Small groups also rely on the physical memory triggers of names on gravestones in order to spark the story-telling and delineation of heritage and history. The locus of memory has shifted into physical tokens and symbols.

When the Catholic and Anglican churches came to the Arctic, they needed to effectively gain control over the collective memory of the community to establish power (Olick and Robbins 1998, 127). The existence of records is important for collective memory (Josias 2011; Lang & Lang 1988, 88; Maoz 2011). How, one might ask, did those in traditional times keep records? They wrote songs for the drum dances. By ousting drum dances, the churches effectively put a ban on the transmission of oral history and the performance of shamanistic rituals. In essence, the churches threw out the records along with the drum.

Arviat was one of the last hamlets to be settled and remains one of the most traditional. In many places across Northern Canada, drum dancing was lost entirely. Despite the return of drum dancing as a recreational art form, many songs containing these "records" have been lost. While drum dancing did persist in some continuous form in Arviat, the churches severely curtailed the activity which could no longer fulfill its role as memory-keeper. Mary, a middle-aged woman, patiently tells me, when I ask about where they are holding a drum dance, that they do not drum dance in the church building. She, however, will not elaborate, and the discussion of traditional activities and the church in the same breath is uncomfortable for her (Field notes). This ban was so forcefully adhered to that, even in 2007, when I accompanied a group of young throat singers and drum dancers to a choral festival in New-foundland, Canada, the youth had great difficulty performing drum dancing when the venue was a church, despite the fact that the churches now officially support the resurgence of throat singing and drum dancing as a performance art.

It should be noted, however, that through the label of "traditional arts," the churches have not allowed these forms of culture to enjoy the same status they had before their being cast out. There is still no drum dancing or throat singing actually occurring inside the churches (Field notes). The churches took control of the community's ability to remember, and to forget, thus transmuting the collective memory according to the interests of the churches.

Houses provided a new locus for collective memory—particularly family memories. While there are stories of drum dances' occurring on the land fairly continuously (Field notes), they did not occur with sufficient regularity to preserve all the songs, nor to remain the locus of memory. My spouse, the music teacher in the community, frequently spoke to me about the challenges he faced with such a small compendium of saved songs. Today, for example, while the news on the radio or CB of a drum dance occurring will summon a crowd, several elders and a few others cycle through only a handful of songs. Often a song will start and only one elder will know the words, or will get partly through and forget the rest of the song. The art form is preserved, but the locus of memory is lost. These drum dances happen fairly infrequently now—sometimes a year's elapsing before someone decides to pull one together.

And yet things continue to happen. Life moves forward. Children are born. People marry and breakup, graduate, experience tragedies, and have hunting or sewing accomplishments. And people remember them. Today, families have come to rely on physical memorabilia which they can both store and display on their walls. These memories fall into several categories; events, reclaiming the past, remembering the recently deceased, and remembering the living.

Events—Commemoration and Souvenirs

How people remember events falls into two main categories, namely photographs and souvenirs. Of course, these photographs and mementos, as all wall artifacts do, serve multiple purposes and contribute to various webs of meaning. The role of wall artifacts in commemoration is to contain memory and inspire remembering. Two of the most common events with clear mnemonic triggers on the wall are weddings and graduations.

The white wedding dress phenomenon is prevalent in Arviat. Serena and Ruby both have wedding photos framed and prominently displayed, each wearing a white wedding dress and holding a bouquet. For those who were married in the early days of the colonization of this region, these memories are intertwined with memories of the Church's shaping of new norms. Lily tells me about how she got married:

> The priest came, like [the local lay-minister], just barged in our house and asked "are you married?" And I said *"Nauk* [no], it's just good to live together." And [the lay minister] said "no, you should get married. I'm gonna announce it this Sunday service." And we had to go to social service 'cause we weren't working. So I barged into the social service and told her "the priest came yesterday and told us that we should get married, but we don't have any money to buy a ring." So she took an Easton's catalogue and she ordered two for 29 dollar wedding rings. So that's how we got our wedding rings. 2 for 29 dollar. [laughter] From Eaton's catalogue. . . . But the teacher told me "you should wear dress" but we couldn't find a fancy dress. So I wear a miniskirt. [laughter] Miniskirt... that I couldn't even bend. I could barely walk. [laughter]. It was her shirt. 'Cause she was longer than me and she said that "it's good for a dress." So I wear it. It looked like a miniskirt, but very, very small. And then her shoes. Her special shoes. I was in size 7, and she was in size 10. [laughter] It was a silver shoes with a big rose on the toe side. [laughter] . . . And then I would [add] Kleenex to make it my size. But they were too big. But we, I wore it. [laughter] *Ii* [yes]. [laughs]

Although Lily finds this memory funny, she also says she was grateful that no one had a camera that day because "we would laugh at it." The experience speaks to the role of the Church and the government, here represented by the social worker and the teacher, establishing wedding norms in the new normal, post-relocation. For most of those married after these norms took root, they took it upon themselves to arrange for white wedding dresses, bouquets, and so on.

Mementos also commemorate other kinds of events. Marg has her dried wedding bouquet prominently displayed, despite the highly organized modern weddings, cradled by the skull and antlers from her son's first successful caribou hunting trip—another event displayed, celebrated, and using the walls to demonstrate good Inuitness. Another home, Oliver's, has several dog team racing awards on display.

It is interesting to note that those in the driving class, having more fully engaged with their walls to resolve their sense of anomie, feel less need to solidify their Inuitness in performance to their walls. They are privileged in having access to resources, such as hunting equipment. They are more confident in their Inuit identity. Similar to when participants answered the question of how traditional they are with claims of *Qablunaaq* fluency, on their walls they often display mementos of trips and activities that demonstrate a knowledge of and participation in *Qablunaaq* practices. Jane has souvenirs from a trip to the United States on display, Madison has pictures of her husband and son on an African safari hunt, and Nadia has one of the rare examples of Southern-style artwork on display.

Graduations are also important community events. Children have lavish graduation ceremonies, even graduating from kindergarten to grade school. Many of the households I visited had graduation caps mounted on the walls, often next to photographs of the child at that time (see figure 4.4). For many children, these early graduations could be their only graduation. Schools make a fuss and families keep these souvenirs to remember the day. It is important to remember these days not only for the achievement itself, but also because these memories help to establish timelines for remembering other events; when a move occurred, for example.

Figure 4.4   Graduation Hats.

Reclaiming the Past

Reclaiming the past is a significant process in which *Arviammiut* engage with
their walls to further overcome anomie. A disruption in the chain of memory
equates to cultural anomie (Newman 2012). Despite the frequency of these
disruptions for Indigenous peoples, scholars rarely work at the intersection
of memory studies and Indigenous studies (Newman 2012). In Arviat, Inuit
agentically engage with their walls, and the symbolic anomie instantiated in
the built environment, to bridge these disruptions in memory.

Early anthropologists in the region took many photos of the *Ahiarmiut*
and *Padlirmiut* groups that now constitute Arviat. Some of these photos are
of living elders as youth, and others are of parents, grandparents, and great-
grandparents who belong to memories of the past. Lily has enlarged some
of these photographs and put them up on the wall behind her sink. Others
have pictures taken in iglus, such as in figure 4.5. Still others have pages
torn or photocopied from old books with pictures of relatives, themselves,
or their namesakes. Lily has a photograph from one of these old books
of her mother in labor and about to give birth to her in an iglu. She has it
framed and displayed in the hallway, just out of view as you enter her home.
She tells me about it, laughing at the craziness of it, and I can't help but be
shocked and distressed at what this photo represents. It reminds me of my
place as white outsider and the historical legacy of "research" in this community. For Lily, however, displaying this photograph is a way to reclaim
her past not only from the break in memory, but from this anthropologist,
from the academy, from others like me. She is proud to have reclaimed
her past, successfully bridging the gaps created by the culture crash. I try

Figure 4.5   Photo in Iglu.

to honor her work at reclamation by including this picture here, and mediate my own positionality as a member of the academy by having taken my photo such as to preserve the privacy of the moment for the woman, her mother, in this picture.

Arviammiut also reclaim the past by displaying early pictures of Arviat, including older houses and buildings (see figure 4.6). Phoebe has a sheet of paper on her fridge, held in place by a magnet. She has drawn, using both sides of the paper, Arviat as she remembers it from roughly the 1960s (see figures 4.7 and 4.8). She tells me this is her "first recollection of Arviat." The few houses were matchbox houses, and she indicates to me where she used to stay in a tent with her family. She includes her footprints and her parents' footprints traveling a well-worn path between the two small lakes to the Anglican church, one of the earliest buildings. Phoebe does the work of reclaiming her past by capturing her earliest memories in this drawing and posting it on her fridge. It is one of the first things one would see on their right-hand side as they enter her home.

Reclaiming the past can include mnemonic triggers for cultural values and practices. A creative storage solution for sunglasses (see chapter 7) reminds inhabitants of the Inuit cultural value of creativity. This display of creativity performs and affirms Inuit identity. Similarly, evidence of hunting, such as animal parts, photographs of hunting, and hunting implements, express the Inuit cultural practice of subsistence hunting. What makes these items look good on the wall is not necessarily the content itself, but the symbolic nature of that content. It feels good to be reminded of, indeed surrounded by, what Inuitness is and one's own successful cultural values and practices.

Figure 4.6   Early House in Arviat.

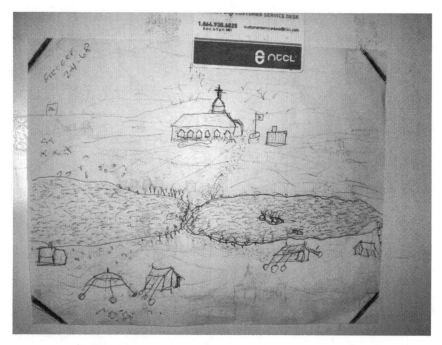

Figure 4.7   Drawn Remembrance of Early Arviat (1).

Recently Deceased

In many homes, I saw pictures of the recently deceased, particularly those who had died suddenly and tragically. When children died, often their school pictures would circulate throughout the town. Other children sometimes carried these photos with them for years. Others would set the photograph in a corner of a framed photo, indicating a relationship between those in the photo and the recently deceased child. Jamie, for example, has the photo of a young girl, who died suddenly in an accident, set in the corner of a photo taken in the very early days of Arviat. She tells me that there is a strong family resemblance between this girl and one of those in the photo. Jamie is both creating a mnemonic trigger for remembering this child, and also reclaiming her past with this action.

Alexis has created a shrine on her wall for her son's partner and their still-born baby, who would have been her first grandchild. The young woman passed away when she was almost to term. I remember the face well as I ask Alexis about the photos; the young woman had attended my program for at-risk youth for a few years and passed away only a week or two after I had moved away.

That's the unknown baby. Her unknown. Not unknown, unborn. Her unborn baby. That was my first one, my first granddaughter.

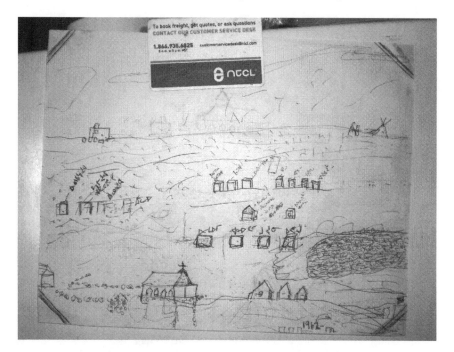

Figure 4.8   Drawn Remembrance of Early Arviat (2).

Alexis tells me that of all the things on the wall, she looks at this shrine the most. While the photos of her son's partner and the still-born child are prominently displayed in the living room, she is unable to put the urn for the grandchild on display because of the pain of loss.

> I told my kids I want to put them somewhere, . . . so my baby got that glass shelf. I tried to put them in there, but bad memory, not bad memory, but my, I think I still have that crying inside in me, so I put them back. Maybe someday, whenever.

The photographs capture the living moments of her son's partner and the short time her granddaughter's form existed in the world. They are frozen in time and despite one of the photographs being of a stillborn, it is better to have a mnemonic trigger to this past, rather than the present which the urn captures and represents. Memory, in this case, is preferable to the present.

Sometimes mementos or other visual cues of lost relatives take the place of photographs. Amber, a walker, does not have any photos of her sister, whom she lost, on display. Instead, she has a rosary through which she remembers and feels a special connection with her sister (see figure 4.9).

> *Amber:* It's a big necklace from the Catholic Church, you know those rosary necklace? It's a big one. And it was, belonged to my late sister. . . . Maybe last

Figure 4.9   Rosary.

year I got it from my niece, her daughter, and when she gave it to me . . . I grabbed that rosary necklace, like, just looking at it, like, it was really beautiful, I liked it. [starts crying] Sorry. When I grabbed it, I felt her presence, like, she was trying to talk to me or trying to be with me. When I grabbed it my hands were full of gold dust. You ever heard of gold dust?

LJ: No.

Amber: Like it's from God, trying to give you something. [still crying] Even though she passed away couple years ago now, [pause, crying] when I grabbed it, I felt her presence. Like, she's still with me. And I saw something white, like an angel. Protecting me and being with me. Sorry.

LJ: Namaqtoq [It's okay]. . . .

Amber: I'm okay. And ever since that time when she gave it to me, I've had it now. Cause when I grabbed it, my hands were, like, sparkle all over my shoulders, I mean my arms and my hands. Like, she was telling me that she loved me. I felt her presence. I miss her, though. Although she was older than me. Yeah. That was the most beautiful experience I ever had.

Amber still poignantly feels this loss. The rosary necklace connects her to her sister through a religious experience, elevating her sister to an angel-like status. This mnemonic trigger allows her to tell this story, to remember this story, and to find comfort in a memory which extends the life of her sister into the present in the form of angelic protector.

The collective memory of those less recently deceased has shifted from an oral tradition to the mnemonic grave markers in the nearby cemetery. Just meters outside of town lies a graveyard with white crosses at each gravesite. Sundays, particularly in good weather, *Arviammiut* flock to the cemetery and take leisurely walks, stopping at graves of their relatives and telling the stories of who is related to whom, how people died, and what they were known for (see figure 4.10).

The Living

Arviammiut also commemorate the living on their walls, creating mnemonic cues for stories and experiences. While those who have passed on primarily dwell in the past, those who are living move forward and sometimes away. Abigail's niece got into some nail polish as a child and left fingerprints on the wall. Rather than clean those off, Abigail preserved them.

> Like, I was going to wash this but my niece, she dabbed them when she was two years old so I, I said "don't wash those off, I don't mind."

She tells me that when she washes the walls, she washes around these fingerprints to preserve them. Like bronzed baby shoes (Kehily & Thomson 2011), these fingerprints preserve a moment in early childhood, both pointing to this state of *nagliginak* (childhood state of adorableness and lovability) as a

Figure 4.10   Cemetery.

desirable state to preserve and, at the same time, holding the growing child in this preferable moment in time.

As Ruby gives me a tour of her walls, amid pointing out gifts from friends and her sister-in-law, she indicates a picture of her husband when he was a young man, "and my husband he was a young, once a young man, young guy, so I just put it there." Ruby works to remember her husband as he was. She superimposes this image of him in the past over his present self. This mnemonic trigger works to frame youth in early adulthood as an ideal time for fellow adults, as opposed to one's grown children, for whom the ideal time is infancy and early childhood. For Ruby, these memories enhance experiences in the present by creating a rosy lens through which to view her spouse.

Gifts that help in remembering the living, such as the poem on Jackie's wall, and family photos, such as the family collage on Jade's wall, jointly work toward spatial fusion as well as locating the self in the family and the family in the community by enacting *aktuaturaunniqarniq amma inuuqatigiitsiarniq* (interconnectedness and interpersonal relationships). Jade's walls tell me, and herself, who her family members are, in both her and other households. If I were to go into those households, I would see Jade's ontological security displayed in pictures of her on her family members' walls.

Walls can also be a place to forget things. Sometimes, as I discuss ahead in chapter 7, walls become places for storage. *Arviammiut* might leave up out-of-date Christmas or birthday decorations to be ignored and forgotten until the next time they are relevant. Brittany even has a broken watch on her wall that never made it to the garbage. It is hanging from a thumbtack that holds up a photograph. Forgotten wall artifacts are often either in places that require more effort to see, that is, not easily in one's view when seated in common places to sit, or in extremely easy places to reach. Brittany was sitting on her couch and reached out, without having to get up or shift her position, and hung the watch on the wall to her right. She would have to turn to look at it, but it was a convenient place to store something temporarily—only she was so successful at forgetting that the watch had been there for months.

CONCLUSION

Walls, as cultural objects, engender norms and practices as objects located at the intersection of society, cultural producers, and cultural consumers. As Inuit in Arviat engage with their *Qablunaaq* walls, overcoming their anomie, they develop uses for the wall that are specific to this unique convergence of *Qablunaaq* cultural objects within Inuit culture and people. Inuit, then, enact Inuitness on their walls and with their walls as they display family and spatially graft the cultural values of *aktuaturaunniqarniq amma inuuqatigiitsiarniq* (interconnectedness and interpersonal relationships) into house spaces. In addition, although the homes do not permit extended family living, *Arviammiut* enact traditional living patterns within unfriendly architecture by accomplishing *spatial fusion*.

As the value of interconnectedness informs the use and placement of wall artifacts, it also transmutes the location of memory from primarily oral practices to mnemonic triggers. Wall artifacts often serve multiple purposes as they illustrate family connections, fuse spaces together, and house memories of stories, people, and times. By approaching walls as cultural objects, one achieves deeper analysis of the uses and meanings of spaces as people move through their everyday lives. In the next chapter, walls, as cultural objects, demand a performance of Inuitness, which I examine in food consumption practices.

Chapter 5

Piliriqatigiingniq [Working Together]
Performing Food Consumption to the Walls

The longer I lived in Arviat, the more *Arviammiut*'s struggle with living within the walls of their houses became apparent to me as an outsider. The link between the built environment and colonial power manifests as spaces within walls become spaces of oppression. Power works through space and place, with the residue of colonialism embedded in the spaces through which Inuit move and live. This engenders strategies of resistance. Inuit transform these spaces into culturally Inuit homes through resistance as identity performance. Consuming Inuit foods with gusto is part of this resistance, a skillful use of weapons of the weak (Scott 2008). It is an identity performance of Inuitness directed at the *Qablunaaq* walls enclosing and watching them. The consumption of food, however, with a hybridization of old and new ways, echoes the cultural changes which the walls bring and demonstrate Inuit ways of *piliriqatigiingniq* (working together).

As I have explained in earlier chapters, groups that experience massive change find themselves struggling to build new authentic selves within unexplored terrain, be it physical, symbolic, or social terrain—or some combination thereof. Dramatic social change throws everything up in the air— collective memory, social practices, norms, hierarchies, and so on. Anomie pervades every facet of life. In instances of relocation and colonization, the fundamental and foundational components of a group's identity are suddenly torn asunder.

Groups and individuals begin to question their identities; discover what is salient to others about themselves, and what they would like to be salient to others. One experiencing what Deborah van den Hoonaard (1997) calls "identity foreclosure" may find themselves asking, "what has changed and how do I make my new life relevant in the greater social context? What is the basis for my identity now?" For many groups, the above experiences

133

involve a process of settling into different routines, different ways of being and thinking, and different performances of identity. Credibility of identity performance, for *Arviammiut*, hinges on space and place and the ways in which newly arranged spaces can and cannot be overcome.

While walled-in, *Arviammiut* must perform identity to that space, to those walls. They are simultaneously pushing back the *Qablunaaq* influence and as the producers of the cultural object of the walls, and imprinting their own identity on those walls, engaging in a process of transforming *Qablunaaq* spaces into Inuit places. This requires *piliriqatigiingniq* (working together). As A. D. King (1989) suggests in his colonial studies, the complexity of our relationship with the built environment and its overlapping symbolic meanings is influenced by the local and the power relations in a given situation. The physical landscapes of our lives, which are structured by power relations, can and should be mapped out as a way of understanding contextual identity performance, particularly in contested colonial spaces (Dorries et al. 2019). Thomas Gieryn (2000) refers to the built environment as a "normative landscape" and indeed, Inuit must navigate whose norms are prioritized in their built environment. But, as Denise Lawrence and Setha Low (1990) point out, the built environment is also interactive.

This is a story of resistance, but not complete resistance. Thomas and Thompson (1972) assert that housing was introduced to Inuit as a colonial project of cultural assimilation; however, walls represent a political project of cultural assimilation that has gone *unfinished*. I argue that people develop strategies to negotiate, navigate, and often to resist the unfolding geographies that bring new cultural paradigms through identity performance. For *Arviammiut*, walled-off from past knowledge means having to come to terms with the new structures and built environment. I argue that groups may do so through the performance of knowledge linked to traditional identity. By embracing and more clearly defining what George Herbert Mead (1934) would call "significant symbols" of Inuit culture, *Arviammiut* infuse their daily performance of self with resistant acts that express their Inuitness.

Inuit tie their traditional knowledge into the land, the place where they have lived over centuries (Takano 2005). Displaced and facing threats to their identity on many levels, one of which is how to maintain a traditional identity when spatially separated from the locus of traditional knowledge, Inuit work together to centralize and heighten the significant symbol of food. The locus of traditional knowledge and food consumption practices is located in the land, not where you inhabit, but where you visit. The *Qablunaaq* homes are raised off the land—creating even more symbolic removal from the land. Traditional knowledge, as what Eviatar Zerubavel (1997) would call a "socially mediated" construct, becomes *overtly tied* to traditional identity as a significant symbol while walled-in. Food, then, becomes a resource for identity performance. Inuit must *piliriqatigiingniq* (work together) to enact strategies to negotiate and resist the power dynamics now inherent to the space and place of their lives. One of the ways they do this is through food.

FOOD AS IDENTITY AND COMMUNITY

As in all cultures, food has a distinct and important role. Studies of other Indigenous groups speak to consistency in the importance of food and food practices, while also indicating a diverse range of those practices. The Wiradjuri in Australia, for example, emphasize that the onus is on individuals to ask when they want or need food shared, rather than the onus being on the giver to give (MacDonald 2000). Sharing among the Aka and the Baka in central Africa maintains two systems of sharing and follows explicit rules (Kitanishi 2000).

For Inuit, food becomes particularly salient as a significant symbol to express cultural identity, embodying expressions of locality, resistance, and vibrancy, displaying a cultural act as symbolic of continued tradition and active cultural practice of *piliriqatigiingniq* (working together). Traditional foods, called "country foods," become a cultural resource (Swidler 1986) with which to respond to and resist encroaching cultural paradigms.

The literature on Inuit food focuses primarily on content and sharing practices. The unfriendly architecture makes it hard to butcher and prepare animals in Arviat homes (Dawson 2004; Marshall 2006; Thomas & Thompson 1972). Sharing practices are widely understood as the traditional approach to traditional food (Uluadluak 2017). Complex rules, however, around social relationships, such as kinship, govern the distribution of food such that this distribution physically reproduces social relationships across space and time (Kishigami 2000; Wenzel et al. 2000). Land-based food consumption entails content (the kind of food itself), practices (awareness and enactment of sharing rules and patterns), and knowledge (how to prepare food) (see figure 5.1).

Some scholars consider the mixed economy today and how different rules apply to traditional food and store-bought Western-style food. Items like sugar and tea have been subsumed into traditional foods and now are subject to traditional sharing practices (Wenzel 2000). I argue that hybridity encompasses how content, practices, and knowledge stemming from land-based food consumption are redistributed and strategically used as forms of resistance, including in instances of extreme poverty.

FOOD PRACTICES

In Nunavut, food is closely associated with hospitality, as in most cultures. Inuit have an informal approach to hospitality. On the land, hospitality is a key Inuit

Figure 5.1   Traditional, Country Foods.

value where to be truly welcome is to be treated as a member of the family. Formality implies distance and can be interpreted as quite rude. When guests come
into a home, an offer of tea or coffee is standard, but guests serve themselves.
Performing informality around food and hospitality is a strategy to access land-
based practices and spatially graft traditional practices into *Qablunaaq* spaces.

> Kim gets up to make tea and then when she sits back down tells me there is tea.
> I get up to get some . . . .(Field notes, May 28, 2012)

I visited Kim regularly throughout my time in the North. In her home, I was
a rare *Qablunaaq* visitor. Had I been expecting her to serve me, it would
have been an offense. Likewise, had she served me, I would have known she
was uncomfortable with me in the home and was distancing herself from me,
invoking *Qablunaaq* behaviors to express distance. In a sense, she would also
be symbolically keeping me distanced from the knowledge and privileges of
traditional *land*-hospitality, reminding me of my spatial place.[1]

While tea and food are made available to guests, *Arviammiut* teach children to fend for themselves at a young age. For many, there are no structured,
set times where parents believe that their children should be eating, regardless
of whether they are hungry or not—the emphasis remains on informality of
practices. As children get older, they begin to prepare their own food. The
age for this varies from family to family, but children as young as 9 and 10
might be kept home from school to care for younger siblings, including the
responsibility of providing food should anyone become hungry. This food is
generally *Qablunaaq* food.

In the walking-class homes, particularly, Western foods are often bought in prepackaged, individual sizes, so what I call *chain reaction eating* is more likely than sharing. One person starts to prepare food. They may offer to open another package of the same thing and microwave it at the same time, or the others may smell the food and wander into the kitchen themselves to prepare their own meals or snacks.

LJ: Do you do, what kind of food do you mostly eat?

Alexis: Just anything.

LJ: Mostly pre-cooked or mostly do you make it yourself?

Alexis: Mostly cooked. My kids. I do cook, when I want to, but it's one of them, it's him who wants to eat this, so he starts cooking. It's her who wants to eat this, so she starts cooking. Like, lunch time or dinner time.

Jasmine relates a similar scenario. *Qablunaaq* food has become the daily food for most of the Arviat population, and it is mostly consumed as a solo, mundane activity.

As a young child, Lily, now an elder, was taken from her family, who still lived nomadically on the land, and brought to a tuberculosis hospital for five years. Now in her sixties, she reflects on her return to her family:

LJ: So when you came back, did you remember being home before, cause you were [away for] five years?

Lily: It was a big difference, like we would have breakfast, lunch and supper at the hospital. But coming back home, they eat anytime. So I would just be mixed up 'cause, why is there no breakfast, lunch and supper? Cause I didn't know that they eat anytime they want.

LJ: Did you just wait a long time till you got too hungry?

Lily: Ii. [yes] [laughter]

LJ: Now, are you eating any time you want?

Lily: Yeah. Anytime we like . . . we just eat whenever we wanna eat.

Lily would have been old enough upon her return to self-regulate her eating habits. Today, this informal self-regulation practice persists as a way to perform Inuitness within a *Qablunaaq* space, although junk food complicates the practice with health concerns.

Scarcity and high costs are also issues; many in Arviat are at their wits' end trying to get enough food for their families. There is an active, informal market which has spawned two Facebook groups entitled "Arviat Sell / Swap Group" and "Arviat SELL/SWAP NO RULES." Among other trades and deals, people visit this website to sell TVs, clothing, furniture, and electronics in order to buy food. The layout of homes often changes in the last week of waiting for the next monthly check, as in Ruby's home.

> I notice right away that the TV is gone and the CB [radio] is sitting on the low make-shift wooden shelf. I ask Ruby about it and she tells me that [her husband] sold it, that they needed money for food. (Field notes, June 3, 2012)

While staying with Bethany, I saw her regularly coming home with fast-food, prepackaged items, what she calls, "Microwavables. Cheap. Cheap cooking."

The cost of food came up regularly in interviews, even when food was not the topic under discussion. During my time spent in walking-class homes, I witnessed the consumption of primarily junk food as well as prepackaged, microwavable food. Some turn to Facebook at moments of desperation.

> I am so tired . . . I mean, I just can't keep up with everything . . . the bills everywhere (few grands each to housing and Northern [store]) trying to keep up with my children's clothes and trying to feed my family, which is sometimes so hard cuz I'm the only one who trying to do everything with no help at all. wish I knew how to solve all my fcken problems cuz I know death is not the answer (which once in a long, long while comes to my mind) I JUST NEED FUCKEN HELP, ok???? bhftkjgyudig!!!!! (Field notes, May 30, 2012)

Although it comes up frequently in informal conversation, some are more reticent and prefer to hide their lack of food. Brittany had been one of my adult education students and was a firm supporter of my transition to researcher in the community. In the midst of that transition, she came up to me after a class and began weeping uncontrollably. She was out of food, with her husband and five kids at home to feed. For the first time in her life, she had had to ask a family member for *Qablunaaq* food, and she felt completely overcome by shame (Field notes, 2007). She did not ask me for food or help, she just needed to share her struggles. Many in the North are malnourished and living lives on the edge of desperation due to the high food costs, combined with the lack of jobs and resources. A 2010 study in the *Canadian Medical Association Journal* found that Inuit in Canada are the most food insecure people in the developed world and this has not changed much. This situation includes access to country food, to which I now turn.

FOOD CONTENT AND KNOWLEDGE: PREPARATION
AS SKILL

The performance of knowledge concerning country food skills helps one demonstrate access to land knowledge, and thus traditional identity, while walled-in to *Qablunaaq* spaces. In Arviat, country foods include caribou, beluga whale, Arctic char, seal, goose, goose eggs, and, for a few select weeks in the summer, cranberries and cloudberries. Occasionally rabbit, muskox, other fish, and ptarmigan make it onto the list. Polar bear meat is usually given to the dog teams.

Depending on the season, different foods receive more or less attention. Goose eggs and berries are only around for a few weeks of the year, for example. *Muktaaq* (whale blubber) can be found most of the year as long as freshness is not an issue; however, it has a peak season as well. Caribou is the most ubiquitous of the foods. It is often eaten frozen and raw or dried into jerky called *nipku*. Caribou caught in the winter may be cached until the spring. Fish, raw and dried, called *pipsik*, is also very common, along with seal.

There is skill involved in consuming traditional foods. During one interview at a cabin, I observed elders eating caribou hooves, something rare to see today. As they expertly fished them out of the pot and held them, they turned the part of the hoof where it had been detached to their mouths and sucked out the small bits of succulent flesh, hard to distinguish from the cartilage and requiring knowledge of its texture and ability to be sucked out. They had also made caribou lard from the fat and were spreading that on *nipku* (Field notes, Shannon's Interview).

Often, elders are relied upon to prepare traditional foods. Families with elders still living stand at a cultural advantage. In an interview on the land, Shannon gives me a look into her family's traditional food preparation, done primarily by her mother, Melanie.

> Shannon: it's been, like, over 20 years we've been going here springtime. My mom, she loves it here. She goes, she goes here to dry her meats and cook whatever there is to cook. Before they rot or.

> [Translating for Melanie now] When she was raised up, *illa* [I mean] back then, my grandparents used to make *nipku tuktu*. She likes that every spring. It's her generation. She'll keep going on.

Melanie is applying for money to teach preparation skills. There is a skill-based mentality of traditionality and traditional activities. Being separated from the land means *Arviammiut* need to develop strategies to develop these skills, as well as to actively demonstrate them to enact traditional identities.

Shannon continues by emphasizing the teaching of the skill and mentions a few things one would need to know in order to engage in the proper and safe preparation of these foods. She speaks about worms, bugs, caching techniques, and how to cook the leg, hoof, head, and neck.

It can certainly be challenging to get the food just right. To cut the caribou meat to make *nipku*, one must take a large piece and begin by slicing a thin piece off, but stop cutting just before hitting the bottom, being careful not to cut it right off. One then turns the meat upside down and again cuts a slice, but twice as wide as the last, so that the first piece is still attached, but now there is a second segment as thin as the first. Again, one stops just before the bottom and turns the meat over. One repeats this process until one has an accordion of meat, which one can then stretch over the drying racks. This skill, Inuit aver, can only be learned on the land.

There is also a spatial component to eating traditional foods in the home. *Qablunaaq* food lives on countertops and is prepared in microwaves and eaten on laps or at tables. For country foods, however, participants often place the meat on a piece of cardboard on the floor, around which groups can gather and eat together. This practice physically mimics the experience of eating on the land.

Even though many consider Arviat as one of the most traditional communities in Nunavut, country food, while more highly valued in the community than *Qablunaaq* food, is becoming less available. While most *Arviammiut* try to eat traditional foods as much as possible, linking that activity to traditionalism, only 13 of the 50 homes I visited during the interview phase had cardboard out for country food. Of these homes, six were the homes of elders and another five were homes of participants who identified themselves as particularly traditional.

While many still prepare traditional foods, a surprising amount of the dialogue around country foods consists of lack of knowledge. Jason, for example, lists several things as distancing contemporary *Arviammiut* from their history and specifies buying "store bought food" as a key factor in this loss of knowledge. Indeed, when we were visiting a friend and decided to buy an Arctic char to share, she did not know how to prepare it:

> We plan to have a barbeque. [We go buy char] None of us know how to filet it. She says there is a part you have to remove carefully or you will lose all your hair. (Field notes, June 9, 2012)

My friend has some lore that she has heard, but knows only that she has to be careful, not which part to fillet. Her definition of the situation is that specialized skills are needed to avoid bad things—more skill than is required for *Qablunaaq* foods.

Survival was key and often knowledge around food preparation involves safety. When Nadia, for example, showed me how to extract bone marrow as a snack, she was very clear about how to crack the bones and wash the marrow in water before trying it, as shards of bone could easily be missed otherwise (Field notes, June 2008).

Felix also points out the knowledge gap and how this has meant his family bears a higher burden as ones who prepare meat:

> When we started drying meat, there was quite a few, *illa* [I mean], there was very few people drying their own. And so, of course, when relatives want or when guests want and people want, we just gave it up so it was going pretty fast. And the kids, of course, always want. . . . I think even lot of people don't know how to make bannock anymore, which almost was a given for anybody and everybody to know how to make, right? So even a simple product like bannock is, people don't make that anymore. I mean, everything else is so easy to get. We just have to open a package, I mean. So I think that's partly why I think a lot of them will be traditional when they visit somebody.

Here Felix uses the term "being traditional" interchangeably with eating country foods. For him, this is a profound act of traditionality, the preparation for which takes skill. But, as he acknowledges, many people now lack the basic skills, not necessary for survival within homes and the hamlet, even while they embrace the activity of consuming the food as an expression of resistance and of their traditionality and Inuitness.

SUPPLY

Supply is a challenge. Hunting takes time and resources. Those who have the financial resources to pay for snowmobiles, gas, guns, bullets, *kamutik* [sleds], and so on, are often busy working jobs which severely limit their hunting time, leaving weekends crammed with land trips. Indeed, a segment of the population has never learned to hunt.

> I work. Um, my mom had two husbands. First one was early 80s, . . . but both of them, my fathers, were elderly and I never got around to get hunting. So, I don't really, I'm more of a city guy, you know. [laughter] I never really learned how to hunt. But it would be nice to learn something new. (Brandon)

Because Brandon does not hunt, his family rarely eats country food. He continues on saying that they do eat the country foods when we get the chance to eat it, or someone gives us. Like, we have *muktaaq* right now that I got from my work. My boss gave me a small piece, a small slab, for free.

Despite being dependent on the generosity of others for supply, Brandon still finds it important to stress that they will eat traditional food when given a chance. He still connects to these foods as part of his Inuitness despite being a "city guy."

When women talk about the supply of country foods, some, such as Nina and Emily, refer to the capacities and accomplishments of their spouses or common-law partners. Often one man will become the supplier for his extended family.

When the male hunter passes away, this can often leave families in the lurch. This is particularly the case for relatives who were not well off and depended on that food for their families. Serena's father passed away roughly a year prior to my interview with her. When the topic of food came up, she became emotional, weeping openly as she told me about her father and how hard it was now that the hunter in the family was gone.

> *Mamarit taima* [indeed, it tastes so good]. *Qangakkiaq* [when was it?]? Couple days ago we had caribou meat from my friend. Last long*ngitoq* [not long]. My kids, they love to eat *tuktu* [caribou]. . . . So, she brought us *tuktu* and that didn't last a day. *Tauka* [just because], we don't have transportation to go hunting, so we just wait. . . . It's hard without dad, *illariq* [for sure]. [tears up] That's what I miss the most. It's like he was there . . . as if he's telling somebody, "they're out of meat again." Then other person *qaujimangi* [would know] [and] would bring us [meat]. We mostly had our food caribou from my dad. Now that he's not there, August*mi* [in August] he died. That's why I miss having dad. *Illarit* [for sure].

Her husband fills the role of father to her children, but he does not hunt and provides no meat. Serena's uncle has started to give them some more regularly, but it is not enough to compensate for how much her father could spare. She struggles both with having less access to country food, and with that country food having come to symbolically represent the presence of a father and male caretaker in her life.

Many families no longer have any hunter connected to them. These families are predominantly walkers. While most share food intrafamily as a given, more and more are willing to sell it interfamily. Brandon finds this a sorry state of affairs and blames the new *Qablunaaq* style of living.

> When they lived in iglus, they were pretty much as a sharing family, you know. They would share pretty much their knowledge, their food, that kind of stuff.

And, uh, I can only say when we got the *Qablunaaq* walls, it's pretty much started to become kind of concentrated, like it's for ourselves only, not sharing.

He specifically links ways of being with the environment in which one lives. And traditional foods should be treated according to traditional practices which are part of the land, that is, sharing.

More and more, however, over the years I spent in the community, selling country foods on the radio became more popular. Not only were hunters (sellers) and buyers participating in the traditional activity of interacting with traditional foods (despite the *Qablunaaq* activity of paying for it), but hunters can recoup some of the cost of gas and bullets while buyers who previously had less access to country foods can now access traditionality and traditional practices more easily, although at a price. These purchases primarily occur over the community radio, but Facebook has become a trading ground as well. Movement of food through relatives, friends, or even strangers is not uncommon, mirroring social forms. I had the privilege of trying *igunak*—aged, raw walrus meat—which had been sent through family networks (Field notes, 2008).

Of course, these trends do not apply to all. Some become known for their generosity, such as Kathy and Lucia who both report that they are frequently asked for food because they are willing to share. Families, such as Felix's and Shannon's, become suppliers for wider groups and struggle with the demand. Frequently at the end of an interview, participants would send me home with chunks of fish or caribou. However, it never occurred to them to share *Qablunaaq* food in this symbolic way.

Two participants took advantage of the concept of indoor space to work against the rhythm of food preparation for the year. They hung drying racks inside.

When we tried drying meat with it, we were making it a little too thick for indoor, so we made it thinner pieces. And during the winter-time everything changes and meat doesn't go bad. . . . There was a lot of, ah, times we were running out of dry meat real fast, even if we made quite a volume in spring. (Felix)

CULTURAL EXPRESSION

Alignment with traditionality is the dominant concern. Eating traditional food with exuberance is a way to express and align oneself with traditionality. Samuel tells me in an informal conversation about how he went to another community in Nunavut as a drum dancer and attended a community feast. While there, he went straight to the traditional food and then sat on the floor to eat it. He tells me how many people there commented to him that he was a "real Inuk" and that they wished more were like him, in touch enough with their traditional culture to go straight to the country food and eat it on the floor. When attending traditional feasts, most sit with their family groups on the floor or with a few in chairs. The meat is served on cardboard on the floor. *Arviammiut* eat this food with gusto, often talking about the food as they eat, highlighting the consumption as an event.

Posts on Facebook about wanting *nipku* "so badly" not only speak about the supply issues within the community, but are also a way for *Arviammiut* to demonstrate their alignment with country food. Participants talked exuberantly about eating traditional foods. Samuel made the most defining reference. Samuel makes a direct link between traditionality and food, as I noted in chapter 2:

> We're very traditional, *tia'na* [for sure]. For example, like, right now social assistance and *hunaiqua*, *nutaqanu*—how do I say it? Child something—child tax, our main *kiinaujak* [money], money, *kihiani* [but] today we just had, we just had our child tax and my children would be very happy to have sour chewy things. Good. And at the same time, if I catch seal, caribou, fish, bring it in, they would stop eating what they're eating and then they would go for fresh blood right away. . . . Now I wish my children to keep them in mind at least you, you fed fresh blood, fresh blood, fresh blood. Best of my ability, fresh blood, fresh blood.

Here, Samuel not only appeals to a particular activity to align himself with traditionality, but he refers to the specific activity for which Inuit are most harshly judged. Samuel invokes exuberant consumption of food powerfully with his repetition of the words "fresh blood." In the face of his location in a Western space, he turns to performance of traditionality for strength of identity.

Other participants also routinely expressed purposeful enthusiasm for traditional foods. As Serena said above:

> Couple days ago we had caribou meat from [my friend]. Last long*ngitoq* [did not last long at all]. My kids, they love to eat *tuktu*. . . . [My friend] brought us *tuktu* and that didn't last a day. (Serena)

> Carl: [re: muskox] We didn't eat it constantly, *not like caribou*. Maybe once a weekend. *We can eat caribou every day.* [Author's emphasis]

Many, like Alice, were eager to tell me their favorite way to eat *tuktu*, "Fat. He loves frozen. She loves the fat and raw. Me, I like it with the rotten fat. I dip it in there. *Igunak*."

Eating traditional foods is a cultural expression and a display. Shannon assures me when I try the caribou butter that, "mostly with this, you won't stop if you try once, and you'll keep wanting."

Eating traditional foods has become a collaborative event of piliriqati-giingniq *(working together), rather than a mundane activity.* Emma, for example, says that she eats traditional foods at drum dances. For her, it is part of the cultural event of the drum dance. Nina tells me that she eats traditional foods after her common law has a successful hunt. These times stand out for her as events, rather than everyday practices. Bethany talks about the effort involved with procuring traditional foods since she has no hunter in her family. Felix, at the other end of the spectrum in terms of socioeconomic class, also tells me about the considerable effort and skill it takes to prepare and have available traditional foods, saying that it takes "an organized crew to produce a volume." As such, the effort and skill associated with traditional foods, particularly in contrast to fast-food from the grocery store, invests the act of eating with particular meaning and importance.

In contrast, *Qablunaaq* food consumption reflects a mundane everyday-ness. *Qablunaaq* food belongs to the downtime, as a solo activity for the most part, versus the group activity of eating traditional foods. As Lily mentioned above, it is a traditional practice for individuals to simply eat solo whenever they feel like it. This practice has become detached from the actual traditional food and has carried over with the treatment of day-to-day mundane foods. *Qablunaaq* foods are often consumed in individual, chain-reaction eating.

In short, traditional and *Qablunaaq* foods involve different practices, knowledge, and skill. In particular, the realms of practice have become most involved in the mechanism of hybridity (see figure 5.2). Eating country food is a display of cultural expression. Today, consumption of that food is an event that often occurs while visiting and with others, while the consumption

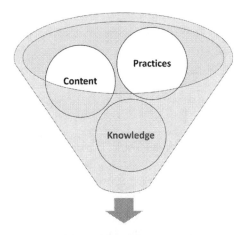

Land-Based Food Consumption

Figure 5.2   Elements to be Redistributed, Contributing to Hybridity.

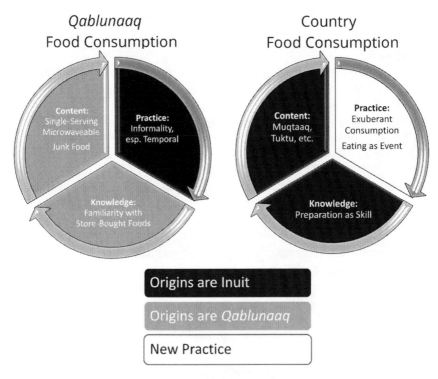

Qablunaaq
Food Consumption

Content:
Single-Serving
Microwaveable
Junk Food

Practice:
Informality,
esp. Temporal

Knowledge:
Familiarity with
Store-Bought Foods

Country
Food Consumption

Content:
Muqtaaq,
Tuktu, etc.

Practice:
Exuberant
Consumption
Eating as Event

Knowledge:
Preparation as Skill

Origins are Inuit

Origins are *Qablunaaq*

New Practice

Figure 5.3   Hybridity and Food Consumption: Inuit Identity in *Qablunaaq* Spaces.

of *Qablunaaq* food is mundane and often occurs alone or as a solo activity—a more traditional practice (see figure 5.3). Whichever food is being consumed, *Arviammiut* strategically perform Inuit identity through the consumption of food, a "significant symbol" of Inuitness, most overtly with the exuberant consumption of traditional foods.

CONCLUSION

There are strong links among the built environment, colonial power, and resistance through identity performance. As A. D. King states, "in a Foucauldian sense, the socially constructed environment is not simply an unpeopled 'landscape' acquiring an 'imperial print' but becomes a disciplinary terrain, a mechanism for inducing new practices, an arena around which new discourses are created [think of Sherry Turkle's (1995) 'evocative objects'], a resource for some, a weapon for others, with which to harass, reclassify, categorize, and control" (1989, 15).

Identity performance through food consumption is one way in which Inuit cope with and resist the repercussions of the colonial project within their built environment, echoes of their history within their walls. With the removal of Inuit from the land, access to the locus of their knowledge is structured by their walls, which have become symbolic of *Qablunaaq* ways of being. Thus, performing their Inuit identity inside these walls, *to* these walls, is a key component of their resistance to encroaching cultural paradigms. Space and place is inherently connected to colonial power and, for Inuit, to the meaning and consumption of food as a "significant symbol."

Figure 5.3 presents contemporary food consumption in Arviat and demonstrates how hybridity works as a mechanism of resistance through identity performance. Three areas contribute to food consumption; practices, content, and knowledge. *Qablunaaq* food consumption has different content and knowledge attached to it. Inuit, however, demonstrate flexibility and agency in the way that they practice consuming that food. Thus, the diagram illustrates that "practice" is the sphere in which identity performances are heightened and performed emphatically to the walls. When consuming land food, the content and knowledge remain more constant, while the practice has changed, becoming more exuberant. *Arviammiut* eat their food, talk about eating their food, and display love of country food exuberantly to their walls as an act of *piliriqatigiingniq* (working together). This hybridity, rather than preserving a practice, has enabled the realm of practice to become one of resistance through identity performance. *Arviammiut* demonstrate that *Qablunaaq* walls have not curbed food culture in Arviat, yet again agentically spatially grafting their culture indoors in creative ways, navigating living within *Qablunaaq* walls.

NOTE

1. I should note that Elders are the exception in that people do serve them food.

Part III

WALLS AS TECHNOLOGICAL OBJECTS

It struck me often, the similarities between buildings and people;
not that they resemble us, but that we resemble them.

—Jacqueline Baker, *The Broken Hours*[1]

When imagining new technologies, people often think of cell phones or machines of great import, of whizbang technologies or "epochal" technologies (Michael 2000). Latour (1992), among others (Arnold & DeWald 2011; Bijker 1997; Michael 2000; Taylor 2012), asserts the need to take a closer look at technologies often overlooked for their banality but which have deep consequences and complex meanings attached to them. Walls, for example, lack the obvious innovative flair of the wheel, the lightbulb, or the automobile, but they shape our lives in profound ways. While a small, yet significant, literature has grown up following Latour's (1992) lead, those studies that do exist focus almost exclusively on the Western context. Arnold and DeWald (2011) highlight this limitation and issue a call for studies of mundane technologies particularly in non-Western contexts.

MUNDANE TECHNOLOGY IN NON-WESTERN CONTEXTS

In 1948, Siegfried Giedion issued a call to historians to take up the study of "anonymous history." Among other commonplace items, Giedion delves into the history of the spoon, the chair, and the drawer. Few stop to consider these everyday items as inventions in the first place. They are, nonetheless, forms of technology deeply rooted in our daily lives. Giedion's call, however, went unanswered for many years.

In the early 1980s, technology studies took off, growing out of science studies, suggesting theoretical models which include Actor Network Theory (ANT) (Callon 1986; Latour 1983) and the Social Construction of Technology approach (SCOT) (Bijker et al. 1987), among others. Initially, those who developed these approaches were interested in unraveling the mysteries of impressively flashy technologies, or technologies of tangible import. By the early 1990s, scholars began to emphasize the importance of studying more banal, mundane technologies (Bijker 1993; Latour 1992; Mukerji 1994). As Mukerji (1994) avers, "material culture" shapes our everyday lives in profound ways. Michael (2000), for example, illuminates how walking boots changed our relationship with nature in unexpected ways. "Invisible technologies," as he terms them, can have more ramifications in our daily lives than more epochal technologies.

Mundane technology carries with it moral implications (Latour 1992). As items in our world with moral prescriptions, it is important to study these "missing masses." Latour (1992) uses the example of door hinges to delineate moral prescriptions. Hinges are a form of leverage which allows a small item to do what would take a great deal of work by humans. This substitution comes with prescriptive messages. The door now discriminates against the aged or the very young, for example. Doorknobs restrict those with disabilities. Thus, there is a moral ideology attached to the hinges. Power relations are reflected and carried out in the spread and use of (mundane) technology as a facet of material culture.

Arnold and DeWald (2011) argue that scholars must move away from diffusionist models which privilege Euro-American innovation and entrepreneurship in favor of attention to the "social life of things" (Appadurai 1986) *within* a colony or non-Western context (Arnold & DeWald 2011, 971), attending to local agency (Arnold & DeWald 2012). Arnold and DeWald (2011) maintain that colonizing regimes have less control over mundane technology than over epochal technology, and although this technology is still inflected with moral prescription, a study of "everyday" technologies exposes the researcher to a user-based, person-oriented level of analysis (Arnold & DeWald 2012). They call for researchers to look beyond

> dominant paradigms of colonialism, nationalism, and development, to explore the multivalent nature of 'everyday life' and enquire into 'the social life of things' as locally constituted, to examine modernity's diverse material forms, technological manifestations, and ideological configurations. (Arnold & DeWald 2012, 1)

Mundane technologies in non-Western contexts must be studied in their local context, on the ground.

While studies have long acknowledged that technologies are both constraining and enabling (e.g., Bijker, Hughes, & Pinch 1987; Mukerji 1994), recent work (Collyer 2011) stresses the importance of turning attention to reflexivity. The concepts of "passive engagements" and "active engagements" offer a way to examine reflexivity more closely. Thus, the everlasting ebb and flow continues. The sands of the shore shape the waves, and the waves shape the shore.

PASSIVE/ACTIVE ENGAGEMENTS

Mundane technology does shape everyday lives and does carry moral prescriptions, but people also exercise agency. It is not mere recursiveness that arises, but reflexivity in the sense that, while there is a recursive relationship, participants are also consciously active in shaping their own norms and patterns of use of the mundane technology according to their cultural preferences. Attention to reflexivity, however, is eclipsed in literature dealing with non-Western, and particularly colonized, locales. Groups, like Inuit, are too often regarded either as helpless victims constrained by imported technologies or completely agentic with no attention to the structural impacts of technology. While colonized groups are victims and have experienced constraint, they are also agentic, creative, and innovative. Passive and active engagements are concepts that allow for a recognition of impact, constraint, and oppression, while at the same time honoring agency and recognizing the strength and resiliency of non-Western groups.

New technologies, mundane or not, are engaged with previously existing cultural resources. Charles Taylor stresses that, while there are some homogenizing aspects, cultural adaptations to modernity (in this case, technologies of modernity) are not identical across civilizations and that "a given society will, indeed must, adopt the mode for which it has the cultural resources" (1999, 164). This study finds that reflexivity emerges as particularly salient in the relationship between *Arviammiut* and exogenous walls.

Interpretive flexibility (Bijker 1993; Pinch & Bijker 1984) constitutes a key tool in considering walls because it chronicles the flux of the polysemic nature of symbols (Schudson 2002). Different relevant social groups (RSGs) negotiate shared meaning or meanings for the technological artifact through use (Bijker 1997). When a technology develops its *technological frame*, the set of congealed meanings, uses, practices, and norms surrounding a technological object, it achieves *closure* (Bijker 1997), but not before previously existing schemas, or ways of thinking (DiMaggio 1997), influence the technological frame. The previous model of the relationship of new technologies to RSGs did not account for reciprocal relationships and multiple forms of interaction.

Figure C.1 extends this model to account for various power dynamics as well as passive and active engagements.

By conceptualizing passive and active engagements, purposely anthropocentric, not only can we investigate the technological frame in the full glory of its relative firmness and fluidity, but we can dig right into the reflexive process, sorting the sand from the waves while still viewing them as part of one social process.

Passive Engagements

Passive engagements:

1. *are those in which individuals, at the micro level, and societies, at the macro level, are affected by the technology.* They are not actively engaged in shaping the technology, but rather bearing the consequences of the technology. Within passive engagements, technology itself, while agentic and part of a social equation, has no motivation—while human beings are laden with motivation.
2. *include unintended consequences.* Telephones changed not only how we communicate but also our social expectations, and the airplane had global ramifications which we, perhaps, have still not entirely understood.
3. *have homogenizing effects.* When a new technology is introduced, there are some ways in which it will reach across cultures to have similar impacts on different societies. The printing press will always make more material more easily accessible and have impacts on the importance of literacy, although in varying degrees across class. Some

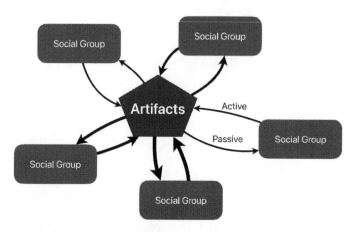

Figure C.1   **Relevant Social Groups, Objects, and Passive and Active Engagements.**

impacts of the technical on the social are quite predictable across societies.

People are not unaware of passive engagements, or how technology has intruded into and changed their lives. As Ralph Schroeder correctly points out, when a new technology infiltrates any given town around the world, it is "initially concerned mainly about the impact on 'morality' and on the disruption of 'tradition'" (2007, 106–107). These concerns are raised in reaction to the homogenizing effects of passive engagements. Rather than implying a technological determinism, however, this concern speaks to the negotiation between passive and active engagements.

Active Engagements

Active engagements *(1) involve some agentic movement or work on the part of the human component to engage with the technology,* either as an individual or an RSG. This can occur *(2) either consciously or unconsciously.* These engagements are the means by which people give the artifact meaning, transform it, establish conscious uses of it, and react to passive engagements, socially constructing the artifact at hand and its technological frame, both in meaning and use. This can be through identity work, boundary work, or emotion work, to name a few, as they construct or reaffirm meaning in the moment.

Telephones provide an excellent example of an active engagement. People actively engage with telephones by creating their own meanings and uses. Before cell phones, people would often call and let the phone ring once to let someone know they had arrived at their destination, or they might call collect and the recipient would not accept the charge. Now people actively engage with cell phones, evident in the meaning that we ascribe to text messaging. New linguistic forms have developed; LOL, OMG, and LMAO. Practices of use develop and texting achieves symbolic, and practical, ascendancy. As a result of the importance we give to texting, we have altered the technology so that cellular phones now cater to texting, specifically. Their keyboards have become easier to use, and we have strengthened the infrastructure needed to support connectivity. *(3) Active engagements entail diversifying effects.* When a new technological artifact is introduced, the preexisting cultural institutions combine with novel agency, and innovative engagements with the object, producing a locally specific, socially constructed use of the technology. At the outset, there are a number of ways in which the object might be used—there is no innate meaning. Which of those uses will surface depends on the schema of the preexisting culture and how they combine it with this new technology. Passive engagements have an indiscriminate effect on culture while active engagements have the potential to vary greatly across societies according to cultural context.

The first chapter in this part examines a passive engagement, namely the changing notions of public and private. Changes in the division of space and, in particular, the creation of interior, divided spaces will inevitably cause a shift in notions of public and private. However, this homogenizing effect interacts with the already existent culture to produce novel understandings. This chapter also discusses overcrowding, which impinges on how Inuit perform privacy.

The second chapter in this part takes the vantage point of an active engagement. Here, I examine the use of the wall as a tool for storage. The mundane technology of the wall is embedded in a specific local context. By studying use, on the ground, the importance of performing Inuitness through the use of the walls emerges. *Arviammiut* actively engage with their walls to give the walls a locally specific interpretation, use, and meaning; that of being a tool for storage.

NOTE

1. Excerpt from *The Broken Hours* by Jacqueline Baker © 2014. Published in Canada by HarperCollins Publishers Ltd. All rights reserved.

Chapter 6

Piniarnikkut Ilittiniq [Learning to Do]

Passive Engagement: Notions of Public and Private

Permanent walls are an "invisible" technology (Michael 2000), slipping in under the radar both theoretically and empirically, tricking us into hardly seeing them at all. Mine is not the first to regard walls as a technological artifact (Adams et al. 2008; Gieryn 2002; Latour 1992), or to assert that one needs knowledge to negotiate walls as a technological system. Marshall, in a study for the Canadian government on policy and housing design, states that "the Inuit are resources-conscious but do not understand their present housing systems and receive no training" (2006, 2). This, of course, implies that Inuit must come to the same understanding Southern Canadians have about housing systems for their understanding to be legitimate, a problematic viewpoint! *Arviammiut* have, however, come to their own understanding of their houses with no help from those who imposed those structures upon them, with heterogeneity across class lines.

In this chapter, I discuss two interrelated passive engagements; changing notions of public and private, as well as newer concepts of what inside and outside mean. In exploring passive engagements, it is impossible for agency not to come up. While the concepts of passive and active engagements help us to separate out two generic social processes in tension with each other, the very fact of their tension means that I must also stray into the realm of agency in this chapter. I will endeavor to make clear, however, the thrust of the passive engagement in forcing this agentic response. In addition, while there are ways an agentic response can work to cope with the changes resulting from passive engagements, the new concepts and definitions of the situation remain firm, and the agency is apparent when adjusting to the results of passive engagement in different ways.

LEVELS OF PRIVACY

Erving Goffman's (1963) concepts of *front stage* and *back stage* can help us understand the varying levels of privacy that *Arviammiut* practice today. We are constantly engaged in performing—to ourselves, to others, to fit roles, to resist roles, and so on. When we know we are being watched, and we are performing accordingly, we are giving a front-stage performance. Things can relax more backstage. Back-stage life can be a relief as we step out of the public eye (even if that public is only a parent or boss), and we can step out of character.

 Arviammiut have two front stages within contemporary architecture. The first and most public is when *Arviammiut* feel as though they are under the gaze of the *Qablunaaq* eye. Kukathas (2008) has called this form of privacy (or lack thereof) in other Indigenous contexts "cultural privacy." In this sense, Inuit must perform Inuitness in the face of Southern judgment, norms, and formality. As a heterogeneous group, some work to perform fluency in the outside world to outsiders, while others perform extreme informality and emphasize elements of Inuitness in which they have previously been judged by these same outsiders, such as the eating of raw meat (see chapter 2).

 The second front stage, in order of publicness, is a more relaxed experience where Inuit are amongst each other. It is still a front-stage performance as each person is now enacting norms for other Inuit, but the intensity of performing *Inuitness* is relaxed. When talking to me, a *Qablunaaq* researcher, about time in this secondary front stage, the storytelling and interactions are pushed to the most public front stage despite my having been accepted in the secondary front stage when with friends *as a friend*, rather than as a researcher.

 Arviammiut negotiate the complexity of their multiple front stages and their backstage with aplomb. I now discuss these levels of public and private as notions introduced by contemporary housing. First I turn to what *Arviammiut* have learned from their walls about how to be in their houses, where the front and backstages are, and how they navigate *Qablunaaq* and Inuit levels of formality associated with publicness. Note that even in this passive engagement, *piniarnikkut olittiniq* (learning to do) is an Inuit value connected with resilience. I then discuss some of the issues that challenge new privacy practices, such as overcrowding and transient living (or what we might call houselessness). I should note that while some did share memories of living in "matchbox" houses, this chapter focuses on contemporary houses.

MAIN ROOM AS FRONT STAGE WITH NORMS

The second front stage in Arviat is spatial. When entering a house in Arviat, there is usually a cold porch (an unheated buffer porch) from which one enters directly into the large main room of the house. Generally, the front door to the house is kept unlocked during the day, and people come and go from each other's houses without knocking. This main room is accessible to the community public. I have noted many times in my field notes when I, or others, have gone into homes, stood in the entryway and asked those in view if so-and-so was home. Often this happens without taking one's boots off since it can be cumbersome to take winter clothing off and on, so it is best to be sure your intended visitee is home before getting too comfortable.

I noted once when I tried to go visiting, "still a locked door, which means no one is home. I don't bother knocking" (Field notes). When the door is unlocked, I and other visitors can go right in. Some walkers do emphasize in their interviews that they most definitely do keep their front doors locked at night because they have neighbors who drink too much and may be unsafe. A handful who are in the midst of abusive situations may also keep their front doors locked in the day, but this is a rare occurrence and indicative of trouble.

Upon entering the house, I find the clash of the first front stage and the second front stage. The first front stage, rather than being spatial, is conditional on those present. When I first dropped by Abigail's home to interview her, there was laundry on the floor in the hallway. She was not home. When I came by an hour later, she was home and the laundry had been pushed into piles. Often when I would go visiting, I would be warned, in slightly embarrassed tones, about the state of the house as I entered. My friend Brittany was quite candid about her nervousness of letting a *Qablunaaq* see her home.

> I debate going straight to Brittany, but decide to wait. Mostly I can just show up at people's houses now, and Brittany got to be okay with me coming over when I lived here, but I know that she is particularly shy to show her house to *Qablunaaq*. I think I might be the only one she has let in at all. I decide to wait and call her because I know she will want to clean a little. We had talked about it when I lived here and she had stopped cleaning for me, but I have been away two years since my last visit, so just in case. (Field notes)

Many participants point out tidiness as a major difference between *Qablunaaq* and Arviat homes, although in my last visit the show *Hoarders* had somewhat complicated this understanding. Still, when I entered a home as a researcher, suddenly the eyes of the South turned upon them and their regular front stage became a new kind of front stage. I was quite aware of this as I entered homes and had to work to mitigate my status as a researcher as I was aware that the mere presence of a researcher can be a form of violence.

Varying standards in the state of undress also demonstrate a learned norm from their walls. As with the South, a state of undress among one's family is more acceptable; however, the main part of the house is a public area. Abigail tells me,

> My nieces, when they finish taking a bath they're just like, ah, no clothes on, run around, and if the parents say they "should put their clothes on" I just encourage, I always say "no! Let them be like that. They're kids one time. When they become adults, they're gonna always have to wear clothes so just let them be if they want to be, *illa* [I mean] no clothes on.

Children can stretch the time that they are allowed to appear naked. The two front stages, however, would come into tension when I would appear. I write several times in my field notes that when I arrived, the husband would have his shirt off, and he would casually get up and go put a shirt on. This level of undress was acceptable in front of other Inuit visitors, but not in the more public front stage that I unwillingly carried with me. When I stayed with Bethany, I note,

> [My friends] are comfortable among themselves with a state of undress, but they are not sure how to feel around me. . . . The other night [my first night there], Martha knocked on my door [already very formal and unusual in an Inuk house]. . . . Her common-law, with his shirt off, now kind of stands behind her and it seems he is being modest about having his shirt off, although later it is just too challenging for him to hide that and he lets go worrying about that.

While I stayed with Bethany and her family, the real challenge was the bathroom door. They had learned that they "should" keep the bathroom as a private, backstage, space. What that means to *Arviammiut*, however, varies. Many close bathroom doors, but many do not. Privacy is accomplished through civil inattention (Goffman 1963), that is, ignoring and pretending not to hear. Bethany's family only needs one lightbulb in their small space of a main area, a bedroom, and a large pantry/closet-like area. They keep the bathroom door closed. When someone is in there, the door is open which acts as a signal. People know not to walk past or to look in while the door is open. The first day I stayed with this family, while I was still a *Qablunaaq* to them, and not yet "Lisa-Jo," was a challenge for all as we navigated together this awkwardness.

> There is no working light in the bathroom so she leaves the door open. I try not to think how I will go to the bathroom when my bladder is ready for it. (Field notes)

> I turn to go into my room [the storage closet room], but realize the bathroom door is wide open and I can hear peeing. I decide to go back to the couch until the girl is done. She hears my movement and asks the baby boy, who is standing

in the doorway of the washroom "*nau Qablunaaq?*" [Where is the white person?] He gestures towards me. I try to look as if I have no idea someone is going to the washroom, just to be helpful. (Field notes)

Ultimately, things relaxed. When I indicated I was going to shower the next day, however, they were kind enough and attentive enough to subtly put the lightbulb in the bathroom that morning so I could close the door.

There are, of course, heterogeneous responses to the understanding that bathrooms are private areas. As Abigail tells me,

Even when we're in the washroom we don't close the door. We're just open, pretty open. *Ii.* [Yes.] Like, Inuit, *we're all different.* Like, my sister-in-law's niece, when she's in the washroom, she closes the door. She's only eleven, so. But when my daughter goes to the washroom it's open when we all, the rest of us we just keep the door open. And it's in the corner too so it's not like we're there to see. [Author's emphasis]

There are a variety of practices in Arviat regarding bathroom etiquette, but all stem from the understanding of bathrooms as backstage, private areas.

BEDROOMS AS BACKSTAGE

Bedrooms are also more private areas, a learned construction of privacy. Deborah, Kathy, Jane, and Ellen, among others, mention the lack of privacy in an iglu. As one open space, with one sleeping shelf, the family would all sleep together, and there was no expectation of privacy. Houses, with their internally divided spaces, teach that bedrooms "should" be separate. Again, there is agency and diversity in how *Arviammiut* implement this concept; however, this is a homogenizing concept as it brings understandings of public and private into closer alignment with mainstream, dominant norms, even through *piniarnikkut olittiniq* (learning to do).

Roughly a third of participants told me they slept with the bedroom door open. A less formal interpretation of privacy, as well as open bedroom doors, correlated with the walking class. Some treated time in bedrooms as they would have time in iglus. Ellen, an elder who lived in iglus until her early 20s, tells me that cooking would generally be done outside the iglu, as does Felix, a relatively young elder who represents traditionality within the community.

You're hardly in them. Iglus, tents. You didn't really spend that much time in them. I mean, you ate and slept in them. You didn't hang around, you know? You always had to be doing something to get ready for whatever season you were in and whatever you're gonna encounter and everything is, um, not set up, so you're doing everything all the time, all the time, all the time. (Felix)

Samuel reinforces this perception, telling me, "In an iglu, they used to go inside the iglu just to sleep and to eat. Besides that, they would not try to be inside the iglu, they try to keep walking or doing things."

Most, such as Brittany, Abigail, and Lily, tell me that they only go into the bedrooms to sleep. Children, as so often happens, are often exempt from this norm and several, such as Abigail, Beatrice, and Ruby, tell me that although the bedrooms are only for sleeping, the children go in there to play with visiting friends or, in the case of Beatrice who can afford computers for the daughters' bedroom, "Twelve o'clock, they eat fast and then they go to their room. Something about Facebook and Bebo." Trevor tells me his daughter usually takes her friends to her bedroom.

Often, when I would go visiting, someone would come sleepily out of the bedroom, regardless of the time. This was more common in walking and riding class families. In instances of overcrowding, which I will discuss in more detail below, bedrooms become convenient spaces when people want to engage in different activities. At Lucia's home, those playing bingo via the radio stay in the bedrooms.

We head in and I ask if Lucia is here. One of her daughters goes to check and says she is in her room. I ask if I should go back. She says to do what I want and motions that I can go back. . . . There are two rooms to the right with the doors right next to each other. Lucia and her husband are in the second one. They are lying on the bed, a mattress on the floor, Lucia on her stomach, her husband on his side. He has no shirt on, Lucia has on a shirt and underwear. They both have bingo cards in front of them with their dabbers, a bright pink. Marie sees me and hands her dabber to her husband and, with some effort as her legs have been bad, gets up and comes to hug me. I tell her she does not have to get up, gesturing to her legs, but she does. He husband dabs her card while she is up. She tells me to make myself at home. I say we need to talk about when I should come stay for a few days. She says she will call me and I can call her after bingo if I am not still there [i.e. if I am done visiting at her home before bingo is done]. She gets back on the bed. We exchange a few more words, but she is back into the bingo and clearly wants to only be doing that. We head back out to the main room. . . . Soon, her husband comes out, buttoning up a shirt.

In this crowded house, there is no space to lay out bingo cards while others are also hanging out doing other things. Norms around privacy are thrown into a more formal level when I visit, but I am also very close with this family and so I am allowed into the back bedrooms to visit even though they are normally reserved for sleeping. In this home, the younger members of the household often go back and forth to the bedrooms because there is not enough room for everyone to sit comfortably in the main room. One exception to the rule was a differently organized house where one could not see the entrance from the main room. The elder who lived in this house told me that he spends most of his time in the bedroom when he is home alone because that way he can have a better view of the porch, the doorway, and whoever may be coming in.

Figures 6.1 and 6.2 show the walls in the main room and a bedroom of the same home, a common pattern across classes, although children have begun decorating their bedrooms more. This is interesting in and of itself. The contrast in decorations reflects both notions of public and private, as well as time spent in the various areas of the home. Several participants, such as Nadia, Lauren, Carmel, and Emma expressed a desire for bigger living rooms. Nadia says that

> *Qablunaaq*, in South, like to have very big bedrooms. Having a bigger living room or a bigger kitchen doesn't matter to them as much. But for Inuit, having a bigger kitchen and a living room matters more than having a great big bathroom or a great big bedroom. So that's how a lot of our new houses are designed now too. The kitchen and the living room are bigger. The bedrooms

Figure 6.1   Public Space in the Home.

Figure 6.2   Private Space in the Home.

are probably a bit smaller than they should be. That's because we made the kitchen and living room bigger and the bathroom a bit smaller. Cause down South, when you're down South you like great big bedrooms and very big bathrooms. [laughs]

In addition, while many contemporary homes in mainstream Canada have prescribed uses for many rooms, such as offices or workrooms, in *Arviat*, a vernacular use of space as multipurpose pervades. Bedrooms can become sewing rooms, but main rooms can become gathering places, offices, spaces to butcher animals, spaces for drum dances, sewing rooms, and so on. The furniture is light, sparse, and easily and often moved to accommodate all kinds of activities.

Seating in the main areas of the home reflects status within the family and among family and visitors. While I was visiting for tea, we were seated around the kitchen table at the outset of my visit. When the matriarch of the family entered the room, she was immediately given a chair.

When Ruby comes into the room (the mother), [the eldest daughter] promptly gets up from the chair and Ruby sits there. No physical acknowledgment is made about the move. Within a minute or two, [the younger daughter] vacates the stool and [the eldest daughter] moves there. (Field notes, June 1, 2012)

Ruby did not have to ask, and no acknowledgment was required. In another visit, my husband came into the home shortly after I did and sat next to me, asking me if he was taking anyone's seat. I told him no. Ruby asked what he had said and I responded that he was worried he had taken someone's seat. She said that "it's okay and that they all just take whatever seat when someone gets up, always just taking whatever seat" (Field notes). Over the course of routinely visiting this home, however, it was clear that the preferential behavior noted above was typical.

PURSUING PRIVACY

The bottom line of this passive engagement is that the houses have taught that privacy, for sleep, for sex, and for time alone, is desirable. Many consider heightened privacy practices as healthier. Kathy, for example, when asked the difference between an iglu and a house, tells me that there is a "big difference" and that more privacy is "healthier" because "in iglu, there's no privacy at all." Emma, Ruby, Phoebe, and others make general statements that privacy is a good thing.

> Right now, I prefer my privacy. Back then I wouldn't have minded, but I'm, I'm catching up with the times. [laughter] I prefer, I think it's more appropriate to have your own room and not a whole one space. Yeah. (Phoebe)

As for many groups, when camping or spending time at a cabin, those privacy expectations are relaxed, but when in a home, *Arviammiut* view privacy as a more comfortable state of being and part of norms and desirable practices.

Participants listed sleep most often as an important element of privacy. Oliver, an elder, says directly that "it's better for Inuit to have their own space. Like, whenever they're going to bed, they have their own privacy and they would, they would go to sleep into their bedrooms." Lily remembers a time when she lived in a matchbox house:

> Lily: *Iingugaluak*. [Yes, for sure]. Cause one time when we were told to move when we had our first child, it was just open. Like when you come inside you would see everything. So it was a little embarrass[ing] to see someone, someone seeing our *bed*. So he had to cover that area only. But everything open. Cause visitors, when they come in, they would not sit in a couch or chair where table was. They would just sit in the *bed*. So it was not comfortable.

LJ: So you like having privacy for your bedroom?

Lily: Ii. [Yes]. . . . But in a cabin we don't mind having it like that, all one. You could see everything. But [to have a bed] in public, it's a little uncomfortable.

Not only does Lily expresses a sense of correctness in having private sleeping areas, but she refers to the main area of the house as a public area. She continues that even in her next house with bedrooms;

In those days we would be nine in three bedroom. We would just sleep in a bedroom and stay in the living room all day. Till we go back to bed. That was our way. In those days.

There is also a feeling today that people are healthier when they have a space for themselves, that it is a proper expectation. This is an entirely new facet of Inuit sensibilities, brought on by the houses and the internal organization of the walls in combination with other influences, such as television. *Arviammiut* are *piniarnikkut olittiniq* (learning to do) in new spaces. Jane tells me that "everybody needs their own little space," and Emma stresses that bedrooms are good because they mean "we don't have to be together 24–7. We can have time being away." Hyacinth tells me it is good to have a break from each other now and then. Lauren likes that she can see into her boys' room from the main room, but laughs as she tells me that "the bathroom is the best place to hide from them. You can lock it and say you're busy."

Only the occasional male participant, such as Marcus, did not stress the benefits of time to oneself as emphatically. These men, however, would have much more time to themselves because much of the "men's work" would happen outside of the home with plenty of space and time to themselves.

Occasionally, other elements of privacy come up. While tidiness is not necessarily expected, Ruby does express concern that her laundry machines are on her front porch. When she tells me she would prefer to have a laundry room, she elaborates that "I don't like my dirty laundry to be seen by everyone."

Expectations of cleanliness also changed with the introduction of the indoor plumbing aspect of the technological system of walls. For many, this is an essential difference between then and now. When asked what is the most different today, Carmel emphasizes cleanliness, saying, "We got school and we have to be clean, *illa* [I mean], our body. And health, we have to be healthy. *Ii.* [yes]." Others support this sentiment:

It's, it's messy and dirty and too, I mean, it's too, space is too open. No rooms, no bathroom. . . . I even tell them, "I'm glad I wasn't born that early." [laughter]

When they're used to being all pampered, no pads, no kleenex. Eweogh. [yuck] I wasn't born that time, so I'm always eogh. (Lucia)

One thing I wouldn't want is, uh, . . . to wear all the same clothes all year until you outgrow it or until they get ripped and you get new one. My parents, they tell a lot of stories from the past, and they were saying Inuit had *irqits*, uh, bugs, or I don't know what they're called. . . . On top. Their hairs, stuff like, uh, lice. And they would, uh, even their caribou parka would have it so they would have do that [makes the wrist snapping motion of shaking out a fabric] and they would come off and then crawl for a bit and then they would die. So that's one thing I wouldn't want. (Abigail)

It is not only that new levels of cleanliness became possible, but, as Trevor states, it is also the feeling that one "should" be clean, "Like we had, we start feeling that we see that we need to be clean."

Sex is also an issue. When I ask how things are different now, Madison leans in to me and says,

Maybe that's why there's high rate in births. [laughter] Cause I don't know how people did it back then in iglus, and those are questions you don't wanna ask. Everybody needs privacy.

Madison, however, does continue on to raise a problem with privacy. While she stresses that things are, generally, better with more privacy, she also tells me that "you don't know what goes on behind doors." Lucia also tells me how walls make "trouble" easier. She continues that notions of privacy and the structure of the houses;

It changed everything. In good ways and some bad ways. Both, good and bad. But it's good to sleep in your bedroom, put the door closed, with nobody watching you sleep, but then it's not good for some people who might want to do something bad. You know. Like, anything bad. Like, we never know what's to happen, *illa* [I mean], it's, it's good and bad to have walls. But it's good to have wall. And not so good for other people, I think.

Her daughter, Jill, chimes in that

it's good cause we get to have our own space, sleeping in our rooms. Long time ago, they used to sleep in just iglu and they would all be lined up, sleeping all together.

Still, the references to "trouble" and "something bad" are community euphemisms for domestic abuse. There are no therapists in town and, as Emma stresses, "we need therapists in here once in a while."

For many, this issue is closely tied to overcrowding. While *Arviammiut* strive to pursue privacy, considering it good, preferable, and generally healthier, as Carmel points out, "big families have problems." This is not surprising considering Gasperini (1973) found that overcrowding of more than two people per room increases quarrelsomeness and that the amount of space in the home affects the nervousness of children between 6 and 11 years old. While abuse is not relegated to large families, fitting five or more into bedrooms does not have a positive impact on "trouble" in the community. Doors, however, may in fact hide much more in an under-filled home than an overcrowded one where people cannot get away from each other and bedroom doors are left open for air quality.

Overcrowding is one of the more serious housing issues facing *Arviammiut* today. There are not enough houses for every family to have one, despite them being built to only accommodate one immediate family. Housing is unevenly distributed across class. In part, this is because, as in mainstream Canada, often elite classes have fewer children. In addition, nepotism is not entirely absent from how resources are distributed, particularly when it comes to jobs that have housing allotments. *Arviammiut* have adapted brilliantly to difficult conditions, but however agentic, talented, and creative a group is, when overcrowding becomes so extreme, it creates a serious crisis.

The most overcrowded house I encountered had 21 people in a four-bedroom house. This situation had recently been slightly relieved when a daughter got her own small house. Her sister would often sleep over, and sometimes others, which relieved some of the pressure—but 19 remain in a crisis-level of overcrowding. Many shared their struggles candidly with me, hoping my research might influence policy.

> *Serena:* We're so crowded that we have to put the double bed there [indicates the living room] and some sleep there.
>
> *LJ:* Does everybody have a spot on a mattress?
>
> *Serena:* Too many. *Illari.* [Yeah].

Many parents report sharing their room with not only infants, as Jamie does, but also with other older children. In the walking-class home, where I stayed for some time, there was one queen-sized bed in the bedroom. This was shared by the mother, daughter, son, grandson, and son-in-law. While the son and his sometimes-there girlfriend would often sleep on top of each other on the narrow couch, during the day, anyone could nap in the bedroom whenever there was room. The only time I saw the bedroom door closed was when the couple who usually slept on the couch retreated during the day for a brief interlude.

Comments such as the following were all too common:

Two bedroom, seven in the house. We all share, like we're five here, three in the other room. (Beatrice)

Eleven people living at my parents' before I moved out. (Deborah)

Seven people sleep here. The son is in a single bed in his own room, two daughters are in a double bed in their own room, she (the mother) sleeps with two more daughters in a double bed in the third bedroom, and her husband sleeps downstairs. Seven people in a three-bedroom house. (Notes from Interview with Brittany)

When talking about these backstage struggles in the first front stage, Lucia, a close friend with whom I could talk about such private matters, explains that dealing with overcrowding, 15 in her home, the resulting sleeping arrangements are Inuit-style:

Lucia: Me and my kids and my, sometimes my two boys sleep on the couch cause there's no room. . . . We live our lives the way we do, like Inuit style. Sometimes we can't, *illa* [I mean], we can't do how *Qablunaaq* do, we don't know how, so it's our Inuit way of doing, you sleep there, you sleep there, so we can fit in each other.

Numbers above 10 in a two-to-three-bedroom house are common. It is less the number of people in the houses and bedrooms, than the size of the houses that is problematic. Larger or more bedrooms would accommodate Inuit families in Arviat much better. But the living spaces also need to be large enough for the entire family to be in the space together without creating air-quality problems. As it stands, the bedrooms are often designed for only one or two people.

Arviammiut are frustrated, and while there is an almost fatalistic sense of acceptance, they wish to be part of the solution by *piniarnikkut olittiniq* (learning to do). The only agency they have, however, is to adjust sleeping arrangements. Many sleep on couches, as Lucia referenced. Sophie, Bethany, Jade, among others, tell me that the sleeping situation in their home routinely has one or more sleeping on the couch.

Some, such as Deborah and Evelyn, who have come from overcrowded homes and have recently moved into their own units, continue to sleep on the couch because they are not used to being alone in a bedroom. Kim, whose home is overcrowded, posted on Facebook that she has goosebumps because she has suddenly found herself alone in the house. In fact, when Kim was younger, I traveled with her for medical appointments and when we were stranded overnight away from Arviat, we shared a hotel room. I asked her whether she wanted her own room, but the then-ninth grader looked at me and shyly told me that she had never been alone in a room before. There will be fresh adjustments if and when this housing crisis is resolved.

One coping mechanism is to have fluid sleeping arrangements. Deborah's sister and niece often sleep at her home (increasing the sense of spatial fusion). They sleep wherever there is room for them within the family houses, rather than in a fixed bed every night. Jasmine sometimes sleeps at her mother's house, even though she has her own home. Emma tells me, "my son got his room, but most of the time my mom sleeps in my bed, I sleep on the couch." Felix is not able to tell me how many people live in his home. He says, rather, "We have, I think on average, eight to ten people here almost all the time."

Other problems, such as air quality, water supply, and illness, accompany these housing issues. Mold is a rampant problem. Samuel generously shares his family's experience.

> We got first here, we were happy. *Kihiani* [however], we had only two children when we moved in here. And for the past 15 years, uh, *kanukia* [what is it?], 7 boys and 2 girls today. And we still live in this 2-bedroom unit. And my older one, my older children, sleep over at my parents. And the next day or two, the older ones stays home and the younger ones take over, ah, sleep over at my parents. And during weekends, my older ones stays whoever their friends are and the other younger ones, one, every weekend one of my boys always stays at my sister's. And some of them at my parents. *Kihiana* [but], we cannot, we really cannot sleep here, the whole family. *Aijoktok* [it doesn't work].

Flexible sleeping arrangements, turn-taking, and sleeping over with family or friends have become necessary for this family. Overcrowding constrains even day-to-day movements in the house. Samuel continues;

> Living room*mi* [being in the living room], we take turns. Like, for example *manna* [right now] my *panik* [daughter], the younger ones, are up there [in the bedrooms] right now. They come down as the older ones go up. Just take turns. Ah, lunchtime, when it's lunchtime, lunch hour, *uvani* [here it] gets really hot from body heat. Really hot. Small, many people. So we try not to be, like, everybody in the room, everybody in the living room. We try, we always trying to be, like, at least few in the upstairs and most of us in the living room. *Ii* [yeah]. . . . We try to manage. Sometimes it's hard. And I had to pay to, uh, get our ventilator fixed. Uh, they fixed it last year, and I had to pay it, *kihiani* [but], they did not fix it. They said they, they're waiting for the part. And I kept going back and they keep telling us it was fixed. It's reported it's already fixed. *Kihiani ajoktok* [But it is not working]. Right now it cannot run and my youngest, my son, he's three years old, *nuvatua* [he is sick with coughing], constant *nuvuq* [cough] from lacking air. *Kihiani* [but], we keep the fan running in the winter to keep air circulation. North wind, keep it in the window. When it turns like South wind, put it by

the door and let the fan run. And so we can have air circulation, *kihiani* [but] it's not too good like that. Window or the door fan, not too good for air circulation.

The hamlet delivers water daily or every other day to most homes. Houses have water tanks and sewage tanks for indoor plumbing, but Arviat does not have an outdoor plumbing system in place. Water tanks, then, are sized to Southern expectations of two parents and two children in a nuclear family. Samuel has 11 people in a two-bedroom house, but also has 11 people trying to survive and stay clean with water for four:

> If our older ones need to take a shower or a bath, mostly at my parents. And my daughter goes to my wife's other sister, to go for a shower or a bath. And the younger ones here. And we always try to give them a bath two at a time. . . . So we can have, like, conserve more water. *Ii* [yes]. Two at a time. Bath, two at a time. (Samuel)

In such cases, illness spreads easily. Lucia tells me;

> *Lucia:* Or when one gets sick and it spreads so fast. Next day the other one is sick and then it goes really fast, *illa* [I mean], the sickness spreads very easily and fast. If I had diarrhea, somebody would get it within the next three, four hours. It's very contagious.
>
> *LJ:* And only one bathroom, hmm?
>
> *Lucia:* Yeah. We always wash it, like every second day.

These conditions surely contribute to the walking-class restlessness previously noted.

While some families struggle under dire conditions, the unequal distribution of housing means that some homes have empty bedrooms. While this is not in itself problematic, it does contribute to some friction among social locations. Of these empty bedrooms, most are sewing rooms, although in one family the daughter has two bedrooms to herself and would like to knock down the wall so that she has one large room. One result of having a lot of room can be that relatives wind up sleeping over a lot, particularly those from overcrowded homes. In one home, each family member has his or her own bedroom, and then a second family with no home stays all together in a previously empty bedroom. There does not appear to be any animosity toward the guest family. The hosts are generous and glad to help. But this is not an entirely comfortable situation for anyone.

Although I mentioned this briefly when discussing anomie, a state of confusion resulting from a dramatic loss or change in norms, in chapter 2, there are some in the walking class who do have enough room in their homes, but the walls remain uncomfortable symbols of anomie and seem to press down on them with *Qablunaaq* eyes in their own homes. These families tend to pull a mattress into the living room, the biggest room in the house, and center it. The whole family sleeps on this mattress together, not only performing a "spatial expression of Inuit closeness" (Dawson 2008), but also shrinking from their walls and the anomie they represent even when they did not grow up before these walls enveloped them. Jasmine, Serena, and Brandon all have a mattress that they store in a bedroom during the day and slide out at night into the more open space for the whole family. This is less and less common as notions of privacy become privileged, but the anomie and the unfriendly architecture (Dawson 2008) create a challenging environment for those without cultural resources to engage actively with their walls and overcome that anomie.

With limited housing, and the majority of housing as government housing with little home ownership, the wait list can be long. Bethany tells me it took 9 to 10 years for her to get her house, which is a two-bedroom house in which six people share one queen bed and a couch. A queen-sized bed would not even fit in the second "bedroom," even if they had another.

When I drop in to the Housing Corporation office, they tell me that there are 155 names on the waiting list and that it currently takes 5–6 years to get a house once you get on the list. Rent is based on income, and most pay around $60 a month. In order to get on the list, including to transfer to a larger home, one has to be fully paid up—not only on rent, but also on any repairs the home may have needed. The woman who administered these lists at the time of my research told me that arrears severely exacerbate overcrowding in Arviat. This has certainly been Melissa's experience. Her small home is big enough for her and her children, but it is in shockingly poor structural condition.

I have to pay, first I have to pay off my bills from the housing. From the damaging, someone breaking and damaging my windows. And my toilet. I don't know how many times the toilet, it's broken. And the bathtub is almost down [falling through the floor]. Maybe you'll take a look after. And the sink, in winter, it get frozen, there's some ice. . . . That's why [the man from Housing] told me to move out of this place. He said it's not healthy. He said that old house is not good for me. But I told him I'm happy to have my own place and I can be myself. I told him that. And he told me to apply right away at the Housing. But I tried, but they said I have to pay my bills first and I can move out to the new place, he said. I mean, yeah, I was told by Housing.

Participants often reference the cost of houses and housing when reflecting on how things are different from before aggressive colonization. Emma complains that "houses are expensive." This is a common complaint.

Big difference. It costs a lot to live in a house, where it used to be free in an iglu or tent. Cause you had to pay for electricity, rent, phone, cable, broadband, food, almost everything. Big difference. (Lucia)

Arrears, like albatrosses, hang around the necks of those suffering in over-crowded homes.

CONCLUSION

New notions of privacy are a by-product of permanent walls, particularly when those walls are designed by people from a culture which highly values privacy. The resultant structures communicate these values and impinge on Inuit culture. New privacy practices emerge around sleeping and the relationship of backstage spaces (bedrooms and bathrooms) and front stage more public spaces in the home. Privacy became desirable, for sleep and also for time alone. This change brings Inuit views more in line with dominant worldviews in the homogenizing process of passive engagements. Agency, however, allows for heterogeneity in the world, and among groups, for how they implement and cope with new values.

Front stages and backstages, however, are complex processes. In Arviat, Inuit consider the main space of the home much more public than someone from mainstream Western culture might. Spatial considerations, such as the division of rooms, determine the locus of the front stage; the main areas of the home for *Arviammiut*. There is, however, an overriding front stage, conditional on those present, which rises above spatial considerations. *Arviammiut* operate with a front-stage understanding when relating to *Qablunaaq*. With such a strong history of *Qablunaaq* judgment of Inuit practices, *Arviammiut* have two front stages, one in relation to Southerners, and one in relation to each other.

The next chapter moves from passive engagements to active engagements, where agency and creativity reign supreme.

Chapter 7

Qanuqtuurungnarniq [Being Resourceful to Solve Problems]

Active Engagement: Walls as Storage

Permanent walls, as an "invisible" technology (Michael 2000), slip under the radar both theoretically and empirically.[1] Although Marshall states that "Inuit are resources-conscious but do not understand their present housing systems and receive no training" (2006, 2), Inuit are just as capable and agentic as any other group in devising their own meanings and uses of their houses. While the previous chapter discusses ways in which the walls impress certain Western notions and understandings upon Inuit, with a homogenizing effect, this chapter discusses the diversifying effects of new technologies.

In the case of Arviat, passive engagements include; radically changed relationships with the weather and the idea of *inside* and *outside*; novel notions of public and private as internally divided spaces, bedrooms, and doors are introduced; and the transmission of family knowledge changes in gendered ways which make more difficult the passing-on of skills, such as sewing, from mother to daughter, some of which I discuss in other chapters. I now turn to a specific active engagement, the wall as a tool for storage and expression of the Inuit value of creatively using everything.

ACTIVE ENGAGEMENT: WALL-AS-TOOL

Active engagements involve a relationship with the technical artifact, in this case the wall, mediated by time, needs, perceived needs, and resources. This is where "work" on the part of the user happens and the social affects the technical and the technological frame surrounding it. This work occurs within the social and cultural context of the users. For the *Arviammiut*, this context involves a focus on creativity and ingenuity.

Inuit Identity: Creativity and Ingenuity

Although the introduction of a new technology might inspire any group to reach new creative heights, the Inuit are actively striving toward this in performance of their Inuit-ness. Creativity and adaptability are part of Inuit self-image (Berkes and Armitage 2010). They greatly value *qanuqtuurungnarniq* (being resourceful to solve a problem), *aturunnarniqasiajungaaq* (improvisation), and *asiajuuqsaraittunnarniq* (resourcefulness), three IQ principles. As *Arviammiut* engage in boundary work to maintain their hold on a distinctive and solid identity, they espouse these values, in particular, as Inuit values.

This is the schema, historically and socially informed, with which *Arviammiut* approach a new artifact. The resources available to Inuit of this area changed dramatically and unpredictably, and the schemas extant from previous living conditions and material resources are now being transposed to make sense of permanent walls.

By exercising resourcefulness, an individual can perform positive Inuitness and boundary work. These values, therefore, play a significant role in how *Arviammiut* relate to objects in their lives. Walls are not exempt. Individuals actively and purposefully invoke these values as "strategies of action" (Swidler 1986), attempting to maximize them in their relationship with walls. Traditionally, when living nomadic lives centered on basic survival, there was a great need to make use of everything possible. The wall cannot simply stand there. It presents a problem of meaning and action. It must serve an active purpose, it must be used in all possible ways. This is *qanuqtuurungnarniq* (being resourceful to solve a problem). By engaging with the wall and determining ways to make it more useful, the wall itself is subsumed into everyday life, normalized within the community, and, in its usefulness, becomes a tool. In short, walls are made over as tools to practice traditional cultural activities and values, such as creativity and ingenuity.

Active engagements which emphasize these, among other, Inuit values include; the enaction of Inuit value of *aktuaturaunniqarniq*, "interconnectedness," through elaborate gifting of items to be displayed on others' walls; the performance of personal and family identity through the display of family photographs; wall-as-tool for remembering with the new ability to collect and maintain souvenirs such as graduation caps; and the reclamation of history through the appropriation of photographs of relatives taken by early explorers and mounting these photographs along with contemporary photographs of family inset in the frame, as in chapter 4.

This chapter now focuses on the specific active engagement "wall-as-tool" for storage. This use of the walls in this way provides an opportunity to actively perform Inuit-ness. There are different levels of storage for which the wall can be used. These range, temporally, from rarely touched articles stored over long periods of time to often-used articles stored on the wall for easy access. I shall proceed through the continuum from long-term to short-term storage of artifacts on walls and connect each to the performance of Inuit values.

Wall-as-Tool: Long-Term Storage for Important Documents or Mementos

There are different levels of storage for which the wall can be used. These range from rarely touched articles stored over long periods of time to often-used articles stored on the wall for easy access. The homes in Arviat have little storage space. Often spaces intended by the architect for storage are redefined into other kinds of spaces. A larger space might be used as a sleeping space, for example. There are few arrangements inside the home for storage, in particular for items such as papers or other miscellaneous small items that one might collect over the years.

When the owners are at a loss for how to store articles which they do not want ruined, they invoke the wall as a useful space. Several participants explained that they had put certain artifacts on the wall to keep them from getting destroyed either from lying around the house or the presence of several children. Nadia, for example, explains why a small rose painting is not framed, "I wanted to put the frame in it, but before somebody wrecks it, I just put it up there."

The desire to keep things safe on the walls comes up across the board.[2] Oliver, a widowed elder who did not move into permanent structures until he was a young adult, also expressed to me that "whatever you leave anywhere in the house, it would get wrecked, so [I] decided to put them [certificates] up on the wall." Phoebe, who frequently has grandchildren present, echoes this sentiment. The wall is, thus, a very useful place to put up anything that the participant would like to keep from getting damaged or destroyed.

There are some, however, who find the determined little fingers of children too daunting. Brandon, for example, is much more cautious. Both of his children are under the age of five and he and his wife have almost nothing on the walls save the drawings by the children directly on the wall. While I am there, the children run loose through the small unit, tiny forces of destruction and chaos. Brandon refers to them as maniacs and says:

> Yeh. I got [my father's] certificates and other important, *qanu* [how do you say it?], documents, maybe? I had them on the wall there, but with this guy around [indicates older child], he's a [shakes head]. (Brandon)

For most, however, the wall is considered the safest place for important documents, certificates, or mementos. Hallways are often a convenient

Figure 7.1   Hallway as Storage for Certificates.

location for the accumulation of such storage (see figure 7.1), which is not frequently accessed. Once "in storage" many of these certificates will be forgotten about in the same way that more Southern filers might forget about a certificate sitting in a filing cabinet.

Other articles may also be stored on the walls for the long run. Phoebe, for example, has a plastic floral arrangement that reads "Mom," which she is storing on her wall until she passes away, when it will be placed at her grave site. Marcus has tacked a lock of his son's hair to the wall. For *Arviammiut*, this is a creative solution to a problem. How does one keep important documents or mementos safe? Where? The solution of using the wall is an active engagement with that wall.

"So I Just Put It Up"

For some, wall storage is more of a last resort. When confronted with small gifts, the participants often turned to the wall as a tool to be used in the resolution of the storage dilemma.

LJ: What made you put it [a plaque with a photograph of a sunset] there?

Jaimie: When they gave it to me *I just hung it up.* [Author's emphasis]

LJ: And how 'bout the basket?

Ruby: Um, somebody gave it to me and I didn't know where to put it *so I just put it there.* [Author's emphasis]

My brother-in-law, someone's husband, made me a knife one day, *so I just.* [indicates where knife is hanging on a nail on the wall] [Author's emphasis] (Felix)

Participants faced with a dilemma conceptualized of the wall as a storage area to "just put" things which needed to be kept and needed to find a home. In many of these cases, the wall could then serve the dual purpose of storage and display. The above quotations are but a selection of similar responses; "I just put them up" (Gabriella), "I just hanged it out there" (Ruby), "It's just up there" (Phoebe), and "Don't know where else to put it so they put it on the door" (Gabriella).

Some gifts on the wall are unwanted gifts. Carmel, for example felt bound to accept a gift from the visiting priest, while Ruby was not sure what to do with a gift of wind chimes. Gifts make up the majority of this category, but there are a range of items that were "just put up" on the walls for storage. Marge knew that she wanted to keep her wedding bouquet and so it rests cradled by caribou antlers on the wall:

That's from my wedding too. Like, I didn't know where I should put my bouquet, *so I just put it there.* [Author's emphasis] (Marge) (See figure 7.2)

Display as Use: Maximizing Use for Otherwise Useless or Broken Artifacts

The desire to make use of things facilitates the transformation of the wall into a tool for storage. It is also a tool for display, and there is some overlap.

Figure 7.2 Marge's Bouquet.

An object that is broken or has served its purpose will not immediately be thrown out. If a use can be conceived of for this object, it will be put to that use. Display is a valid use for an object, and thus some of these items end up on the wall and out of the way in storage, and also on display.

Oliver automatically tries to make use of everything, having grown up "on the land" and having had to make use of everything for basic survival. On his wall is a rifle:

> Oliver [through translator]: When it stopped working, um, he put it up on the wall *cause it won't be any use if he just left it on the ground.* So when it stopped working he put it up on the wall for decoration. [Author's emphasis]

Through this use, Oliver is indirectly performing his Inuit-ness. While consciously adapting the utilization of the gun in order to ensure its continued value as a useful item, Oliver demonstrates his ability to be resourceful and creative in his approach to solving the "problem" of the non-working rifle. Isabella solves the problem of a broken harpoon similarly.

These wall artifacts are not merely out of the way, they are now serving an aesthetic purpose. There is a conscious "re-engagement" happening. Marge, for example, has a spatula that is no longer usable for its intended purpose. It now sits in her window sill serving an ornamental function (see figure 7.3). Part of what is aesthetically pleasing about this object is that it demonstrates obvious ingenuity in action. She has re-engaged with this artifact. Abigail underscores this point when I ask her about the stickers on her range hood. She tells me that her mother decorated the range hood and then continues:

> Yeah, *my mum's pretty creative.* She even put a sticker, *illa* [I mean], she received the card and she cut it, birthday card, and she, uh, taped it on her helmet. Something different, she said. [Author's emphasis] (Abigail)

An old birthday card could not simply be thrown out. If a use can be found, or invented, it is hailed as creative, recognized as such by the community, and valued as something Inuit. While some cultures may not see the meaning behind a decorated spatula or a cut-out from a birthday card taped onto a helmet, within the community these acts are quite meaningful. In this way, *Arviammiut* are actively engaging with the wall and using it as a tool to enable these acts—as a locus, it is the medium through which an aesthetic purpose for an artifact can be accomplished.

Lily's home is the most extreme example within the community. Explaining to me an old flour sack she has framed on the wall, Lily accentuates the importance of display as a valid aesthetic purpose and a way to keep old items, which are no longer useful in their intended purpose:

Figure 7.3 Spatula and Lace.

So my husband, Brennan, found that between the stuff and "look what I found!" And then . . . I said "I'm gonna keep it. I'm gonna put it in the wall." I was so surprised cause it has the price in there, four dollars thirty-one cents, but the English part, they use it for repairing a canoe. When there's a hole, they have to repair, so it's only in French. [laughter] (See figure 7.4)

This flour sack has undergone not two, but three stages of usefulness—twice re-engaged.

Figure 7.4   Framed Flour Sack.

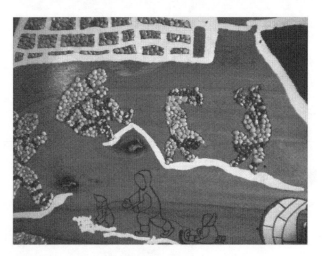

Figure 7.5   Lily's Wall.

The centerpiece of Lily's home is her wall (see figure 7.5), also discussed in chapter 2. In 1990, Lily and Brennan chartered a helicopter and went back to where her family had lived on the land before she was born. They saw white rocks there and began to collect them. Over the years, and several trips later, they have amassed quite a collection. Today the rocks reside on the

wall. Lily draws traditional scenes and then Brennan cuts them out and creates a sort of mosaic with the rocks, with Lily gluing them and then Brennan
lacquering them in place. As she tells me about the wall, Lily says:

> First, at home, we kept them in the jar. But *it doesn't look like any use*, so I
> sketch on a paper and ask my husband, "if I large my sketching, could you
> please cut the ones that I need you to cut?" And he said, "yes." . . . So instead of
> displaying the rocks [in] the jar, we wanted to do something special with those
> rocks. [Author's emphasis]

Not only do these scenes serve to connect her to her past, but she is actively,
viscerally, engaging with the wall to create an aesthetic use for rocks which
were serving no purpose stored in a jar.[3]

Occasional Access: Christmas Decorations

Along the continuum, there are also items which are stored for occasional
access, such as Christmas decorations. In some homes, Christmas decorations
stay in place year-round, "stored" in plain view on the walls; however, they
are only "used" during Christmastime. How are they used? They are attended
to only during the Christmas season. For the rest of the year, residents and
visitors are "clutter blind" to these items on the wall. At Christmastime, these
ornaments and signs may be accented with other pieces of decoration so that
they will be noticed and appreciated. When I questioned participants on these
decorations in the summer, Ellen, Marcus, and Oliver gave similar responses
to Trevor:

> Uh, Christmas decorations, like during the Christmas time of the season. Maybe
> most of us put some decorations inside the house and so we feel that there's a
> meaning to a Christmas, is what it means to us too, so we can show it to other
> peoples, like, from outside of this house, so we can tell those people too that we
> feel the Christmas spirits, so some, we decorate our house too, like during the
> Christmas time of the season. (Trevor)

While not all participants have Christmas decorations up year-round, in
storage for part of the year and in use during the month of December, most
have some articles whose "away" place is on the wall and which are used
occasionally. The knife on Felix's wall is one example of this. Other examples include notepads, pin cushions (see figure 7.6), schedules, fly-swatters,
and backscratchers. Ruby explains about the pin cushion, "We always use it
for sewing, needles, pins. [It's on the wall] so that it will be easy to take and
it's far from the children."

Figure 7.6   Pin Cushion Stored on a Wall.

Easy-Access Storage: Keys, Sunglasses, and Knives

There are also easy-access storage solutions on the walls. These include hooks for keys, which are almost without exception hand-made, and other more creative displays of resourcefulness. Sunglasses, for example, need to be easy to access, and yet will get scratched if they are not stored safely. Sunglasses are quite important because they prevent snow-blindness in the spring. By implementing creative storage areas on the wall with string or wire, *Arviammiut* are enacting their Inuit-ness by practicing what they are known for; ingenuity. Tori takes pride in her solution for sunglasses (see figure 7.7). New ideas, new ways of doing things are a part of her member-ship in the community and her own expression of her personal identity as an Inuk.

Innovation is tied in with practical purpose. Tori did not sit down and think about how she could be innovative that day, and thus more Inuit. When presented with a problem, she found a solution. Inuit find solutions. This is a treasured part of their cultural tool-kit (Swidler 1986). Tori, and others, pride themselves on their solutions. The wall provides another avenue for solutions.

Ruby has found a solution for the easy-access storage for knives which might make Southern housewives swoon. No one has told *Arviammiut* about the socially accepted norms concerning the treatment of walls in the South.

Figure 7.7   Sunglasses Storage.

Figure 7.8   Ruby's Knives.

For Ruby, the trim above the counter provides an ideal location for knives (see figure 7.8).

Other items stored on walls for quick and easy access are CDs, bills, scissors, pens, and phone numbers. House or phone numbers may be taped up, on a post-it note, or even written directly on the wall such as at Deborah, Oliver, Ruby, Hyacinth, Gabriella, Elise, and Felix's homes.

These uses of the walls are active engagements in action. Walls came with no handbook of uses and meanings. Inuit were able to approach them with fresh eyes and to determine a meaning, through use, which, while not entirely unique, consciously reflects their firm practice of and belief in resourcefulness and practicality. They accomplished this by *qanuqtuurungnarniq* (being resourceful to solve a problem). The wall becomes a convenient location in a way that would not have occurred to these participants had they been restricted to the layered and historical meanings others, from a more Southern background, give to walls. Wall-as-tool for storage is one of the meanings which *Arviammiut* have ascribed to the technological artifact through their use of that artifact, a use thatwas mediated through the social; through the performance of their definition of Inuit-ness in their intentionally and consciously creative and innovative uses for the new technology.

CONCLUSION

A special kind of technology, mundane technology, banal and demure, can be found woven into the fabric of our lives. These technologies are not immediately understood as invented, and yet technological innovation and change can apply just as equally. It is important to pay attention to these banal technologies if we wish to understand the full spectrum of our relationship with technology and technological artifacts. Studying mundane technology grants us access to the day-to-day, taken-for-granted aspects of technology that affect, and are affected by, greater proportions of the population. This work, however, has mainly been carried out in Western contexts. These two chapters about technological objects offer a glimpse into mundane technology in a non-Western context, with an analytical focus on the use-level.

Reflexivity emerges as an important facet of mundane technology. By including both passive and active engagements in my analysis and by focusing on use, I tease out how the technological artifact of walls affects Inuit, and how Inuit, in turn, do have agency and shape the technological frame of the wall. By examining passive engagements and active engagements, we also create room in technology studies for a deeper understanding of the role of culture and of the work performed within active engagements.

Walls interrupt life-as-it-was and bring consequences to bear on Inuit culture, profoundly changing their relationship with the weather and yet walls fly under the radar as a technology and their massive consequences have passed largely unnoticed or have been ascribed to other cultural changes. These are passive engagements *Arviammiut* have with their walls. As Inuit find new ways to make the wall useful, they find new ways to relate to the wall, to make it their own and to assert and affirm their identity as Inuit through the creative and innovative uses they find for their walls. These are the active engagements *Arviammiut* have with their walls. By pairing active engagements with passive engagements, we can account for the dual recursive and reflexive nature of the relationship between the social and the technical.

There are implications of passive and active engagements that warrant further study. Passive engagements, for example, seem to pull cultures toward cultural convergence. Active engagements, on the other hand, seem to encourage the kind of identity and boundary work that fosters unique cultural identities and cultural divergence. It is possible that these concepts may be transposed into studies of modernization to help us discover which processes boost cultural diversity, and which lead to homogeneity.

NOTES

1. This chapter is a slightly modified reprint of a previously published chapter I published: van den Scott, Lisa-Jo K. 2016. "Mundane Technology in non-Western Contexts: Wall-as-Tool." Pp. 33–53 in *Sociology of Home: Belonging, Community and Place in the Canadian Context*. Laura Suski, Joey Moore, and Gillian Anderson, eds. Toronto: Canadian Scholars Press International.

2. Keep in mind that many of the items that *Arviammiut* are storing on their walls, such as documents and photographs, are also new to them. They are, at the same time, engaging with these new objects as well, forming new meanings, finding new uses for them, and learning of their consequences.

3. This intersects with another active engagement at play: reclamation of the past, which is primarily through the display of old photographs that early explorers took on their travels, covered in chapter 4.

Conclusion

I had two main goals with *Walled-In*. The first was to present a sociology of walls that offers a new lens for understanding power, colonialism, contestation, resistance, and resilience in our built environment. I argue for the importance of studying the mundane, and the role of walls in our everyday lives. The second was twofold. I wanted to honor participants and the elders who invited me to do this work by not glossing over the horrors of their past, while also bringing attention to their resilience and agency. Too often when scholars discuss the catastrophic impact of colonization, they reduce Inuit to a victimized group. Too often when they recognize agency, strength, and adaptability, they dismiss colonization as having been dealt with and mentally imagine that Inuit are now "okay" and all is well. The truth is a combination of these things. I hope that after reading this book, you, dear reader, have a new appreciation for the insidiousness of walling Inuit into Western spaces (which demands constant performance of Inuit identity) beyond and in addition to the more overt elements of colonization, as well as a new respect for the ingenious ways that Inuit, as an agentic, resilient, and heterogeneous group, have performed resistance, overcome some elements of their built environment, and altered the meaning and use of their walls to bring them under their own command, reshaping the walls of their homes into tools for Inuit expression, with varying degrees of success across class.

And yet, their housing situation is dire. Inuit cope with overcrowding and often dilapidated housing. It is difficult to balance highlighting their challenges and strengths at the same time; Inuit struggle with needing help with housing, but *not* needing patronizing judgment for a housing crisis brought on by the Canadian government and other collaborators of colonization.

A SOCIOLOGY OF WALLS

By now the theoretical significance of walls, and how we use walls, should be evident. Walls come up again and again in our literature and arts because the sheer impassibility and opaqueness of walls present a powerful metaphor. One "hits a wall" or "throws up walls" to shut people out. Stories such as *The Cask of Amontillado* and *The Secret Garden* imply that behind walls lie beauty or terror—but certainly nothing banal. If it is behind a wall, it must be worth it! This fascination with walls comes up again and again despite the fact that in our everyday lives, we cannot even really see the walls around us most of the time. We take for granted how our office buildings flow, how our bedrooms are walled-off from the rest of the house, and so on. It is only when something is not working well that we notice the walls. And yet, their impact is as powerful as the metaphors would suggest.

But how to theorize walls? By looking at walls through three different lenses, we can gain analytic purchase. First, walls are boundary objects. They are objects located at the center of group relations. By thinking about which groups are involved with walls, we can map out the relationships of these groups. Consider a family home—how do walls help or hinder the relationships (power and otherwise) of children and parents, parents and the government, the family and neighboring families, and so on.

Second, walls are cultural objects. Walls exist within a culture or society. They have cultural producers and receivers. Think, for example, of decorating trends that come and go. These are tied to the economy, to the urban growth machine (Logan and Molotch 2007), to class status and performance, to doing family and displaying family, and so on and so forth. Cultural trends, such as increasing pressure on the nuclear family and a change in expectation for whether or not strangers (in the guise of servants, staff, or boarders) should reside in the home with the nuclear family, have impacted architecture and even what we show in family photographs on display (Halle 1993).

Third, walls are also technological objects. The field of technology studies has a rich history of dealing with materiality. While I drew on helpful concepts from the culture literature, understanding the social construction of technology offers the concepts of *technological frame*, *interpretive flexibility*, and *closure* (Bijker 1997). Walls, as technological objects, have a socially constructed meaning for those who introduced them; their technological frame. Users, however, are not bound to these same understandings, meanings, or uses. As users begin to interact with a technology, and with each other about that technology, there is flexibility in how they interpret it; interpretive flexibility. Over time, the ways that people interact with a technology, especially a mundane one, settle into patterns that now seem unremarkable to users. Use and interactions generate norms, and the meanings and uses; the technological frame achieves closure. Walls go through a similar process and it helps to step back and see how users have interpreted walls differently from designers' conceptualizations.

This sociology of walls offers a lens through which to study other walls across time and place. For example, what can we learn about border walls when we consider them from each conceptual standpoint; as boundary objects, cultural objects, and technological objects. Even white-picket fences could benefit from this approach. Fences, as boundary objects, make statements about what kind of people we are to the neighbors. As cultural objects, we present and perform the ideology of the perfect family home through fences, as well as reify notions of capital and ownership. As technological objects, we define norms for entering and exiting the property. Each object type overlaps with the others, but by taking the time to consider walls from each vantage, much can be learned.

A sociology of walls does not generalize one theory to all walls, but rather offers a process-driven view of how to do research on the walls of any home in any place. The meanings, practices, and symbolism would be completely different. And yet, the walls still play a cultural role, for example, and it is important to consider what that might be. They act as boundary objects and their use implicates them in identity work. As technological objects, they have multiple meanings, often not foreseen by architects and designers.

I introduce three concepts to further this theory of walls. When we interact with something new, particularly a new technology introduced from another culture or representing a dramatic change or advance, there are two social processes in play. First, there are *passive engagements*. Objects, technologies, or new ways of organizing impact people, and some of those impacts occur in homogenizing ways. There are unintended consequences. They affect people differently across class. The concept of passive engagements allows for the researcher to examine these impacts while escaping a deterministic view of the world. The second concept, that of *active engagements*, provides a way to conceptualize of the flip side of the coin; the ways in which people practice agency when relating to this new object or idea. The resulting technological frame is not determined. The previous mental schema, or cultural toolkit, come to bear on figuring out this new thing. People interact and react with agency. They resist. They embrace. They reimagine. Active engagements entail diversifying effects. Both of these social processes are simultaneously in play.

The third important concept emerges from considering active engagements, resistance, and the built environment. I introduce the concept of *spatial fusion* to refer to the social process of constructing multiple, distinct spaces as part of the same place. Several houses may come to stand as one "home." Offices in various buildings or parts of buildings may be seen as one collective place of work. The bathroom attached to a master bedroom may be fused with the bedroom, and inhabitants view the space, as a whole, as their bedroom area. We exercise spatial fusion, at its most basic level, when we see the separated rooms in a house as part of the same place.

These three social processes; *passive* and *active engagements* and *spatial fusion* add to the symbolic-interactionist literature, as well as the more specifically oriented fields of culture and technology studies. Symbolic interactionism (SI) offers a lens through which to view the empirical world. Symbolic interactionists, myself among them, see that we socially construct the meanings we have for things, ideas, people, places, and so on, through our interactions. These meanings can change over time through further interactions and experiences. SI offers a bevy of concepts with which to study the social world. Many of these concepts are *generic social processes* (Prus 1987), processes that occur across social settings. Rather than seeking generalizable facts in a fluctuating and dynamic world, we seek to understand how meaning forms, and what generic social processes underpin how we operate in our worlds of meaning. Power and the impact of macro structures, of course, are key parts of what SI finds in everyday micro situations (Fine 1991, 2012).

CASE STUDY

Arviat, Nunavut, was one of the last places in which Southern traders established regular contact with Indigenous people in Canada. The accelerated, rapid colonization process meant that the Canadian government walled-in *Arviammiut* in the late 1950s and early 1960s. Their walls are still relatively new and bear great consequences, despite the agency and adaptability of Inuit. David Damas (2004) provides an excellent history of the area and the complexities of the initial transformation from nomadic migration to community-dwelling. Other work has focused on the cultural impracticalness of the new houses in Nunavut (Collings 2005; Dawson 2004, 2008; Duhaime et al. 2004; Gareau & Dawson 2004). Peter Dawson (2004, 2) noted that Inuit "spatially graft" cultural practices into the new "unfriendly architecture." I followed up on his observations to more closely learn about reliance, resistance, and reimagining use from Inuit, as well as to learn about what social processes were in play.

It seems there are unending things outsiders, like me, can learn from Inuit. I first discussed the complex relationship of knowledges and geographies in Arviat. *Arviammiut* found themselves in a state of anomie after the relocation into housing and colonization and a landscape that rewards willingness to be disciplined. Their walls became symbolic of that anomie, and by engaging with their walls, they were able to face, and overcome, some of that anomie. The successes, in large part, are correlated with social class. In Arviat, there are three distinct social classes; drivers, riders, and walkers, as discussed in chapter 2. Class is, in effect, played out through the use of space. Upper classes, however, have more resources with which to come to terms with their anomie. Their relationship to space, the hamlet, and the land also relates to their sense of traditionality. I explore a geography of knowledge and the nuances that accompany it. Being walled-off from the locus of one's knowledge and traditional identity requires constant negotiation of group boundaries and what it means to be Inuit and traditional.

From there, I demonstrate how time spent on the land comes to represent access to learning and knowledge. Knowledge within walls, however, is another matter. The interior division of spaces and community living impact the cross-generational transmission of knowledge. I use sewing as the example. There is also a gendered dynamic such that "women's knowledge" and "men's knowledge" are differently affected, with women's knowledge more likely to be lost.

Turning to walls as cultural objects, I demonstrate how Inuit use walls to spatially graft the cultural value of interconnectedness indoors. By displaying family pictures, *Arviammiut* locate themselves in their families and in their community. The walls have also become a place to remember by displaying photos and mementos. These wall artifacts also serve as a mechanism to accomplish spatial fusion. By extensively giving gifts and, thus, decorating each other's walls, *Arviammiut* work to accomplish extended family living despite the nuclear-family-oriented houses. They establish space across houses as part of the same home, thereby enacting spatial fusion.

Walls, however, keep a symbolic Western eye present in the community, and in the homes. As a result, Inuit identity is constantly under watchful threat and *Arviammiut* must perform Inuit identity *to* their walls. They accomplish this through the exuberant consumption of traditional foods, and the solo practices of eating Southern foods. These practices result in a cultural hybridity in their approach to food.

The relationship with their walls and the Western spaces also creates complex front and backstages—some which are spatially fixed and others which depend on who is present in the room. The interior division of spaces "teaches" new conceptions of public and private, a passive engagement. By contrast, as an active engagement, *Arviammiut* use their walls for storage, for demonstrating creativity, and interconnectedness.

Walls interrupt life-as-it-was. There is no easy way to present the complexities which this interruption brings on. Anomie vies with spatially grafting Inuit culture indoors. Class resources increase the disparity of success in coming to terms with anomie, the walls, and traditionality under contemporary circumstances. The housing crisis of supply and quality complicates life further. The overall character of strength, resilience, and agency, however, serves *Arviammiut* well as they move forward.

References

Aarluk Consulting Inc. 2011. *Infrastructure of a Sustainable Arviat: Vol. 2 Consultation Report.* Government of Nunavut.

Abulof, Uriel. 2014. "National Ethics in Ethnic Conflicts: The Zionist 'Iron Wall' and the 'Arab Question.'" *Ethnic and Racial Studies* 37(14): 2653–69.

Adams, Annmarie, Kevin Schwartzman, and David Theodore. 2008. "Collapse and Expand: Architecture and Tuberculosis Therapy in Montreal, 1909, 1933, 1954." *Technology and Culture* 49(4): 908–42.

Akittiq, Atuat, and Rhoda Akpaliapik Karetak. 2017. "*Inunnguiniq* (Making a Human Being)." Pp. 102–111 in *Inuit Qaujimajatuqangit: What Inuit Have Always Known to Be True*, edited by Joe Karetak, Frank Tester, and Shirley Tagalik. Winnipeg: Fernwood Publishing.

Alfred, Taiaiake, and Jeff Corntassel. 2005. "Being Indigenous: Resurgences against Contemporary Colonialism." *Government and Opposition* 40(4): 597–614.

Alkon, Alison Hope, and Michael Traugot. 2008. "Place Matters, But How? Rural Identity, Environmental Decision Making, and the Social Construction of Place." *City & Community* 7(2): 97–112.

Anderson, Nels. 1923. *The Hobo: The Sociology of the Homeless Man.* Chicago: University of Chicago Press.

Appadurai, Arjun. 1986. *The Social Life of Things: Commodities in Cultural Perspective.* Cambridge; New York: Cambridge University Press.

Archibald, Jo-Ann. 2008. *Indigenous Storywork: Educating the Heart, Mind, Body, and Spirit.* Vancouver: UBC Press.

Arms, Myron. 2004. *Servants of the Fish: A Portrait of Newfoundland After the Great Cod Collapse.* Hinesburg, VT: Upper Access.

Arnold, David, and Erich DeWald. 2011. "Cycles of Empowerment? The Bicycle and Everyday Technology in Colonial India and Vietnam." *Comparative Studies in Society and History* 53(4): 971–96.

———. 2012. "Everyday Technology in South and Southeast Asia: An Introduction." *Modern Asian Studies* 46(1): 1–17.

As It Happens. 2013. "Hudson Bay Hunters Rescue." CBC. This interview aired on CBC radio and is available at: https://www.cbc.ca/player/play/2324628099. Last accessed August 20, 2020.

Associated Press. 2009. "Man Convicted of In-Home Indecent Exposure." *NBC News*. https://www.nbcnews.com/id/wbna34483145#.XlF15Up7nIU%20Last%20accessed%20February%2022,%202020.

Attfield, Judy. 1999. "Bringing Modernity Home: Open Plan in the British Domestic Interior." Pp. 73–82 in *At Home: An Anthropology of Domestic Space*, edited by Irene Cieraad. Syracuse: Syracuse University Press.

Ayalik, Alice. 2017. "*Inutsiapagutit* (Inuit Teachings)." Pp. 89–101 in *Inuit Qaujimajatuqangit: What Inuit Have Always Known to Be True*, edited by Joe Karetak, Frank Tester, and Shirley Tagalik. Winnipeg: Fernwood Publishing.

Bartlett, Cheryl, Marshall, Murdena, and Marshall, Albert. 2012. "Two-Eyed Seeing and Other Lessons Learned Within a Co-Learning Journey of Bringing Together Indigenous and Mainstream Knowledges and Ways of Knowing." *Journal of Environmental Studies and Sciences* 2:331–340.

Becker, Jessica. 2021. "Speaking to the wall: Reconceptualizing the US–Mexico Border "Wall" from the Perspective of a Realist and Constructivist Theoretical Framework in International Relations." *Journal of Borderlands Studies* 36(1): 17–29.

Bennett, John, and Susan Rowley (Eds.). 2004. *Uqalurait: An Oral History of Nunavut*. Montreal: McGill-Queen"s University Press.

Berger, Peter Ludwig. 1963. *Invitation to Sociology: A Humanistic Perspective*. Garden City: Doubleday.

Berkes, Fikret, and Derek R. Armitage. 2010. "Co-Management Institutions, Knowledge, and Learning: Adapting to Change in the Arctic." *Inuit Studies* 34(1): 109–31.

Bijker, Wiebe E. 1993. "Do Not Despair: There Is Life after Constructivism." *Science, Technology, & Human Values* 18(1): 113–38.

———. 1997. *Of Bicycles, Bakelites, and Bulbs: Towards a Theory of Sociotechnical Change*. Cambridge, MA: MIT Press.

Bijker, Wiebe E., Thomas P. Hughes, and Trevor J. Pinch. 1987. *The Social Construction of Technological Systems: New Directions in the Sociology and History of Technology*. Cambridge, MA: MIT Press.

Bikard, Arielle Fridson. 2011. "Reading Mirrors: Reception of the Israeli Wall in the German Media, 2003–2004." *German Politics & Society* 29(1): 25–57.

Bissonnette, Andréanne, and Élisabeth Vallet, eds. 2020. *Borders and Border Walls: In-Security, Symbolism, Vulnerabilities*. Routledge.

Blumer, Herbert. 1969. *Symbolic Interactionism: Perspective and Method*. Englewood Cliffs, NJ: Prentice-Hall.

Bourdieu, Pierre. 1977. *Outline of a Theory of Practice*. Cambridge, UK; New York: Cambridge University Press.

———. 1979. *Algeria 1960: The Disenchantment of the World; The Sense of Honour, The Kabyle House or the World Reversed: Essays*. Cambridge, UK; New York: Cambridge University Press.

Brindley, Tim. 1999. "The Modern House in England: An Architecture of Exclusion." Pp. 30–43 in *Ideal Homes?: Social Change and Domestic Life*, edited by Tony Chapman, and Jenny Hockey. London: Routledge.

Brook, Ryan K., and Stephane M. McLachlan. 2005. "On Using Expert-Based Science to "Test" Local Ecological Knowledge: A Response to: Gilchrist et al. 2005. "Can Local Ecological Knowledge Contribute to Wildlife Management? Case Studies of Migratory Birds"." *Ecology and Society* 10(2): r3.

Bugni, Valerie, and Ronald W. Smith. 2002. "Designed Physical Environments as Related to Selves, Symbols, and Social Reality: A Proposal for a Humanistic Paradigm Shift for Architecture." *Humanity & Society* 26(4): 293–311.

Bushnell, John. 1990. *Moscow Graffiti: Language and Subculture*. Boston: Unwin Hyman.

Byford, Andy. 2014. "The Mental Test as a Boundary Object in Early-20th-Century Russian Child Science." *History of the Human Sciences* 27(4): 22–58.

Caine, Ken J., Colleen M. Davison, and Emma J. Stewart. 2009. "Preliminary Field-Work: Methodological Reflections from Northern Canadian Research." *Qualitative Research* 9(4): 489–513.

Callon, Michel. 1986. "Some Elements of a Sociology of Translation: Domestication of the Scallops and the Fishermen of St Brieuc Bay." Pp. 196–233 in *Power, Action, and Belief*, edited by John Law. London: Routledge & Kegan Paul.

Castleden, Heather, Vanessa Sloan Morgan, and Christopher Lamb. 2012. "'I Spent the First Year Drinking Tea:' Exploring Canadian University Researchers Perspectives on Community-Based Participatory Research Involving Indigenous Peoples." *The Canadian Geographer / Le Géographe canadien* 56(2): 160–79.

Chan, Angela Fung-Chi. 2008. "Shadow of the Wall." M.Arch., School of Architecture, University of Waterloo, Waterloo, ON.

Chapman, Tony. 1999. "Spoiled Home Identities: The Experience of Burglary." Pp. 143–46 in *Ideal Homes?: Social Change and Domestic Life*, edited by Tony Chapman, and Jenny Hockey. London: Routledge.

Chevalier, Sophie. 1999. "The French Two-Home Project: Materialization of Family Identity." Pp. 83–94 in *At Home: An Anthropology of Domestic Space*, edited by Irene Cieraad. Syracuse: Syracuse University Press.

Christensen, Julia. 2017. *No Home in a Homeland: Indigenous peoples and Homelessness in the Canadian North*. Vancouver: University of British Columbia Press.

Clarke, Adele. 2002. "Taste Wars and Design Dilemmas: Aesthetic Practice in the Home." Pp. 131–52 in *Contemporary Art and the Home*, edited by Colin Painter. Oxford: Berg.

Coburn, Elaine, Ed. 2015. *More Will Sing Their Way to Freedom: Indigenous Resistance and Resurgence*. Halifax: Fernwood Publishing.

Collings, Peter. 2005. "Housing Policy, Aging, and Life Course Construction in a Canadian Inuit Community." *Arctic Anthropology* 42(2): 50–65.

———. 2009. "Participant Observation and Phased Assertion as Research Strategies in the Canadian Arctic." *Field Methods* 21(2): 133–53.

Collyer, Fran. 2011. "Reflexivity and the Sociology of Science and Technology: The Invention of "Eryc" the Antibiotic." *Qualitative Report* 16(2): 316–40.

Cooper, Richard. 2011. "In Praise of the Prescription: The Symbolic and Boundary Object Value of the Traditional Prescription in the Electronic Age." *Health Sociology Review* 20(4): 462–74.

Coser, Rose Laub. 1961. "Insulation from Observability and Types of Social Conformity." *American Sociological Review* 26(1): 28–39.

Coulthard, Glenn Sean. 2014. *Red Skin, White Masks: Rejecting the Colonial Politics of Recognition*. Minneapolis: University of Minnesota Press.

Cresswell, Tim. 1996. *In Place/out of Place: Geography, Ideology, and Transgression*. Minneapolis: University of Minnesota Press.

Damas, David. 1988. "The Contact-Traditional Horizon of the Central Arctic: Reassessment of a Concept and Reexamination of an Era." *Arctic Anthropology* 25(2): 101–38.

———. 2004. *Arctic Migrants/Arctic Villagers: The Transformation of Inuit Settlement in the Central Arctic*. Montreal: McGill-Queens University Press.

Dangwal, Dhirendra Datt. 2009. "The Lost Mobility: Pastoralism and Modernity in Uttarakhand Himalaya (India)." *Nomadic Peoples* 13(2): 84–101.

Darke, Jane. 1996. "The Englishwoman"s Castle, or, Don"t You Just Love Being in Control." in *Changing Places: Women"s Lives in the City*, edited by Chris Booth, Jane Darke, and Susan Yeandle. London: Sage.

Darke, Jane, and Craig Gurney. 2000. "Putting Up? Gender, Hospitality and Performance." Pp. 77–99 in *In Search of Hospitality: Theoretical Perspectives and Debates*, edited by Conrad Lashley, and Alison J. Morrison. London: Butterworth-Heinemann.

Davis, Reade. 2006. "All or Nothing: Video Lottery Terminal Gambling and Economic Restructuring in Rural Newfoundland." *Identities* 13(4): 503–31.

Dawson, Peter Colin. 2003. "Analysing the Effects of Spatial Configuration on Human Movement and Social Interaction in Canadian Arctic Communities." Pp. 1–14 in *4th International Space Syntax Symposium*. London.

———. 2004. "An Examination of the Use of Domestic Space by Inuit Families Living in Arviat, Nunavut." edited by Canada, Mortgage Housing Corporation, and External Research Program. Ottawa, ON: Canada Mortgage and Housing Corp.

———. 2008. "Unfriendly Architecture: Using Observations of Inuit Spatial Behavior to Design Culturally Sustaining Houses in Arctic Canada." *Housing Studies* 23(1): 111–28.

de Certeau, Michel. 1984. *The Practice of Everyday Life*. Berkeley: University of California Press.

Delanoë, Alexandre. 2015. "Data on Quantified Self as Boundary Objects: A Case Study on Households" Electricity Consumption." *Rassegna Italiana di Sociologia* 56(3–4): 503–28.

Denis, Jeffrey S. 2015. "Contact Theory in a Small-Town Settler-Colonial Context: The Reproduction of *Laissez-Faire* Racism in Indigenous-White Canadian Relations." *American Sociological Review* 80(1): 218–242.

Dennis, Wayne. 1940. *The Hopi Child*. New York; London: D. Appleton-Century Co., for the Institute for Research in the Social Sciences, University of Virginia.

Department of Education, Nunavut. 2007. *Inuit Qaujimajatuqangit: Education Framework for Nunavut Curriculum.* Iqaluit: Nunavut Department of Education.

Department of Human Resources, Nunavut. 2013. "Inuit Qaujimajatuqangit (IQ)." http://www.gov.nu.ca/hr/site/beliefsystem.htm. Last accessed February 27, 2013. Now available at: https://web.archive.org/web/20120214115337/gov.nu.ca/hr/site/beliefsystem.htm. Last accessed August 20, 2020.

Dermott, Esther, and Julie Seymour. 2011. *Displaying Families: A New Concept for the Sociology of Family Life.* New York: Palgrave Macmillan.

DiMaggio, Paul. 1997. "Culture and Cognition." *Annual Review of Sociology* 23: 263–87.

Dorries, Heather, Robert Henry, David Hugill, Tyler McCreary, and Julie Tomiak. 2019. *Settler City Limits: Indigenoush Resurgence and Colonial Violence in the Urban Prairie West.* Winnipeg: University of Manitoba Press.

Duffles, Marilia. 2005. "An Elegant Dedication to Ancient Crafts After Years of Neglect, Japan is Rediscovering its House-Building Traditions." Pp. 12 in *Financial Times.* London.

Duhaime, Gérard, Edmund Searles, Peter J. Usher, Heather Myers, and Pierre Fréchette. 2004. "Social Cohesion and Living Conditions in the Canadian Arctic: From Theory to Measurement." *Social Indicators Research* 66(3): 295–318.

Durkheim, Émile. [1933] 1964. *The Division of Labor in Society.* New York: Free Press of Glencoe.

Eber, Dorothy. 1975. *People from Our Side: A Life Story with Photographs by Peter Pitseoliak.* Hurting Publishers

Fairhurst, Eileen. 1999. "Fitting a Quart into a Pint Pot: Making Space for Older People in Sheltered Housing." Pp. 96–107 in *Ideal Homes?: Social Change and Domestic Life,* edited by Tony Chapman, and Jenny Hockey. London: Routledge.

Ferrell, Jeff. 1993. *Crimes of Style: Urban Graffiti and the Politics of Criminality.* New York: Garland.

Finch, Janet. 2007. "Displaying Families." *Sociology* 41(1): 65–81.

Fine, Gary Alan. 1991. "On the Macrofoundations of Microsociology." *Sociological Quarterly* 32(2): 161–77.

———. 1996. *Kitchens the Culture of Restaurant Work.* Berkeley, CA; London: University of CA Press.

———. 1998. *Morel Tales: The Culture of Mushrooming.* Cambridge, MA: Harvard University Press.

———. 2012. *Tiny Publics: A Theory of Group Action and Culture.* New York: Russell Sage Foundation.

Fortin, David T. 2022. "Lessons from Cahokia: Indigeneity and the Future of the Settler City." In *The Routledge Handbook of Indigenous Development,* edited by Katharina Ruckstuhl, Irma Alicia Velásquez Nimatuj, John-Andrew McNeish, and Nancy Grey Postero, 392–401. Routledge.

Foucault, Michel. 1977. *Discipline and Punish: The Birth of the Prison.* New York: Pantheon Books.

Fox, Nick J. 2011. "Boundary Objects, Social Meanings and the Success of New Technologies." *Sociology* 45(1): 70–85.

Frake, Charles O. 1975. "How to Enter a Yakan House." Pp. 25–40 in *Sociocultural Dimensions of Language Use*, edited by Mary Sanchez, and Ben Blount. New York: Academic Press.

French, Laurence, and Jim Hornbuckle. 1981. *The Cherokee Perspective: Written by Eastern Cherokees*. Boone, NC: Appalachian Consortium Press.

Gareau, Marcelle, and Peter C. Dawson. 2004. "An Examination of the Use of Domestic Space by Inuit Families Living in Arviat, Nunavut." Pp. 1–8 in *Socio-Economic Series*. Ottawa: Canada Mortgage and Housing Corporation (CMHC).

Garvey, James. 2007. "The Moral Use of Technology." *Royal Institute of Philosophy Supplement* 82(61): 241–60.

Gasparini, Alberto. 1973. "Influence of the Dwelling on Family Life: A Sociological Survey in Modena, Italy." *Ekistics* 216: 344–48.

Giddens, Anthony. 1990. *The Consequences of Modernity*. Stanford: Stanford University Press.

Giedion, Siegfried. [1948] 1969. *Mechanization Takes Command*. New York: W.W. Norton & Company Inc.

Gieryn, Thomas F. 1983. "Boundary-Work and the Demarcation of Science from Non-Science: Strains and Interests in Professional Ideologies of Scientists." *American Sociological Review* 48(6): 781–95.

———. 2000. "A Space for Place in Sociology." *Annual Review of Sociology* 26: 463–96.

———. 2002. "What Buildings Do." *Theory and Society* 31(1): 35–74.

———. 2008. "Cultural Boundaries: Settled and Unsettled." Pp. 91–99 in *Clashes of Knowledge*, edited by Peter Meusberger, Michael Welker, and Edgar Wunder. Dordrecht: Springer.

———. 2018. *Truth-Spots: How Places Make People Believe*. Chicago: University of Chicago Press.

Gilleard, Chris, and Paul Higgs. 2002. "The Third Age: Class, Cohort or Generation?" *Ageing & Society* 22(03): 369–82.

Goffman, Erving. 1959. *The Presentation of Self in Everyday Life*. Garden City, NY: Doubleday.

———. 1963. *Behavior in Public Places: Notes on the Social Organization of Gatherings*. New York: Free Press of Glencoe.

Goldsack, Laura. 1999. "A Haven in a Heartless World? Women and Domestic Violence." Pp. 121–32 in *Ideal Homes? Social Change and Domestic Life*, edited by Tony Chapman, and Jenny Hockey. London: Routledge.

Gomez, Victoria, and Jessica St. Clair. 2008. *Tag You"re It!: The Subculture and Controversy of Graffiti*. Raleigh, NC: Lulu Publications.

Griswold, Wendy. 1987. "A Methodological Framework for the Sociology of Culture." Pp. 1–35 in *Sociological Methodology*, edited by Clifford Clogg. Washington, DC: American Sociological Association.

———. 2008. *Cultures and Societies in a Changing World*, 3rd ed. Thousand Oaks, CA: Pine Forge Press.

Halle, David. 1993. *Inside Culture: Art and Class in the American Home*. Chicago: University of Chicago Press.

Harpending, Henry, and Renee Pennington. 1990. "Herero Households." *Human Ecology* 18(4): 417–39.

Harré, Rom. 2002. "Material Objects in Social Worlds." *Theory, Culture & Society* 19(5–6): 23–33.

Harris, Michael. 1998. *Lament for an Ocean: The Collapse of the Atlantic Cod Fishery: A True Crime Story.* Toronto: McClelland & Stewart.

Haynes, Jo, and Esther Dermott. 2011. "Displaying Mixedness: Differences and Family Relationships." Pp. 145–59 in *Displaying Families: A New Concept for the Sociology of Family Life*, edited by E. Dermott and J. Seymour. Hampshire: Palgrave Macmillan.

Heaphy, Brian. 2011. "Critical Relational Displays." Pp. 19–37 in *Displaying Families: A New Concept for the Sociology of Family Life*, edited by E. Dermott, and J. Seymour. Hampshire: Palgrave Macmillan.

Heyman, Josiah McC. 2008. "Constructing a Virtual Wall: Race and Citizenship in U.S.-Mexico Border Policing." *Journal of the Southwest* 50(3): 305–33.

Hicks, Jack, and Graham White. 2005. "Building Nunavut Through Decentralization or Carpet-Bombing it into Near-Total Dysfunction? A Case Study in Organizational Engineering." in *Annual Meeting of the Canadian Political Science Association*. University of Western Ontario, London, ON.

Hornblower, Simon. 1991. *The Greek World, 479–323 BC*. London; New York: Routledge.

Hughes, Everett C. [1945] 1984. *The Sociological Eye: Selected Papers*. New Brunswick, NJ: Transaction Books.

Hunt, Pauline. 1989. "Gender and the Construction of Home Life." Pp. 66–81 in *Home and Family: Creating the Domestic Sphere*, edited by Graham Allan, and Graham Crow. Basingston: Palgrave.

Hurdley, Rachel. 2006. "Dismantling Mantelpieces: Narrating Identities and Materializing Culture in the Home." *Sociology* 40(4): 717–33.

Jackson, John Brinckerhoff. 1994. *A Sense of Place, A Sense of Time*. New Haven: Yale University Press.

Johnson, Elmer H. 1952. "Family Privacy in a Multi-Unit Dwelling." *Marriage and Family Living* 14(3): 219–25.

Josias, Anthea. 2011. "Toward an Understanding of Archives as a Feature of Collective Memory." *Archival Science* 11(1): 95–112.

Kalluak, Mark. 2017. "About Inuit *Qaujimajatuqangit*." Pp. 41–68 in *Inuit Qaujimajatuqangit: What Inuit Have Always Known to Be True*, edited by Joe Karetak, Frank Tester, and Shirley Tagalik. Winnipeg: Fernwood Publishing.

Karetak, Joe, Frank Tester, and Shirley Tagalik, eds. 2017. *Inuit Qaujimajatuqangit: What Inuit Have Always Known to Be True*. Winnipeg: Fernwood Publishing.

Kehily, Mary Jane, and Rachel Thomson. 2011. "Displaying Motherhood: Representations, Visual Methods and the Materiality of Maternal Practice." Pp. 61–80 in *Displaying Families: A New Concept for the Sociology of Family Life*, edited by E. Dermott, and J. Seymour. Hampshire: Palgrave Macmillan.

Kelly, Benjamin. 2017. "The Social Psychology of Compromised Negotiations: The Emergence of Asymmetrical Boundary Objects Between Science and Industry."

in *Microsociological Perspectives in Environmental Sociology*, edited by Brad Brewster, and Anthony Puddephatt. New York: Routledge.

Kenyon, Gary M., and William Lowell Randall. 1997. *Restorying our Lives: Personal Growth through Autobiographical Reflection*. Westport, CT: Praeger.

Kershaw, Peter G., Peter A. Scott, and Harold E. Welch. 1996. The Shelter Characteristics of Traditional-Styled Inuit Snow Houses. *Arctic*, 49(4): 328–338.

Kinberg, Clare. 2008. "Notes on Border Walls and Cultural Exchange: From Conversations with Wendy Kenin." *Bridges: A Jewish Feminist Journal* 13(2): 32–39.

King, A.D. 1984. "The Social Production of Building Form: Theory and Research." *Environment and Planning D: Society and Space* 2(4): 429–46.

———. 1989. "Colonialism, Urbanism and the Capitalist World Economy." *International Journal of Urban and Regional Research* 13: 1–18.

Kino-Nda-Niimi Collective. 2014. *The Winter We Danced: Voices from the Past, the Future, and the Idle No More Movement*. Winnipeg: ARP Press.

Kitanishi, Koichi. 2000. "The Aka and Baka: Food Sharing among Two Central Africa Hunter-Gatherer Groups." Pp. 149–70 in *The Social Economy of Sharing: Resource Allocation and Modern Hunter-Gatherers*, edited by George W. Wenzel, Grete Hovelsrud-Broda, and Nobuhiro Kishigami. Osaka: Museum of Ethnology.

Kopytoff, Igor. 1986. "The Cultural Biography of Things: Commoditization as Process." Pp. 64–92. In *The Social Life of Things*, edited by Arjun Appadurai. Cambridge: Cambridge University Press.

Kublu, Alexina, F. Laugrand, and J. Oosten. 2017. "The Nunavut College Oral Traditions Project." Pp. 1–18 in *Inuit Worldviews* by Saullu Nakasuk, Herve Paniaq, Elisapee Ootoova, and Pauloosie Angmarklik. Iqaluit: Nunavut Arctic College Media.

Kukathas, Chandran. 2008. "Cultural Privacy." *The Monist* 91(1): 68–80.

Kusenback, Margarethe, and Krista E. Paulson. 2013. *Home: International Perspectives on Culture, Identity, and Belonging*, 3rd ed. Frankfurt: Peter Lang.

Kwint, Marius. 1999. "Introduction: The Physical Past." Pp. 1–16 in *Material Memories: Design and Evocation*, edited by Marius Kwint, Christopher Breward, and Jeremy Aynsley. Oxford: Berg.

Kwint, Marius, Christopher Breward, and Jeremy Aynsley. 1999. *Material Memories: Design and Evocation*. Oxford: Berg.

Kyser, J. 2011. *Sustainable Aboriginal Housing in Canada: A Case Study Report*. Toronto: Housing Services Corporation.

Lachmann, Richard. 1988. "Graffiti as Career and Ideology." *American Journal of Sociology* 94(2): 229–50.

Lamont, Michele. 2000. "Meaning-Making in Cultural Sociology: Broadening Our Agenda." *Contemporary Sociology* 29(4): 602.

Landry D. 2019. "'Stop Calling It Graffiti': The Visual Rhetoric of Contamination, Consumption and Colonization." *Current Sociology* 67(5): 686–704.

Lang, Gladys Engel, and Kurt Lang. 1988. "Recognition and Renown: The Survival of Artistic Reputation." *American Journal of Sociology* 94(1): 79–109.

Langerbein, Helmut. 2009. "Great Blunders?: The Great Wall of China, the Berlin Wall, and the Proposed United States/Mexico Border Fence." *History Teacher* 43(1): 9–29.

Latour, Bruno. 1983. "Give Me a Laboratory and I Will Raise the World." Pp. 141–70 in *Science Observed: Perspectives on the Social Study of Science*, edited by Karin D. Knorr-Cetina, and Michael Mulkay. London: Sage.

———. 1990. "Technology Is Society Made Durable." *Sociological Review* 38: 103–31.

———. 1992. "Where Are the Missing Masses? The Sociology of a Few Mundane Artifacts." in *Shaping Technology, Building Society: Studies in Sociotechnical Change*, edited by Wiebe. E. Bijker, and John Law. Cambridge, MA: MIT Press.

Lawrence, Denise L., and Setha M. Low. 1990. "The Built Environment and Spatial Form." *Annual Review of Anthropology* 19: 453–505.

Lee, Molly, and Gregory A. Reinhardt. 2003. *Eskimo Architecture: Dwelling and Structure in the Early Historic Period*. Fairbanks: University of Alaska Press.

Le Guin, Ursula K. 1974. *The Dispossessed: An Ambiguous Utopia*, 1st ed. New York: Harper & Row.

Leuenberger, Christine. 2006. "Constructions of the Berlin Wall: How Material Culture is Used in Psychological Theory." *Social Problems* 53(1): 18–37.

Linebarger, Christopher, and Alex Braithwaite. 2020. "Do Walls Work? The Effectiveness of Border Barriers in Containing the Cross-Border Spread of Violent Militancy." *International Studies Quarterly* 64(3): 487–98.

Liu, Sida. 2015. "Boundary Work and Exchange: The Formation of a Professional Service Market." *Symbolic Interaction* 38(1): 1–21.

Logan, John R., and Harvey L. Molotch. 2007. *Urban Fortunes: The Political Economy of Place*. Berkeley: University of California Press.

Macdonald, Gaynor. 2000. "Economies and Personhood: Demand Sharing among the Wiradjuri of New South Wales." Pp. 87–112 in *The Social Economy of Sharing: Resource Allocation and Modern Hunter-Gatherers*, edited by George. W. Wenzel, Grete Hovelsrud-Broda, and Nobuhiro Kishigami. Osaka: Museum of Ethnology.

Macdonald, Nancy. 2001. *The Graffiti Subculture: Youth, Masculinity, and Identity in London and New York*. New York: Palgrave.

Madigan, Ruth, and Moira Munro. 1999. ""The More We are Together": Domestic Space, Gender and Privacy." Pp. 61–72 in *Ideal Homes? Social Change and Domestic Space*, edited by Tony Chapman, and Jenny Hockey. London: Routledge.

Mallett, Shelley. 2004. "Understanding Home: A Critical Review of the Literature." *Sociological Review* 52(1): 62–89.

Maoz, Azaryahu. 2011. "The Politics of Commemorative Street Renaming: Berlin 1945–1948." *Journal of Historical Geography* 37(4): 483–92.

Marks, Paul. 2010. "Sensors and Robots Aim to Bolster Border Security." *New Scientist* 205(2742): 20–21.

Marshall, Sandra. 2006. "Arviat Community and Housing Design Charrette." Pp. 1–10 in *Technical Series*. Ottawa: Canada Mortgage and Housing Corporation (CMHC).

Mauss, Marcel, and Henri Beuchat. 1979. *Seasonal Variations of the Eskimo: A Study in Social Morphology*. London: Routledge & Kegan Paul.

McAllister, Patrick. 2004. "Domestic Space, Habitus, and Xhosa Ritual Beer-Drinking." *Ethnology* 43(2): 117–35.

Mead, George Herbert. 1934. *Mind, Self & Society from the Standpoint of a Social Behaviorist*. Chicago, IL: University of Chicago Press.

Meier, Ninna. 2015. "Collaboration in Healthcare through Boundary Work and Boundary Objects." *Qualitative Sociology Review* 11(3): 60–82.

Merkur, Daniel. 1992. *Becoming Half Hidden: Shamanism and Initiation Among the Inuit*. Stockholm: Almqvist & Wiksell International.

Michael, Mike. 2000. "These Boots Are Made for Walking. . .: Mundane Technology, the Body and Human-Environment Relations." *Body & Society* 6(3–4): 107–26.

Miller, Daniel. 2001. *Home Possessions: Material Culture Behind Closed Doors*. Oxford; New York: Berg.

Moore, Barrington. 1984. *Privacy: Studies in Social and Cultural History*. Armonk, NY; New York: M.E. Sharpe; Distributed by Pantheon Books.

Moreton-Robinson, Aileen. 2016. *The White Possessive: Property Power and Indigenous Sovereignty*. Minneapolis: University of Minnesota Press.

Morgan, David H. J. 1996. *Family Connections*. Cambridge, UK; Cambridge, MA: Polity Press; Blackwell Publishers.

Morton, Christopher. 2007. "Remembering the House: Memory and Materiality in Northern Botswana." *Journal of Material Culture* 12(2): 157–79.

Mukerji, Chandra. 1994. "Toward a Sociology of Material Culture: Science Studies, Cultural Studies and the Meanings of Things." Pp. 143–62 in *The Sociology of Culture: Emerging Theoretical Perspectives*, edited by Diana Crane. Oxford: Blackwell.

Munro, Moira, and Ruth Madigan. 1999. "Negotiating Space in the Family Home." Pp. 107–17 in *At Home: An Anthropology of Domestic Space*, edited by Irene Cieraad.

Needham, G.H. 1968. *Living in the New Houses*. Ottawa: Indian and Northern Affairs Canada.

Newman, Andrew. 2012. *On Records: Delaware Indians, Colonists, and the Media of History and Memory*. Lincoln, NE: University of Nebraska Press.

Olick, Jeffrey K., and Joyce Robbins. 1998. "Social Memory Studies: From 'Collective Memory' to the Historical Sociology of Mnemonic Practices." *Annual Review of Sociology* 24: 105–40.

Ore, Janet. 2011. "Mobile Home Syndrome: Engineered Woods and the Making of a New Domestic Ecology in the Post–World War II Era." *Technology and Culture* 52(2): 260–86.

Owens, Kellie. 2015. "Boundary Objects in Complementary and Alternative Medicine: Acupuncture Vs. Christian Science." *Social Science & Medicine* 128(Supplement C): 18–24.

Parin, Paul, Fritz Morgenthaler, and Goldy Parin-Matthèy. 1986. *The Whites Think Too Much: Psychoanalytic Investigations among the Dogon in West Africa*. New Haven: Human Relations Area Files.

Peña-Alves, Stephanie. 2020. "Outspoken Objects and Unspoken Myths: The Semiotics of Object-Mediated Communication." *Symbolic Interaction* 43(3): 385–404.

Pile, Steve, and Michael Keith. 1997. *Geographies of Resistance*. London; New York: Routledge.

Pinch, Trevor J., and Wiebe E. Bijker. 1984. "The Social Construction of Facts and Artefacts: Or How the Sociology of Science and the Sociology of Technology Might Benefit Each Other." *Social Studies of Science* 14(3): 399–441.

Prince, Raymond. 1964. *Indigenous Yoruba Psychiatry*. Human Relations Area Files.

Prus, Robert. 1987. "Generic Social Processes: Maximizing Conceptual Development in Ethnographic Research." *Journal of Contemporary Ethnography* 16: 250–93.

Radcliffe-Brown, A. R. 1952. *Structure and Function in Primitive Society: Essays and Addresses*. Glencoe, IL: Free Press.

Rahn, Janice. 2002. *Painting without Permission: Hip-Hop Graffiti Subculture*. Westport, CT: Bergin & Garvey.

Rapoport, Amos. 1982. *The Meaning of the Built Environment: A Nonverbal Communication Approach*. Beverly Hills: Sage Publications.

Rentetzi, Maria. 2008. "Configuring Identities Through Industrial Architecture and Urban Planning: Greek Tobacco Warehouses in Late Nineteenth and Early Twentieth Century." *Science Studies* 21(1): 64–81.

Riesman, David. 1950. *The Lonely Crowd: A Study of the Changing American Character*. New Haven: Yale University Press.

Robarchek, Clayton Allen. 1978. *Semai Nonviolence: A Systems Approach to Understanding*. Ann Arbor, MI: Xerox University Microfilms.

Rosenberger, Robert. 2020. "On Hostile Design: Theoretical and Empirical Prospects." *Urban Studies* 57(4): 883–93.

Rybczynski, Witold. 1986. *Home: A Short History of an Idea*. New York: Viking.

Saunders, Peter, and Peter Williams. 1988. "The Constitution of the Home: Towards a Research Agenda." *Housing Studies* 3(2): 81–93.

Sapsed, Jonathan, and Ammon Salter. 2016. "Postcards from the Edge: Local Communities, Global Programs and Boundary Objects." *Organization Studies* 25(9): 1515–34.

Schroeder, Ralph. 2007. *Rethinking Science, Technology, and Social Change*. Stanford: Stanford University Press.

Schudson, Michael. 2002. "How Culture Works: Perspectives from Media Studies on the Efficacy of Symbols." Pp. 141–48 in *Cultural Sociology*, edited by Lyn Spillman. Malden, MA; Oxford: Blackwell.

Scott, James C. 1998. *Seeing Like a State: How Certain Schemes to Improve the Human Condition have Failed*. New Haven: Yale University Press.

———. 2008. *Weapons of the Weak: Everyday Forms of Peasant Resistance*. New Haven: Yale University Press.

Sewell, William. 1992. "A Theory of Structure: Duality, Agency, and Transformation." *American Journal of Sociology* 98(1): 1–29.

Shils, Edward. 1981. *Tradition*. Chicago: University of Chicago Press.

Silverstein, Paul A. 2004. "Of Rooting and Uprooting: Kabyle Habitus, Domesticity, and Structural Nostalgia." *Ethnography* 5(4): 553–78.

Simmel, Georg. 1994. "Bridge and Door." *Theory, Culture & Society* 11(1): 5–10.

Simpson, Leanne Betasamosake. 2017. *As We Have Always Done: Indigenous Freedom through Radical Resistance.* Minneapolis: University of Minnesota Press.

Singh, Chetan. 2009. "Pastoralism and the Making of Colonial Modernity in Kulu, 1850–1952." *Nomadic Peoples* 13(2): 65–83.

Sizemore, Michael M. 1986. "New Age Architecture: The Human Integration of New Technologies." Pp. 58–63 in *The Built Environment: Present and Future Values,* edited by F. O. Bonkovsky. Columbus, GA: University Center Press, Brentwood Publishers.

Smith, Linda Tuhiwai. 2021. *Decolonizing Methodologies: Research and Indigenous Peoples,* 3rd ed. New York: Zed Books Ltd.

Snipp, C. M. 2013. "American Indians and Alaska Natives in Urban Environments." Pp. 173–92 in *Indigenous in the City: Contemporary Identities and Cultural Innovation,* edited by E. Peters and C. Andersen. Vancouver: UBC Press.

Snow, David A., and Anderson Leon. 1987. "Identity Work Among the Homeless: The Verbal Construction and Avowal of Personal Identities." *American Journal of Sociology* 92(6): 1336–71.

Snyder, Gregory J. 2009. *Graffiti Lives: Beyond the Tag in New York"s Urban Underground.* New York: New York University Press.

Soja, Edward W. 1989. *Postmodern Geographies: The Reassertion of Space in Critical Social Theory.* London; New York: Verso.

Star, Susan Leigh, and James R. Griesemer. 1989. "Institutional Ecology, "Translations" and Boundary Objects: Amateurs and Professionals in Berkeley"s Museum of Vertebrate Zoology." *Social Studies of Science* 19: 387–420.

Starolis, Haley. 2020. "Hostile Architecture: The Death of Urban Spaces." *Crit* 86(1): 53–55, 57.

Statistics Canada. 2007. Arviat, Nunavut (Code6205015) (table). 2006 Community Profiles. 2006 Census. Statistics Canada Catalogue no. 92-591-XWE. Ottawa. Released March 13, 2007. https://www12.statcan.gc.ca/census-recensement/2006/dp-pd/prof/92-591/index.cfm?Lang=E (accessed May 27, 2024).

Statistics Canada. 2023. *Census Profile*: 2021 Census of Population. Statistics Canada Catalogue no. 98-316-X2021001. Ottawa. Released November 15, 2023. https://www12.statcan.gc.ca/census-recensement/2021/dp-pd/prof/index.cfm?Lang=E. Last (accessed January 15, 2024).

Steele, D. H., R. Andersen, and J. M. Green. 1992. "The Managed Commercial Annihilation of Northern Cod." *Newfoundland Studies* 8(1): 34–68.

Stewart Patrick Robert Reid. 2015. "Indigenous Architecture through Indigenous Knowledge *Dim Sagalts'apkw Nisiṁ* [Together We Will Build a Village]." Dissertation University of British Columbia.

Strong, Mary Clare. 1981. "An Ethnography of New Yorican Mural Communication." Thesis. Ann Arbor, MI: Temple University.

Sudjic, Deyan. 2005. *The Edifice Complex: How the Rich and Powerful Shape the World*. New York: Penguin Press.

Swidler, Ann. 1986. "Culture in Action: Symbols and Strategies." *American Sociological Review* 51(2): 273–86.

Tackett, Nicolas. 2008. "The Great Wall and Conceptualizations of the Border under the Northern Song." *Journal of Song-Yuan Studies* 38(1): 99–138.

Takano, Takako. 2005. "Connections with the Land: Land-Skills Courses in Igloolik, Nunavut." *Ethnography* 6(4): 463–86.

Tamez, Margo. 2013. "Place and Perspective in the Shadow of the Wall." *Aztlán: A Journal of Chicano Studies* 38(1): 165–88.

Tamplin, Andrea K., Sabine A. Krawietz, Gabriel A. Radvansky, and David E. Copeland. 2013. "Event Memory and Moving in a Well-Known Environment." *Memory & Cognition* 41(8): 1109–21.

Taylor, Charles. 1999. "Two Theories of Modernity." *Public Culture* 11(1): 153–74.

Taylor, Jean Gelman. 2012. "The Sewing Machine in Colonial Era Photographs: A Record from Dutch Indonesia." *Modern Asian Studies* 46(Special Issue 01): 71–95.

Tester, Frank. 2017. "Colonial Challenges and Recovery in the Eastern Arctic." Pp. 20–40 in *Inuit Qaujimajatuqangit*. Winnipeg: Fernwood Publishing.

Tester, Frank, and Peter Kulchyski. 1994. *Tammarniit (Mistakes): Inuit Relocation in the Eastern Arctic, 1939-63*. Vancouver: University of British Columbia Press.

Th Baigent, Sibley Qúy. 2004. "First Words of a Native Daughter." *Michigan Quarterly Review* 43(4): 679–85.

Thomas, D. K., and Charles Thomas Thompson. 1972. *Eskimo Housing as Planned Culture Change*. Ottawa: Northern Science Research Group, Department of Indian Affairs and Northern Development.

Tönnies, Ferdinand. [1957] 1964. *Community and Society (Gemeinschaft und Gessellschaft)*. East Lansing: Michigan State University Press.

Turkle, Sherry. 1995. *Life on the Screen: Identity in the Age of the Internet*. New York: Simon & Schuster.

Uluadluak, Donald. 2017. "*Pamiqsainirmik* (Training Children)." Pp. 147–73 in *Inuit Qaujimajatuqangit: What Inuit Have Always Known to Be True*, edited by Joe Karetak, Frank Tester, and Shirley Tagalik. Winnipeg: Fernwood Publishing.

van den Hoonaard, Deborah K. 1997. "Identity Foreclosure: Women''s Experiences of Widowhood as Expressed in Autobiographical Accounts." *Ageing & Society* 17(5): 533–51.

van den Hoonaard, Will C. 1997. *Working with Sensitizing Concepts: Analytical Field Research*. Thousand Oaks: Sage Publications.

van den Scott, Jeffrey, and Lisa-Jo K. van den Scott. 2019. "Imagined Engagements: Interpreting the Musical Relationship with the Canadian North." *Qualitative Sociology Review* 15(2): 90–104.

van den Scott, Lisa-Jo K. 2009. "Cancelled, Aborted, Late, Mechanical: The Vagaries of Air Travel in Arviat, Nunavut, Canada." Pp. 211–26 in *The Cultures of Alternative Mobilities: Routes Less Travelled,* edited by Phillip Vannini. Surrey: Ashgate.

———. 2017. "Collective Memory and Social Restructuring in the Case of Traditional Inuit Shamanism." *Symbolic Interaction* 40(1): 83–100.

———. 2018. "Role Transitions in the Field and Reflexivity: From Friend to Researcher." *Studies in Qualitative Methodology: (Special Issue) Emotion and the Researcher: Sites, Subjectivities and Relationships* 16: 19–32.

———. 2019. "Symbolic Interactionism." In *SAGE Research Methods Foundations*, edited by Paul A. Atkinson, Sara Delamont, J.W. Sakshaug, and Richard Williams. Sage.

Vowel, Chelsea. 2016. *Indigenous Writes*. Winnipeg: Highwater Press.

Wagner-Pacifici, Robin, and Barry Schwartz. 2002. "The Vietnam Veterans Memorial: Commemorating a Difficult Past." Pp. 210–20 in *Cultural Sociology*, edited by Lyn Spillman. Malden, MA; Oxford: Blackwell.

Watts, Vanessa. 2013. "Indigenous Place-Thought and Agency Amongst Humans and Non-Humans (First Woman and Sky Woman go on a European World Tour!)." *Decolonization: Indigeneity, Education, & Society* 2(1): 20–34.

Wenzel, George W. 2000. "Sharing, Money, and Modern Inuit Subsistence: Obligation and Reciprocity at Clyde River, Nunavut." Pp. 61–86 in *The Social Economy of Sharing: Resource Allocation and Modern Hunter-Gatherers*, edited by George W. Wenzel, Grete Hovelsrud-Broda, and Nobuhiro Kishigami. Osaka: Museum of Ethnology.

Wenzel, George W., Grete Hovelsrud-Broda, and Nobuhiro Kishigami. 2000. "Social Economy of Modern Hunter-Gatherers: Traditional Subsistence, New Resources." Pp. 1–6 in *The Social Economy of Sharing: Resource Allocation and Modern Hunter-Gatherers*, edited by George W. Wenzel, Grete Hovelsrud-Broda, and Nobuhiro Kishigami. Osaka: Museum of Ethnology.

Williamson, Robert G. 1974. *Eskimo Underground: Socio-Cultural Change in the Canadian Central Arctic*. Uppsala: Institutionen för allmän och jämförande etnografi vid Uppsala Universitet.

Wong, Sabrina, Leena Wu, Brooke Boswell, Laura Housden, and Josee Lavoie. 2013. "Strategies for Moving Towards Equity in Recruitment of Rural and Aboriginal Research Participants." *Rural and Remote Health* 13(2).

Wright, Melissa W. 2020. "Border Thinking, Borderland Diversity, and Trump's Wall." Pp. 211–19 in *Environmental Governance in a Populist/Authoritarian Era*. Routledge.

Wycherley, R. E. 1976. *How the Greeks Built Cities*. New York: Norton.

Yaneva, Albena. 2008. "How Buildings "Surprise:" The Renovation of the Alte Aula in Vienna." *Science Studies* 21(1): 8–28.

York, Abigail M., and Michael L. Schoon. 2011. "Collaboration in the Shadow of the Wall: Shifting Power in the Borderlands." *Policy Sciences* 44(4): 345–65.

Younging, Gregory. 2018. *Elements of Indigenous Style: A Guide for Writing by and About Indigenous Peoples*. Canada: Brush Education Inc.

Zerubavel, Eviatar. 1997. *Social Mindscapes*. Cambridge, MA; London: Harvard University Press.

Index

Page numbers in italic indicate figures.

About the Author

Lisa-Jo K. van den Scott is an associate professor of sociology at Memorial University of Newfoundland, having obtained her PhD from Northwestern University. Before that, she lived in Arviat, Nunavut, with her spouse (Jeff, "the music teacher"). Her research interests include space and place, time, symbolic interaction, culture, and science and technology studies. Dr. van den Scott coedited *The Craft of Qualitative Research* and coauthored *Qualitative Research in Action,* beginning with its fourth edition. She has published articles in such journals as *American Behavioral Scientist, Journal of Contemporary Ethnography,* and *Qualitative Sociology Review.* She currently serves as the editor-in-chief of *Symbolic Interaction,* the lead journal of the Society for the Study of Symbolic Interaction (SSSI). van den Scott received SSSI's Helena Lopata Mentor Excellence Award in 2019 and Kathy Charmaz Early-in-Career Award in 2022. She has long been involved as an organizer of the Annual Qualitative Analysis Conference, affectionately known as "the Qualitatives," an international, interdisciplinary conference based in Canada.

RELEVANT BOOKS

van den Hoonaard, Deborah K., and Lisa-Jo K. van den Scott. 2021. *Qualitative Research in Action: A Canadian Primer,* 4th edition. Oxford University Press.
Kleinknecht, Steve, Lisa-Jo K. van den Scott, and Carrie B. Sanders, eds. 2018. *The Craft of Qualitative Research.* Toronto: Canadian Scholars Press.